Writing for the Media

Writing for the Media

Martin Maloney *Department of Radio, Television, and Film*
Northwestern University

Paul Max Rubenstein *Department of Radio, Television,*
and Film
Northwestern University
and Columbia College, Chicago

prentice-hall, inc. englewood cliffs, n.j. 07632

Library of Congress Cataloging in Publication Data

Maloney, Martin Joseph, 1915-
    Writing for the media.

    Includes index.
    1. Mass media—Authorship. 2. Mass media—
Handbooks, manuals, etc. I. Rubenstein, Paul,
joint author. II. Title.
P91.M317   808'.066'791   79-20810
ISBN   0-13-970558-9

Printed in the United States of America

10   9   8   7   6   5   4   3

Editorial/production supervision and interior design by Douglas Kubach
Manufacturing buyer: Anthony Caruso

Prentice-Hall International, Inc., *London*
Prentice-Hall of Australia Pty. Limited, *Sydney*
Prentice-Hall of Canada, Ltd., *Toronto*
Prentice-Hall of India Private Limited, *New Delhi*
Prentice-Hall of Japan, Inc., *Tokyo*
Prentice-Hall of Southeast Asia Pte. Ltd., *Singapore*
Whitehall Books Limited, *Wellington*, *New Zealand*

To Michelle and Rachel, Katie and Cordee

Contents

Acknowledgments

This part of the book is like putting together a wedding list; you are bound to offend someone by leaving out their name. If we have omitted any names it is an unintentional accident of memory. Writing a book or writing a script is not a singular effort; the process involves people, and we have a lot of them to thank.

First, the hundreds of students at Columbia College in Chicago and Northwestern University, who took our classes rather than sleeping an hour later in the morning. The demands you placed on us to teach you more than just an acceptable level of skill in writing for the media, especially at such an early hour, kept us all awake. Your classes allowed us to test out theories that we later incorporated into this book. You gave us genuine delight while watching your talents grow. And without the willingness of our administrators at both campuses, who gave us some elbow room to finish the manuscript, we'd probably still be on page fifty. The Northwestern University's Evening Division and Roosevelt University's continuing adult education programs helped shape a book that we hope answers the needs of the professional writer.

There were a number of people in the industry who gave us suggestions and criticism during the several drafts of *Writing for the Media*. Thanks to Ira Kerns and Joan Beugen of the Creative Establishment; Gilbert Altschul of Gilbert Altschul Productions; Ken Solomon and Don Ivener of Associated Audio-Visual Corporation; Scott Craig, Jim Coursen, George Baum, and Richie Bernal of WBBM-TV, CBS in Chicago; Les Teichner of the Chicago Group; Cinematographer Steve Golden and film editor Barbara Kaplan; and Robert Hudacek of RAH Productions.

Thanks to Diane Karkyewicz for her initial work on the preparation of the first draft; Deborah Firestone who provided some sunshine and hope when it was needed the most.; our anonymous reviewers, whose suggestions helped us reach the final draft; Cheryl Smith, for her initial copyediting; Stan Lazan, for his encouragement; Ethel and Maury Rosenburg, for all of their help; and Dr. Irv Rein, professor of Communication Studies at Northwestern University, who lead us to Prentice-Hall.

Dick Cosme, our sales and acquisitions representative, lead us to the editor every author dreams of working with, William H. Oliver. His instincts for what is right and his fairness when asking for the best can't be praised enough. Constantly Bill's manner came across as someone who believes that working in the absence of crisis provides the most creative atmosphere. Once the book reached production stage, Douglas Kubach took over. From then on the book was in his hands, and we couldn't have asked for a better pair.

And to Ethel and Maury Rosenberg, you showed the ends parents will go to helping a son get published. Thank you for accepting the long distance calls collect from Universal Studios when one of the authors was out there writing a motion picture, and the postage you spent in mailing printed page proofs from Chicago to Los Angeles.

Finally, we want to thank our typewriters. There is a rhythm and sound in typing that helps a writer hear; this experience might be unknown to people who write in longhand. Hitting the keys, sometimes strongly, sometimes softly, helps to create the flow of the story and the cadence of speech patterns while writing dialogue or narration. Our typewriters, although old and battered by long airplane flights, have given a lifelong relationship, something recognizable, familiar, and warm to the ear.

Introduction

This is a book about writing for the media, some rather specialized kinds of writing created by the demands of still photography, motion picture photography, and audio and visual recording techniques. We address ourselves to people who want to write for motion pictures and television, those who are interested in writing and producing slide films, 8mm and 16mm films for educational and promotional purposes, documentaries for radio, film, and television, television specials, and various kinds of audio and video tape recordings.

There is a considerable market for such writing, far more accessible to most writers than the market for feature film scenarios and network television scripts. In fact, the market for this material is more promising than the market for magazine nonfiction, and at the present time it is much more promising than the market for any sort of fiction. But we have not ignored the area of fiction, that is writing teleplays and feature film scripts, not only because a market for this work exists but because an understanding of dramatic forms and techniques is basic to all media writing.

Writing for the media, as we describe it, is a highly practical affair. Producers of educational films, for example, need someone who can write a produceable script on an assigned topic that can be shot within reasonable time on a pre-specified budget. And they need a writer who can work to a deadline. Much of the same can be said of producers who guide the development of motion pictures for theatrical release.

This does not mean that talent has no value to the media writer. An intel-

1

ligent, imaginative, well-written script makes all the difference between a minimally effective educational film that will bore some thousands of people while doing its pedestrian job of instruction, and one that will not only teach its subject, but also stimulate and excite its viewers. The same holds true for television productions that entertain or inform, and motion pictures that provide nostalgia, adventure, fantasy, or escape.

Because writing for the media is skilled work, and because there has been little if any discussion of this subject in print, we have tried to compile a practical handbook for the prospective writer and the writer and producer with experience in this field. We have, from time to time, touched on the historical development of forms such as the documentary, and on the theoretical reasons why we believe our advice to be valid, but in the main we have tried to describe how-to-do-it: what a writer must know, what the markets are, the various forms of scripts, getting assignments to write, planning and drafting and finally revising the script itself.

Most people who think they might like to write for the media come to the task with expectations formed out of the centuries-old tradition of writing for print. These expectations are often highly romantic and not very realistic, even when measured against the realities of writing for the printed page toward the end of the twentieth century. Measured against the demands of the new media—the often complex communication technologies—they are at times almost ludicrous. Yet the writer's part in these new ventures in expression and communication is no less worthy or interesting than it has ever been. It is, however, different. Our hope is that this book will help you to understand and perhaps live and work in this much altered writer's world.

chapter 1
The Business
of Writing

One of the common notions about writers runs somewhat as follows. You are struck with a fascinating idea. You sit down at your desk and after much travail express this idea in a novel, an essay, or a lyric poem. You then show the manuscript to a publisher (who is always looking for expressions of literary talent without much regard to the form or the subject matter through which it is expressed). The publisher (if he thinks he detects talent or genius in the manuscript) publishes it and presumably makes money from its sale. Some of the money goes to the writer and provides him with a living.

We need not worry about whether this scenario holds true for novelists, historians, poets, or other writers for print. The point to remember is that almost the exact reverse is true for the media writer. You rarely, if ever, develop an idea on your own, without knowing whether or not a producer is interested in it. You are more likely to be asked by a producer to write a script on a specified subject, at a specified length, for a specified budget. You do not just sit down with your notes and write a full script suitable for production. You write a treatment—a narrative summary of the proposed script. You may rewrite it several times to suit the requirements of a producer or client. The treatment is then turned into a first draft of the script, which will certainly be revised at least once and probably several times. Throughout this process, which may involve the producer of the script, the director, a client's representative, and several other people, the production script emerges. Finally, if you are an established professional, you do not do any of this work on speculation; what you are to be paid, and for exactly what work is usually settled beforehand in a written contract.

3

This is why our book on media writing begins with a chapter on the writer as a business person. A good deal of business comes first and accompanies the actual writing of a script.

SCREENPLAYS AND TELEPLAYS

The Los Angeles area has for many years been considered the center of motion picture production in the United States. Many early motion pictures were made in the New York area and in Chicago, but bad weather and the lack of good natural light soon forced the movie-makers to southern California. Hollywood became the much-romanticized center for film production. In the 1950s and 1960s, when network television was done either on film or videotape rather than "live" in the studio, television producers also shifted their activities to the west coast, in large part because talent and production facilities were already concentrated there.

Today "Hollywood" is a misnomer. Only two film studios, Goldwyn and Paramount, remain in Hollywood proper. MGM is in Culver City. Columbia has moved to Burbank and shares space with Warner Brothers. Universal Studios, where more television programs are produced than anywhere else in the country and perhaps the world, is located at Universal City near Burbank, which also happens to be home for Disney Studios and NBC Television.

Nevertheless, all of these production companies and a number of others are clustered together in a relatively small area. The writers who write the scripts for most television programs and some feature films, quite naturally, live and work in the immediate neighborhood. A writer does not have to live in the area in order to work, but distance is a handicap—especially if the writer is not yet well established.

There are two reasons for this. First, there is a great deal of talking involved in the process of successful television and film writing. Writers must talk to their agents, to producers, to their friends in the industry. Otherwise they are simply out of touch with what is going on in a very volatile business. Writers sell their ideas and abilities as much by talking them as by writing them. Second, screenplays are rarely the product of one person. They evolve through a series of revisions prompted by elaborate discussions with producers, collaborators, studio executives, and so on. Writing for the entertainment media is not quite the lonely soul-wrenching affair of romantic tradition; it is much more a sort of social involvement.

Thus being close to the source of buying and production is almost mandatory for the writer, especially when getting established. Nearly all of the teleplays and screenplays produced are written by authors living in the Los Angeles area. Some agents—almost indispensable in this business—want their writers to have almost daily contact with producers and insist that the writers make the rounds of production offices. Certainly getting assignments for a television series will require a number of story conferences with the producers, story editors, or head writers for the series. It is not impossible for a writer to write for television or feature films while living away from the Los Angeles area, but it is difficult. Even if you do write screenplays in another part of the country you'll find commuting by plane to the studios in California a necessity for story and script conferences.

This situation is not the result of a conspiracy to keep aspiring writers from writing for the media. Young writers with little or no media experience can and do go to California to find a career, many successfully, just as young actors used to go to New York in the hope of winning fame and fortune on Broadway. But the fact remains that writers in Kansas City, or New Orleans, or Topeka are being unrealistic if they hope to sell a play for television or motion picture production by traveling no farther than their local post offices.

THE NONFICTION SCRIPT

The writing and selling of nonfiction scripts for use by local television broadcasters, radio stations, business concerns, governmental agencies, schools, and colleges is a very different matter. The demand for scripts of this kind is many times greater than the demand for plays. Moreover, this demand is normally far greater than the output of the relatively few writers who know how to write these scripts.

Radio and television stations interested in producing documentaries and specials must, of course, be large enough to have both sizeable audiences and reasonable production facilities; but there are many such stations spread across the country. Film and tape production agencies may be found in large cities and smaller communities alike. The *Writer's Market* lists several dozen audiovisual markets, located in such places as Lawrence, Kansas; Fort Lauderdale, Florida; St. Louis, Missouri; Detroit; San Francisco; and Elgin, Illinois, in addition to New York City, Los Angeles, and Chicago. As is the case with authors of dramatic scripts, writers must do business with producers in person, rather than through the mail.

The prices paid for nonfiction scripts are variable. As of this writing, the Writers Guild of America has worked out agreements with some of the major PBS stations (including the one in Los Angeles), as well as with the commercial networks and producers, the studios, and the independents. These agreements, of course, include minimum fees for scripts. But as of the present writing, the Guild has no agreements with industrial film and video producers, so that writers must negotiate on their own. You are not likely to be paid as well for such assignments as you might be for a dramatic script. But with hundreds of film-video-audio production companies scattered across the country your chances of getting a script assignment are good.

If your eventual goal is to write for feature films or network television, you might do well to start writing for the instructional-industrial media. The work is there to be done, and the experience and credit can be invaluable to your career. A surprising number of West Coast producers and writers began this way. For example, Mike Gray, who wrote the *China Syndrome*, and Robert Altman both got their start writing documentary and industrial films in Chicago.

*Script Types
and Markets*
The federal law under which operators of radio and television stations are licensed to broadcast specifies that they must operate "in the public interest, convenience, or necessity." This requirement is usually taken to mean that broadcasters, although they may devote almost all of their programming time to entertainment, must also provide a service to the community in their broadcasts. One way of satisfying this requirement is to broadcast documentaries and news specials on local, national, or international issues. Many stations produce such programs or commission outside producers to do them.

The radio documentary during the 1930s and well past the end of World War II was a special form. It was researched, scripted, and produced as a normal studio production, using actors to play the various roles. On-the-spot coverage was severely limited by the crude state of sound technology. Disc recorders— either the 16-inch transcription discs used by radio stations or the smaller ones played on home phonographs—were clumsy to use on location. Wire recording, developed toward the end of this period, could not be edited. Thus it was possible to use some natural sound in documentaries, but only with a great deal of trouble.

Recording on audiotape was a different matter. Recorders became more efficient and manageable during the late 1940s and the early 1950s so that "real life" situations could be covered directly, rather than through the traditional studio interview. Moreover, tape was easy to manipulate. Increased sophistication was now possible through editing, dubbing, and rerecording. The audio documentary at this point changed radically. It was no longer a literary affair, a statement of the writer's views on the world (as was the case with many wartime documentaries produced by Norman Corwin and Arch Oboler); it now became an edited version of tape-recorded events.

Today, audio documentaries for radio usually consist of a series of interviews, carefully edited for time and effect. Authors of documentaries are usually writer/producers. They do the preliminary research on the script, prepare a treatment for the program, edit or advise on editing the tapes, and write what is needed to tie the whole program together. Considering this, it is not surprising that most radio documentaries are staff-written and staff-produced.

There is the added possibility of syndicating audiotapes and offering them for broadcast on a variety of stations. Syndication requires at least a modest investment of time and money on the part of writer/producers. They must produce tapes, see that they are duplicated for broadcast (on cassettes or reels), offer productions for sale or lease to radio stations, and manage their distribution.

The syndication market is somewhat peculiar. There are some syndicates that handle audiotapes, but it is entirely possible for writer/producers to syndicate their own materials by offering them to a list of radio stations. No matter how this is done, stations pay very little for the broadcast rights to the individual program. The profits, of course, mount when a radio series becomes successful enough to be saleable to several hundred stations.

There are other possible markets for the audiotape; for example, some religious denominations commission the production of series on church history or doctrine, and many schools use them as teaching aids. In recent years, thousands of audio cassettes have been produced for instructional purposes, teaching everything from English vocabulary to philosophy. Several publishers, including Prentice-Hall, have a division for audiovisual learning kits. In addition, cassette recording for business is quite profitable.

Television documentaries are done by production teams that usually, though not always, include writers. Network documentaries and specials normally have high budgets and experienced production staffs. Writers may hold staff positions, or may be hired by contract to do whatever writing is necessary. Sometimes writers, as such, may not be engaged at all. Robert Banner, whose California company has produced a great number of television specials, says that the writing was minimal on a program filmed in the USSR featuring Peggy Fleming, the ice skater. The Banner production team went to Russia with no more than a list of the locales in which they hoped to shoot and of people they hoped to meet. Once permission was granted to film in a particular place, or to interview a particular person, Banner says that he and the director would rough out dialogue that seemed appropriate to the situation, and the scene would be filmed. He admits that this procedure was somewhat risky, since it was not possible to tell whether they had a show or not until the team returned to the United States and began to screen their footage.

The nonfiction productions of local television stations follow much the same pattern as we have outlined above, the differences being that the local program usually deals with topics of local interest and has a considerably smaller budget. Writers are usually hired by the producer or drawn from the station's news staff.

Educational films and videotapes all serve the purposes of education, but vary widely in length, style, and topics. An educational film designed for use in a geology class may strive to present clear, limited information about rock formations. Such a film could have a showing time of ten minutes and involve the services of three people in the writing/production process. The three would probably divide up the tasks of research, outlining, shooting, editing, and sound mix. The film itself would probably be expository, showing only samples of the rock formations in question, accompanied by a voice-over explanation.

In contrast, a more elaborate educational film might be developed around the Hopi Indians' struggle to maintain their traditional culture in the face of pressures from the white world. Such a film would be carefully planned and researched, have a fairly high shooting ratio, and call for the services of six or seven people involved in all stages of its production. The development of a suitable scenario or shooting outline would be one of the first steps.

The market for educational films is very large, and opportunities for writers are excellent. Most scripts are done on assignment by the producer or the producing company; it is possible, however, for a writer to prepare a proposal for a film or a series of films and to sell this to the producing agency. If you develop and sell such an idea, be sure to get legal advice in preparing your contract with the producer. You may receive not only a writer's fee and a producer's fee, but royalties on subsequent sales or rentals of the series.

Slide films are probably the most old-fashioned of all the new media; we can even say they are automated versions of the old magic lantern show, or the lecture illustrated with slides. A slide film typically will consist of 8-100 35mm slides projected on a screen and accompanied by a sound track. The slides are changed automatically, synchronized with the sound.

The sound track in a slide film is similar to the sound track in a motion picture; it may include narration, comments recorded in interviews, sound, music, and even dialogue. The slides are carefully edited and arranged. At its most effective, a slide film will use shots and editing patterns very much like those to be found in motion pictures.

To our knowledge, slide films are used exclusively as audiovisual aids in schools and training programs. They are best used to deal with information of a highly visual nature that can be conveyed through still photographs. A slide film on the architecture of Gothic cathedrals would be appropriate; one on the philosophy of Plato, nearly impossible to imagine.

Slide films are usually produced and distributed by the same companies that make educational motion pictures. Scripts—exceedingly important—are sometimes staff-written, sometimes done on assignment by free-lance writers. Work is normally done on assignment, but writers can sometimes develop proposals.

Market Information

Free-lance writers who wish to write for radio or television have no choice but to check the program listings of stations in their localities, to determine which, if any, produce and broadcast television documentaries and special programs. Once they have located the stations that are potential markets, they must check each one thoroughly to see if there is any possibility for local work. For example, in Chicago the *Commercial and Industrial Yellow Pages "C" Directory* has over two hundred listings of motion picture producers and production companies. Some of these companies operate out of garages and apartments, others are much larger, and a few could almost be thought of as communication factories. Even the largest of these companies, however, tend to keep permanent staff trimmed in order to reduce overhead costs. This means that these companies must subcontract for most or all of their creative needs, including writing.

In investigating production agencies, try to see as many of their films, videotapes, and so on as possible. At the very least, study their catalogues carefully. Writers for the media should become as familiar as possible with classic and current nonfiction films, tapes, and slide films. Public libraries often have their own collections of films, which can be viewed or taken home for study. Colleges and universities (and sometimes high schools) have film societies, the main purpose of which is to show films that would not ordinarily be shown at local theatres. More specialized nonfiction materials are more difficult to come by, but it is important that you watch and listen to as much of this sort of material as you can.

<table>
<tr><td>

The Writer's
Credentials
</td><td>

It is difficult to interest a producer in giving you writing assignments or taking your proposals very seriously if you can present no evidence of your writing ability. Any writer who works on assignment or contract should prepare both a portfolio and a resume. The portfolio should be put together in as attractive a fashion as possible; it should show the writer's credits and include samples of his or her work. Particularly for writers new to the media, the portfolio should give an accurate idea of what they have done professionally, even though none of the items may relate to the sort of media writing we have discussed here. The fact that you may not have had much experience in writing for the media need not be detrimental. If you have written magazine articles, newspaper stories, or a play produced by a local theatre, these accomplishments may impress a producer looking for new talent. If you have an opportunity to take writing courses in high school or college—especially those in which you write plays or film or television scripts—by all means do so. Use these courses, not only to give yourself a means of creative expression, but to learn a professional style in preparing treatments and writing scripts. Save the best of your work to use in your portfolio. It may be the means of getting you that all-important first assignment one day.
</td></tr>
</table>

When you have learned the basics of media writing, try to get some assignments writing for local radio or television stations that may pay you little or no money, but will result in production. You will in fact be well paid for such work in experience and writing credit. For instance, nearly all television and some radio stations give free air time to religious groups and public service organizations. The stations supply the director and the various technical personnel required to put the program on the air, but the group involved is usually supposed to originate and produce the program—which means, among other things, writing the script. Since such groups usually do not include anyone who knows much about radio or television production, they extend a warm welcome to a willing writer.

If you take part in such a project, the first scripts that you write will be amateurish, and the productions often less than mediocre—at least, judged by network standards. On the other hand, you will probably write a much better script than the group could get otherwise. For your own profit, you will have the invaluable experience of struggling through a production and learning from everyone's mistakes, and at the end you will have an air credit.

Canvass the local nonprofit organizations in your community, i.e., churches, synagogues, hospitals, libraries, public and private schools, environmental groups, Boy Scouts, Girl Scouts, local heart and cancer associations, the League of Women Voters, men's clubs, women's clubs, theater groups. Call them up or visit; find out what their media needs are. If they have need of your services and can pay, so much the better. If they can't afford to pay a fee and you have the time, help them anyway. In the end, the help you may provide can supply you with invaluable contacts, as well as media experience and something more to show in your portfolio.

The Uses of Agents

A writer's agent is expected to take the burden of business dealings off the writer's shoulders; the agent finds the market, sells the manuscripts, works out advantageous contracts, and understands the various laws that may affect writers. Writers without agents, especially when they have run into a stretch of bad luck, very often feel that their problems would be solved if they could only get a good agent. Even their typewriters would work better.

The usefulness of agents, however, is a variable. Some say "an agent is only as good as the last job he or she has gotten you." A successful novelist may need an agent just in order to function. The agent, in effect, stays on the ground where sales are made and contracts negotiated, so that the novelist may live in Macao or Nice or the upper peninsula of Michigan and transact business by telephone. The person who writes feature films or scripts for network television must have an agent, because producers often refuse to do business in any other way. But our advice, as far as the business of writing and selling nonfiction scripts is concerned, is *forget about agents*. Agents are useful only when they can do things for you that you could not do equally well yourself. In selling nonfiction scripts, there is very little that an agent could do for you that you could not do much better. You, the media writer, must make your own contacts with producers and be available to discuss rewrites. It is possible that an agent might be able to negotiate a large contract for you, but otherwise his or her services would be of small value. In negotiating contracts for nonfiction scripts an attorney knowledgeable in contract law can be useful.

The Author's Rights, and How to Protect Them

There are two basic facts to remember about your property rights in any manuscript that you produce. The first is that when you have written anything you own it as your personal property, just as you own clothes or furniture. All you need to establish legal ownership is proof that the manuscript is original work completed on such-and-such a date. Second, your property rights in the manuscript do not cover the idea, but the physical expression of the idea. In other words, if you write a film script about "a day in the life of a modern rancher," you cannot prevent someone else from writing a different script on the same subject, but you can prevent anyone from copying, publishing, or producing your script without your consent.

Ideas are everybody's property; the specific expression of an idea belongs to the person who creates it. Your property right in your manuscript is called a "copyright." The term comes from the English common law, and was coined long before ideas could be embodied in film or videotape. "Copyright" is, literally, the right to make and distribute copies of a manuscript. Under the law of the United States, there are two forms of copyright available to writers.

Common law copyright

The English common law, which was adopted as a basis of law in the United States, holds that authors have a property right in any work they can prove they have written. They can, therefore, prevent all others from making copies of their work and distributing them. They need not register their work in order to obtain this protection *as long as the work remains unpublished.*

One problem with common law copyright is the matter of proving authorship as of a certain date. Suppose that you have written the treatment for a film, and this treatment falls into the hands of an unscrupulous person who turns the treatment into a film script, and produces it. You see the film, and find in it enough literal uses of material in your treatment to prove that the film script must have been based on your original work. But the person who has pirated your material says quite blandly that he completed his film scenario and registered it on a certain date, and that this script was based on a treatment which he himself had prepared. You must now be able to show that you claimed authorship of the treatment as of an earlier date.

In order to provide such evidence, some writers take the precaution of sealing a new manuscript into an envelope along with a signed statement claiming authorship, and then mailing it to themselves by registered mail. The envelope is then, of course, filed away unopened.

Some writers' organizations—The Writers Guild of America (West and East) as an example—provide a service to accomplish the same end. They accept a copy of the manuscript, seal it, and file it with an affidavit by the author, affirming that the manuscript is his or her original work as of the date on which the material was registered and stamped by the Guild's registrar.

Rights to literary property, under the common law, are permanent, as long as the work in question is not published. Writers could, if they wished, will a warehouse full of unpublished manuscripts to their heirs; and in fact, some valuable manuscripts are so passed along, occasionally for generations. An unpublished Sherlock Holmes novel by Conan Doyle, a previously unknown play by Ibsen, or a secret memoir of the American Revolution by George Washington, if such works should appear, would be enormously valuable literary properties, and would undoubtedly be treated legally as if they had been completed the day before yesterday.

In general, of course, writing is valuable only when it is published or produced, and it is at this point that the common law copyright fails. Unless it is properly registered under the law dealing with statutory copyright, a published work immediately goes into the public domain, and is thereafter the property of all comers.

Statutory copyright

If you wish to retain any property in a published piece of writing you must apply for a copyright from the Bureau of Copyright, Washington, D.C. To do this, you must complete an application form, which can be obtained from the Bureau, and submit it with a copy of the work in question and a small fee. Copyright is then granted automatically, and the published work must include a notice of copyright. In the case of newspaper, magazine, or book publications, the publisher applies for the copyright. It also is possible to copyright some unpublished or produced works such as plays and film scripts, and the author normally makes the application.

The copyright laws were changed in 1978 to increase the protection of an author's work. The new law covers all material published after January 1, 1978, extending copyright protection for the author's lifetime plus a period of fifty years. In the case of multiple authorship, the fifty year term begins with the death of the last surviving author. However, all works published before January 1, 1978 are still covered by the old law, which grants protection for a term of twenty-eight years, renewable for forty-seven years, for a total period of seventy-five years. But once a work enters public domain it cannot be restored to copyright.

Divisible
copyright

The law recognizes that since a piece of writing may be used in a variety of ways copyright must be divisible, and may be disposed of or leased in parts. For example, if you write a novel, you may assign to a publisher only the right to publish it in hard cover in North America. This arrangement would permit you to make a separate agreement with a paperback publisher, a magazine, foreign publishers, film or television producers, and so on. In the case of a novel, it is obviously desirable for authors to relinquish only part of their rights to a publisher; film rights to a successful novel, for example, may be extremely valuable.

Generally speaking, where a script is written on assignment, or where a script has only one or two possible uses, divisible copyright is not especially important. A slide film or filmstrip script, for example, is not likely to be published, or to be useful in some other medium. However, if you intend to complete a large script-writing project that demands considerable research and original thought, it may be desirable to retain some rights in the material.

How Much
Protection?

Some writers, especially the relatively inexperienced ones, tend to be very nervous about safeguarding their literary property. They fear that their ideas may be stolen, or that an unscrupulous producer or editor may use their material without credit and without payment.

Undoubtedly, ideas have been stolen from writers. However, since there is no legal property right in ideas, not much can be done about this situation. Furthermore, as we have noted, almost no ideas are worth stealing. The idea itself may have little value; the execution of it is everything.

It is also true that actual manuscripts have been stolen from their authors and published or produced in slightly altered form. This practice does make somewhat more sense than stealing ideas, but not very much more. For any publisher or producer who has adequate financial support to stay in the business, it is really cheaper and easier to be honest. Moreover, in our experience, producers and editors are more likely to be scrupulously honest than otherwise, whatever their motives. Therefore, we suggest that in most situations you may submit an unpublished work of nonfiction to a producer without taking any special precautions.

The protection of fiction scripts and treatments is a different matter. For a fee of $10.00 for non-members and $4.00 for members, you can register these materials with the Writers Guild of America West, Inc., 8955 Beverly Boulevard, Los Angeles, California 90048.

Obtaining a statutory copyright is certainly neither difficult nor expensive, and the registration does give you full protection of your rights in the work, if you feel that you need such protection.

Assignments and Agreements

Writers may either submit a proposal to producers or accept an assignment from them. In either case an oral or written agreement between writer and producer is made. We now have to look briefly at the nature of these agreements.

Although the signing of a formal contract is a somewhat rare occurrence, you need to learn how to read and interpret such documents. Always study a contract carefully before signing it. If it is a complicated contract, or if you do not understand all of the provisions in it, have a lawyer read it.

Oral agreements with producers, although they are informal and sometimes rather ambiguous, commonly work out well enough. However, you need to be certain that you understand what you are agreeing to do, and when; and what the producer promises to do, and when. It is a good idea to take written notes on such agreements, or to tape record them. You cannot afford any avoidable confusion over the details of an agreement.

IN GENERAL . . .

Business precedes creativity in the sort of writing we are discussing in this book. You do not, as an established media writer, produce a script or anything else unless you are reasonably sure that it will be used and that you will be paid for your time. You must set aside time for business purposes. If you are looking for assignments, you must have regular periods set aside in which you talk to people who may have assignments to make, or who may know of opportunities that are available. If you are making proposals for scripts, you must make them regularly and see that they continue to circulate among producers who may be interested.

Where proposals are concerned, you can expect to write many more than are ever accepted. The mortality rate on ideas, suggestions, and proposals is very high. No matter how successful you are, you will always need to maintain a continuous flow of workable ideas that can be proposed to producers.

You must plan to spend time on conferences with producers and meetings with resource persons as part of your research. Writing is a solitary business, and as a side effect, many writers tend to avoid such meetings. They are, however, essential if you are doing nonfiction scripts. Whenever you attend such a meeting, take careful notes—or better still, take along your tape recorder.

As we have just noted, you must be absolutely clear about the details of any oral agreement with producers: what they want, when they need your material, what they will pay and when. Similarly, you must read contracts carefully before signing them. Ask questions if you don't understand. Consult a lawyer if the contract is a large one and you aren't sure of the details. Use agents only if they can do something for you that you can't do yourself.

Writers are usually thought to have no special talent for business dealings, and no interest in them. In a sense this may be true. Good writers are highly specialized in their interests and abilities, and their sort of specialization does not usually extend to business affairs. Occasionally you may find writers who have become valuable properties because of their names, reputation, and talent, and may consequently be able to turn their business dealings over to another, or even to neglect them seriously. Media writers can never afford either of these alternatives. You must be reconciled to the fact of spending a fair amount of time on the business side of writing.

chapter 2
The Nonfiction
Script-Forms
and Formats

Dwight MacDonald once argued, in a vigorous and entertaining essay called "The Triumph of the Fact," that Americans are compulsively drawn to facts: relevant, irrelevant, important, or trivial, they are all pablum to the national spirit. We show a reverence sometimes bordering on the absurd for news, current information, "keeping up with the world." We like to know how things work. Our fiction and drama are heavily laced with factual material. In the fall of 1978, it was even said that American television networks, having exhausted the possibilities of violence and sexuality as themes, proposed to create dramatic and entertaining shows whose chief charm would be absolute fidelity to life. One of the first of these programs was the 1978 medical documentary series, "Lifeline." It lost its life not too long after the show aired.

MacDonald's error seems to have been his belief that something in the American character prompted this hunger for specific information. An historian might more reasonably argue that the interest in observable, reportable fact has developed, and not in America alone, along with the rise of science and technology. With it in the last century and a half have come such literary and artistic movements as realism and naturalism, as well as the nonfiction forms of the new media.

THE ORIGIN AND DEVELOPMENT
OF NONFICTION FORMS

Probably the last generation in the European tradition to be little concerned with tangible facts lived and died somewhere during the late Middle Ages.

15

Fascination with the world of percepts developed during the Renaissance. Medieval painting, for example, was stylized and decorative; its themes were largely religious, dealing with the observable world in a poetic rather than a realistic way. Early painters of the Renaissance, such as Massaccio, became concerned with the representation of the true proportions of the human body. Renaissance art in general was based on science: the study of anatomy, the development of perspective, the investigation of color. This interest in realism, the factual accuracy of representation, which had not been present in the Middle Ages, goes along with the newly developing sciences, and the tendency to base literature on observation rather than myth.

In the graphic arts, this tendency seems to have reached a high point in France during the early years of the nineteenth century. A painting like Gericault's "Raft of the Medusa" was not merely a form of ultra-realism, it was journalism. Then, in the 1830s, photography appeared. It had its beginnings in DaVinci's *camera obscura*, a room-sized box camera without film. DaVinci learned that if a small hole was drilled into the wall of a darkened room which opened into a sunlit courtyard, an upside-down image of the courtyard would be projected through the small hole onto the opposite wall. In the nineteenth century Louis Daguerre and his colleague Joseph Niepce learned how to sensitize that far wall so it would retain the image. The *daguerrotype* set off a cultural explosion. It created a reproduction of visual "reality" so precise that realistic painters appeared to have been rendered obsolete. They were not, of course, for impressionist painters, among others, explored a kind of realism beyond the range of the camera.

In literature, toward the end of the last century, a school of ultra-naturalism was created, perhaps in response to the new visual truths revealed by the camera. The novel in France went from the romanticism of Dumas and Hugo to the realism of Balzac and Zola. Balzac was one of the first novelists to explain the relationship between the life of an individual and the political and social context of his times. Zola went to extraordinary lengths to document his novels, to make them reflections of the life of his day. The same interests and techniques were passed on to the American social writers of the first half of the twentieth century, among them Sinclair Lewis. Thedore Dreiser and, John Steinbeck. The theater, similarly, went from Dumas and Hugo to Ibsen, Chekhov, and Shaw.

The Documentary   When motion pictures came on the scene in the 1890s, they were devoted principally to recording reality in a way that was impossible with the still camera. They could show real people actually moving, as in life. It is difficult, in the perspective of nearly a century, to understand how the Lumiere film of workers leaving a factory could ever have been interesting to anyone; but that is because we have lost the sense of miracle at being able to preserve a fragment of life, in movement, as it occurred. The alternate function of film—the creation of magical illusions—can be seen in the work of the illusionist, Georges Melies. By combining these two functions, fantasy and reality, film took on its special quality as an artistic medium. The early emphasis on reality in film was later developed in two forms: the newsreel and the documentary.

The film documentary, from its beginnings, was a highly prestigious subgenre, perhaps because there is a tendency to assume that facts and realities are good, and fantasy and dream, at best, are frivolous. Modern, industrialized man does feel a sense of piety when he "faces facts." But it is also true that the film documentary attracted the attention of a number of brilliant and dedicated filmmakers, such as Robert Flaherty, a cinematic poet, and John Grierson. It remains extremely important in both theater and television.

About the time that the documentary and the newsreel were becoming familiar to American moviegoers, radio appeared on the national scene. As Marshall McLuhan says, the content of the new medium is an old medium. Radio proceeded to internalize motion pictures, newspapers, the vaudeville stage, and so on, and transform all this in terms of its own characteristics as a sound medium. One of the features of radio came to be its reporting of "real" events, either historical or contemporary. Thus radio developed its own style of documentary.

Radio documentaries may have been influenced by the naturalist school of novelists; the novel was the important literary form of the period in which radio appeared, and novelists set most of the influential literary styles. But the influence was probably indirect. Radio documentaries seemed to owe most of their philosophy and technique to film documentaries, which in turn were influenced by certain modern theatrical works, such as the "Living Newspapers" of the Federal Theater and the plays written and produced by the German Epic Theater.

Epic Theater was a German creation of the 1920s. It survived in Germany until the advent of the Nazis. Its two major exponents, director Erwin Piscator and playwright Bertolt Brecht, later spent some time in the United States. According to Piscator, the philosophy of the Epic Theater was "content before form, truth before illusion," a philosophy to which any documentary writer could subscribe. Epic Theatre used theatrical, film, and radio techniques (all on the stage) to present "truth"; Brecht's *Threepenny Opera* and *Fears and Terrors of the Third Reich*, and Hasek's *Good Soldier Schweik* were among their outstanding productions.

Despite the fact that Epic Theater was never very widely known to a general public, thus short-lived and not especially prosperous, its influence on the theater was great. The "Living Newspaper" of the American Federal Theater is an example. Also Pare Lorentz's two classics of the documentary form, *The River* and *The Plow That Broke the Plains*, were produced while the Federal Theater was in existence, and appeared under the same general auspices. It is reasonable to suppose that they, like the theatrical productions to which they ran parallel, were formed by similar influences.

The first radio documentary, or "actuality broadcast," was probably "Crisis in Spain," a 1931 BBC production that was based on press materials. *The March of Time* was the earliest (1931-43) successful documentary series offering weekly, dramatized summaries of the news. It ran parallel to the *Time-Life-Fortune* publications and the motion picture *March of Time*, but developed its own distinctive techniques in style, presentation, and pacing. During the 1930s it became a familiar part of American popular culture, although sometimes criticized on the grounds of too much drama and too little "actuality."

The outbreak of the Second World War made the documentary a major radio form, just as it transformed news broadcasting. Public interest in the progress of the war was overwhelming, and the broadcasters became convinced that they had an audience for factual materials presented at the level of dramatized comment, even as they had an audience at the level of plain and fancy reporting.

Up to the 1940s, radio documentary was produced like radio drama, in the studio, with professional actors. Scripts were based on fact and usually included direct quotations taken from the press. The development of portable wire and tape recorders, during and after the war years, changed that situation radically. Unlike the cumbersome and difficult disc recorders, wire and tape recorders could be handled by almost anyone, were portable, and worked satisfactorily under field conditions. With them, it became easily possible to record actual events as they occurred, and with the development of the tape recorder, to also edit and rework them into documentary form. The armed forces, during the war, used documentary teams whose duty it was to report and record landing operations and battles as they progressed. Many documentary programs, both "actuality broadcasts" and those of the dramatic comment variety, were performed during the war.

The habit of documentary radio continued after the war years. One New York station presented a series of dramatizations based on the Congressional Record and called *The Halls of Congress*. Allen Funt seized on the tape recorder and the actuality technique to produce his popular series, *The Candid Microphone*, which later was continued into television and film.

When television became a competitive medium in the late 1940s, it followed the pattern of absorbing older media forms. Television documentary began early and became exceedingly popular; the *Crusade in Europe* series, based on General Eisenhower's book, and *Victory at Sea* are examples. These early series were based on a great deal of film left over from the war. Programs were put together from selections of wartime footage, with voice-over narration and music for a sound track. Shooting new footage, at that time, was regarded as far too expensive and time-consuming a process to consider.

Eventually, of course, broadcasters came to use film as part of their routine operation, with the result that the present-day TV documentary is rather like the tape-recorded radio documentaries of the 1940s and thereafter. However, a number of interesting variations on this pattern have appeared. The highly controversial *American Family*, produced by PBS, is one. In this series, the production crew eavesdropped on the daily life of a chosen family; the programs depicted with a great appearance of candor the personalities of the family members, their emotional interrelationships, and their problems. Another variation was offered by the NBC *Project 20* broadcasts some years ago. These documentaries, produced by a special NBC team, dealt with historical topics ordinarily beyond the reach of true documentary. One of the programs, "The Real West," dealt with the history of the last decades of the American frontier. In a sense it was reminiscent of the earliest radio documentaries; the program was based on contemporary photographs and other artifacts as well as historical documents; Gary Cooper made his final public appearance as a sort of yarn-spinning witness to this phase of frontier history. The technical interest of the series lay in the fact that the producers had borrowed and elaborated an earlier film technique (often used in educational films on art history) for animating still pictures.

Examples of these and other formats may be seen on television today. Probably the most common is the news documentary, which deals with a current issue, sometimes involving investigative reporting, and is perhaps too often limited to edited segments of filmed interviews. These documentaries are common because they can be put together quickly with relative ease, and consequently they are suited both to the handling of current issues and to the budgetary limitations imposed on them. In situations where the demands of time and budget are relaxed, the documentary can be, technically speaking, much more complex and interesting. Without stretching the definition too much, we may take the documentary, in whatever medium it appears, to be a public, generally-circulated form of nonfiction.

Educational
Forms

The same media that make use of the documentary have also been used for various specialized purposes, generally educational in nature. For example, there have been educational radio stations in the United States since the early 1920s, educational television stations since the late 1940s, more recently a public television network, and a variety of closed-circuit and other special television systems. Now with the advent of cable television another door for public or educational television is opened.

Educational radio, like most early radio in the United States, came into being in a rather haphazard manner. The general enthusiasm over radio broadcasting affected academics as well as others. Engineering and technical schools saw the usefulness of having a school or college broadcasting station as a laboratory for their students. Some teachers and administrators imagined that radio might provide a more modern and efficient way of teaching. In the end, after many licenses were obtained and stations built, it was discovered that little or no thought had been devoted to the problems of who was to teach by radio, who was to benefit from the teaching, or how to go about the business. The result was, very often, that teachers went on the air and delivered their classroom lectures, which proved to be neither good radio nor very good education. Twenty-five years later, when television had replaced radio as the newest and most exciting medium, history repeated itself. Television was seen by some as technology's solution to educational problems, vast sums were spent on hardware, and much of the early educational programming consisted of old industrial or educational films, or classroom lectures. Educational radio and television have, over the years, found new ways of making useful statements. In the main, however, most of these are modeled on the documentary or the classroom teaching situation.

Another tradition, *audiovisual education*, has developed roughly parallel to the tradition of educational broadcasting. Audiovisual devices have usually been thought of as complementary to classroom teaching; traditionally they fall into the category of audiovisual aids for education. In recent years, with the appearance of teaching machines and other innovations, it has become possible to teach rather effectively in a teacherless classroom. But the effectiveness of a one-on-one relationship between teacher and student still surpasses whatever the new technology can offer. Machines are void of inflection, emotion, reward, or other spontaneous responses a human can provide.

THE NONFICTION SCRIPT: FORMS AND FORMATS

Now that we have traced the history of media forms and provided some kind of background to set our book against, we can begin examining script types and what goes into writing each of them. There are five types of script formats with which we are especially concerned in this book: the documentary, the educational or industrial film, the slide film, the teleplay, and the screenplay. This section will discuss the first three.

The documentary takes slices of life, traces history, chronicles the perils that befall all humanity; in short, this nonfiction form is a microscope that records all the blemishes and bouquets of life. We suppose that the documentary is a visual conscience of sorts. All we do, see, and think is captured in its light and shadow.

The educational film has been around for a long time and has not changed greatly over the years. Functionally, it may be used for teaching or for enrichment (as a supplement to course instruction).

Instructional or teaching television is systematic, attempting to teach a specific body of information or specific skills. Educational or enrichment television, on the other hand, is nonsystematic, designed to stimulate, to arouse interest; it tends to be a sort of high-grade intellectual/aesthetic vaudeville. Yet it also can evoke, and has, a sense of reality so powerful that it seems to put the viewer into the turomil of ongoing events. What better learning experience than to be a part of the phenomenon studied?

The instructional film will usually deal with a specific body of information, or with well-defined skills it is supposed to teach. An instructional film thus might be devoted to showing in detail an experiment in physics. The film is, in effect, a lesson, and its structure and techniques derive from classroom teaching.

The educational film, on the other hand, may be a documentary, or very like a documentary in general style. Some are done as travelogues. Some are dramas closely based on fact. A film on the life styles and problems of the American

Indian inevitably comes out as a standard documentary, written and produced in much the same way whether it is intended for television broadcast or showing in a classroom. A film on life in the early American colonies could be done in a simple dramatic form.

Industrial films tend to be heavily informational in nature, and often resemble straight instructional films. A manufacturing concern that uses highly specialized equipment to produce machine parts might commission a film to show unique features of its manufacturing process. A drug manufacturer might want a film on methods of quality control. Generally speaking, industrial sponsors are likely to be interested in films that are heavily laden with information—sometimes far too much to be easily digested by the audience.

Next there is the slide film, which has a long ancestry indeed. The magic lantern show, the travel lecture illustrated with slides, and all the other variations on this technique have been part of American culture for well over a hundred years. The idea of the slide-illustrated lecture was quite simple: the prospective lecturer obtained a series of photographic slides, arranged them in some sort of logical order, and then constructed a lecture around the pictures. Originally, of course, this method required the services of a projectionist, who would change the slides on cue from the speaker. More recently, the projectionist has been replaced by the semi-automatic slide projector, which permits the speaker to make changes with a push-button device.

The slide film is a completely automated and comparatively sophisticated version of this old form. The lecturer has now vanished into a recorded sound track, which may include music and sound effects in addition to narration and field-recorded voices. The form of the slide film script has moved away from the illustrated lecture concept in the direction of the documentary. Slides are selected and edited as motion picture film would be, with the same attention to composition and movement.

Slide films today are widely used for educational purposes. They are much less expensive to produce and use than motion pictures and are probably better suited to the presentation of many topics.

The remainder of this chapter will be devoted to the basic technical information you will need in order to write these types of nonfiction scripts: production terminology, script formats, special visual and sound techniques, and so on. The most important fact for you to remember when you are faced with the peculiarities of script format and terminology is this: a script, unlike the manuscript of a short story or a poem, has little particular value in itself. It is usually not meant to be read for pleasure or instruction. It is a chart for production and the final test of the quality of a script is in that production. When you write a script, therefore, you are talking to a director, a sound technician, a cameraperson, a lighting expert, an actor. You must phrase your communication in the forms they understand, and you must use the technical language that will allow you to accurately convey the effects you hope for. As a writer, you need not be a director or an actor, but you must understand what they do, and how they talk about what they do.

Sound Formats
and Terms

The typographical format for audio scripts is the one developed years ago for studio-produced radio broadcasts. Today, of course, technology has changed the methods of studio production considerably, but the script format remains essentially the same. What follows is the opening of a script used in a series called *The Great Ideas*. The series was based on *The Great Books of the Western World*, published by Encyclopedia Britannica. These programs were studio productions done on tape, with inserts of recorded interviews. They were originally broadcast on WMAQ Radio, Chicago, and were later syndicated on tape to various stations around the country.

THE GREAT IDEAS
Program #10: "Man and the Beasts"

READER: What a piece of work is man! How noble in reason! How infinite in faculty! In form and moving how express and admirable! In action how like an angel! In apprehension how like a god! The beauty of the world! The paragon of animals! And yet, to me, what is this quintessence of dust? Man delights not me.

MUSIC *BEHIND . . .*

ANNCR: The words you have just heard are from *Hamlet*, by William Shakespeare. This program is *THE GREAT IDEAS*, presented each week by Station WMAQ in cooperation with the Encyclopedia Britannica, publishers of *THE GREAT BOOKS OF THE WESTERN WORLD*. Tonight's great idea . . . man and the beasts!

MUSIC *CONCLUSION AND OUT.*

NARRATOR: Good evening. It is one of man's principal passions to discover what he *is* . . . what he can be called . . . what creature under heaven or above he most resembles. This passion has expressed itself in a clatter of voices . . .

MUSIC *PRETTY JAZZY, I SHOULD THINK, ESTABLISH AND BEHIND . . .*

READER: (TRY TO VARY ALL THESE VOICES: KEEP THEM ALL SOMEWHAT GROTESQUE.) Man is a political animal!

MUSIC *PUNCTUATION AND BEHIND . . .*

READER: Man is a featherless biped!

MUSIC *PUNCTUATE, AND BEHIND . . .*

READER: Man is a machine!

MUSIC *PUNCTUATE, AND AGAIN BEHIND . . .*

READER: Man is a rational animal!

MUSIC *PUNCTUATE, AND AGAIN BEHIND . . .*

READER: Man is the only animal that blushes—or needs to!

MUSIC *CONCLUSION AND OUT.*

NARRATOR: Man is . . . what? And why should man concern himself with what he is? Well, because names make so much difference to us. Please observe. If you are convinced that humanity, yourself included, is no more than animal, what model have you for your own behavior, except this . . . ?

SOUND   *THE SAVAGE SNARLING OF A GREAT BEAST.*

NARRATOR: And in that case I should prefer to avoid you. But if you suppose that man is a machine . . . in this twentieth century, a computer . . . what is your model then?

SOUND   *THE BEEP BEEP BEEP OF A COMPUTER*

NARRATOR: Well, then, if you are a machine for turning out products, or ideas, or memoranda, I shouldn't worry so much about approaching you. But I don't suppose I should invite you home to dinner either. On the other hand, if you seemed to approach Hamlet's view of man, I might feel otherwise.

READER: What a piece of work is man! How noble in reason! In action how like an angel! In apprehension how like a god! The beauty of the world! The paragon of animals!

MUSIC   *PUNCTUATION AND OUT.*

NARRATOR: Man needs, apparently, to know what he himself is: what his limitations are, what he can do, what he may aspire to. And of course, there are endless differences among the clicking of the computer, the snarl of a beast, and the voiceless song of angels.

Yet to all of these, in the Western tradition, and in the Great Books, man has been compared. Curiously enough, human beings have most often tried to discover their own identity by comparing themselves to animals, by bouncing their own consciousness off animal behavior, so to speak. It occurs to me that this is one reason why we keep animal pets, and tell animal stories, and go to zoos, for that matter. With me in the studio is ———, a man who knows a great deal about animals and human reactions to them. Tell me, Mr.——— , what do you think people learn about themselves by associating with animals?

INTERVIEW: *SEGMENT IN REPLY TO QUESTION: ABOUT ONE MINUTE.*

MUSIC   *PUNCTUATION: MAYBE SOMETHING FROM ST. SAENS' CARNIVAL OF THE ANIMALS.*

First, some simple observations about the format. Note that the names or titles of speakers go in capital letters flush left. Music and studio sound cues are set in italic capital letters. Directions to a performer are set into his speeches at the appropriate point, in parentheses and in capital letters. If any special production devices for distorting sound are used, such as filter or echo, they would similarly be set into the dialogue lines at the appropriate points, in parentheses and capital letters. The same form is used for directions dealing with perspectives, such as *fade in* and *on mike*.

In general, this script format isolates the different elements—sound, music, speech—in the production, in order to avoid confusion. Dialogue lines alone are set in capitals and lower case so that the actor will not inadvertently read a sound cue as part of a speech. When preparing your script for production you would type it double-spaced to allow room for corrections and additions. You would underline all music and sound cues which are set in italics in the example.

Where pre-taped segments are inserted into the program—the one-minute interview segment is an example—the directions are also set in caps and underlined (italic). A documentary script that makes heavy use of edited segments from interviews and other field recordings will consist largely of such directions, since the studio portion of the script may consist of nothing more than a few music cues and a little narration to tie the segments together.

Let us now look more closely at some of the elements in the script format.

First, there is the use of speech. For the moment, we shall make some simple, basic observations on this subject. (The problems of writing dialogue and narration will be dealt with in a later chapter.) The sounds of human voices are obviously the principal language of an aural medium. Human speech can express more meanings, affective or denotative, than can sound effects or music. The basic problem in writing for several voices is to keep the identities distinct. This involves finding a clear-cut role for each voice. If the script is a dramatic one, you have no great problem with roles; your voices will be named Mary, or John, or Ellen, etc., and if you are any kind of dramatic writer, each voice will have its own distinct personality and function. If the script happens to be a documentary, or a dramatized essay like the *Great Ideas* script excerpted above, the problem may be somewhat greater. If you will look back at this script, however, you will notice that there are three roles distinguished in the script: the reader, the narrator, and the announcer. The announcer's role is simple: to identify the program and to briefly explain its content. At the end of the script a similar identification will be made. The narrator is somewhat more complicated. The script is a dramatized essay on an idea, and the narrator is the essayist. The narrator's speeches explain, summarize, and in general present the rationale of the script. The reader, in this series, plays the most complex role of the three; or rather, a series of roles. One moment the reading may be a passage from the New Testament, and the next a quotation from Sigmund Freud.

The problem of keeping various identities distinct in an audio script must always be in the writer's mind. In the days of network radio it was generally thought that soap serials and family comedies were—in this sense at least—ideal radio forms, the reason being that a family naturally provides a range of almost automatically distinguishable voices. But as we have remarked, in scripts like the *Great Ideas* the problem is more difficult. The writer could, of course, select quotations so that they gave the reader the best possible chance for vocal variations, but in the long run the burden was on the reader's skill at fast voice changes.

Sound cues in the audio script refer to studio sound. Sounds that occur on field-recorded tapes, videotape, or film are referred to as *wild sound*, and are not usually mentioned in the script. Although sound effects were, in the early days of radio, done manually (crumpled cellophane created a forest fire, two coconut shells provided horses' hooves, and so on) they are now available in recorded form. Ordinarily, for the purposes of studio production, the exact cues desired will be put on tape cartridges, carefully timed and cued, so that any effect can be brought in with split-second accuracy.

Following are some basic suggestions for writing sound cues.

Be sure that your cue actually describes a sound. Writers new to the audio script will very frequently write a piece of stage business and call it a sound cue, thus:

SOUND: *JOHN SMILES AND PICKS UP THE GLASS FROM THE TABLE,*

instead of the proper way:

SOUND: *DRINKING GLASS PLACED ON TABLE*

or:

SOUND: *DRINKING GLASS SHATTERED ON FLOOR.*

Second, *sound cues must be easily identifiable in the context of a scene.* A few sounds are identifiable, in or out of context—footsteps, for example, or a gunshot. Others are fairly easy to identify once they are set in context—a harbor scene that includes the hooting of boat whistles, the lapping of water, and so on, should offer few difficulties. But a good many sounds have to be identified in words, which accounts for the old and sloppy cliché line from the days of radio melodrama: "Look out, Jack! He's got a gun! Put down that gun, Ralph!" If a little of this sort of thing is followed by a loud, cracking noise, few people will misunderstand what has happened.

A final suggestion concerning sound cues: *use them sparingly.* The purpose of a sound cue is to stimulate the listener's imagination so that he or she can visualize a place or an action.

A look back at the excerpt from the *Great Ideas* script will tell you that music is used in audio scripts for several very specific purposes: to separate scenes or other elements of the script, to suggest or reinforce the emotional content of a passage, to serve as a kind of punctuation, usually exclamatory. The use of music in auditory scripts is unique; in film, the writer rarely if ever includes music cues, since a complete musical score will be prepared and added to the sound track as one of the last stages of production.

Music adds a third language to voice and sound—often more powerful, but less capable of making specific statements. Music in the audio script is an affective language; it speaks almost entirely of feelings.

A good music cue may contain three kinds of information. First, *it should indicate where the writer wants music*—between script segments, behind a speech, and so on. Second, *it may indicate at what relative volume level the music is to be heard*, whether the cue is to be "in the clear," or to fade behind sound or speech. Third, *it may indicate the kind of music desired*. Following are some ways in which music cues may be written.

You may only want to indicate a spot you wish filled with music, or to call for some routine and obvious function of music, the specific type being immaterial or self-evident:

MUSIC: BRIDGE.

In some cases, however, you may wish to describe the mood or sensation you want the music to create in the minds of the listeners. Then you would write the direction this way:

MUSIC: AN OMINOUS STRAIN.

This sort of cue can easily be over-used. Writers, who are normally not musicians, can become intoxicated with the beauty of their own directions and demand of music more than music can reasonably give.

Technical cues (those effects which must be reproduced by the use of sound) purport to describe, in musician's terms, the effect desired. It is somewhat dangerous to write a technical cue if you do not have a knowledge of music. Also the technical cue presupposes a composer and live music available for the production.

Finally, a writer may call for a particular passage from a specific musical composition. Such cues are sometimes very useful; feelings readily evoked by the sound of a familiar theme may not be touched by a new and unfamiliar sound.

In addition to voice, sound, and music, the writer of sudio scripts has available a few special devices for distorting sounds in order to modify meanings.

First, there is the *echo chamber*, or reverberation effect. A soundproofed studio is acoustically "dead"; there is little or no reverberation in the sounds recorded in it, and the effect created is that of sounds heard in an enclosed space. Sometimes, however, the writer may wish to suggest a large, echoing environment, or may simply want to give a general effect of colossal size. In such cases the use of echo is indicated.

Originally, in radio productions, the echo chamber was a real chamber—a tunnel or room that was very live acoustically. Sounds from the studio would be piped into the chamber via speaker, then picked up on a microphone that fed into the studio control board. With this system, of course, there could be only one degree of echo. More recently, reverberation effects have been produced electronically, so it is possible to get any effect from a slight resonance to a heavy, repeated boom.

Whether the echo effect is used impressionistically or realistically, it always suggests great size—a big environment, a big, booming voice, and so on.

The *filter* is a device for eliminating certain frequencies in sound, thereby affecting their pitch and quality. Filter effects are produced electronically, and it is possible to filter out any given range of frequencies in a sound.

In general, the filter gets its effect by contrast with normal voice tones or other sounds. Filtered talk, when contrasted with ordinary speech, suggests *the unreal, the strange, the abnormal*, or—*in the case of the realistic use of the filter—the distant*. Since the filtered effect is one of contrast, the writer must be sure to provide "normal" sounds to create the effect. The extended use of filter is self-defeating; a long, filtered sequence will eventually come to sound like a case of bad recording or bad sound reproduction.

Finally, the writer may at times call for the use of the *dead booth*. The studio itself, as we have noted, has no noticeable reverberation; however, it is possible to create an environment that is completely "dead." (Originally, the *dead booth* was just that—a booth inside the studio that had been so padded as to allow no resonance at all.) Lines spoken from the *dead booth* connote a small, confined space.

These are the languages of the audio script: human speech, sounds, music. The sound-distorting devices serve to modify their meanings in some cases. The basic technique of the audio script at its best is that of suggestion. Sound is a profound stimulus to the human imagination; it is wasted when used to make direct, detailed statements. Even in the case of the modern audio documentary, which consists largely of excerpts from field recordings, the principle of suggestion holds. The voices may be "real" voices rather than those of actors; the sound may be wild sound rather than the recorded effects of the studio production. Nevertheless, the recordings must be edited, juxtaposed, interpreted by narration, and enhanced by music with the principle of suggestion always in mind.

Formats for Film and Video

There are two basic typographical formats used for film and videotape productions, and several variations on each of these. There are also two stages of the film script that should be recognized; they are usually referred to as the action-and-dialogue script and the shooting script. The shooting script is a detailed, completely worked-out statement that details the nature of a film shot-by-shot. The action-and-dialogue script represents an earlier stage in the writing and production process; it includes all spoken lines and all visual business, but is not usually worked out in complete detail.

To understand why film scripts are what they are, you must understand one or two elementary facts about film production. A motion picture is not shot continuously from beginning to end, with each scene photographed in consecutive order, first to last. The script is broken down into a series of shots, a shot being a continuous view filmed by one camera without interruption. A short educational script, for example, may contain fifty or sixty shots. Shots vary in length depending on their content as well as the feeling they are supposed to convey. Directors shoot their films one shot at a time; and they may shoot several versions of a single shot, either to get the precise effect they want or to give their film editors some selection to work with. The film may be shot from beginning to end, but it need not be. Often enough, work on shot #73 will be followed by work on shot #2, which will be followed by work on a sequence of shots from #49 to #55.

Because films are made this way, the film script in its final form must be elaborately detailed, shot by shot. Whether the writer is required to turn out the final shooting script or not depends on the situation; you must be prepared at least to come very close to the final form.

A different script format was developed for television productions. The early television shows were done live rather than on tape or film, which of course meant that they had to be done sequentially. Instead of using one camera taking one shot at a time, the television directors used anywhere from two to five cameras in the studio and got their shot patterns by cutting from one camera to another. As a result, the television script had no reason to be worked out shot by shot. The writer included dialogue, the visual business, and an occasional suggestion for camera work; the director then determined the actual sequences of shots.

The typographical format that evolved from this situation was simple; the script page was divided vertically into two columns. The left-hand column was *video* and included all the visual material, described usually in rather general terms. The right-hand column was *audio* and included the spoken lines plus any sound and music cues. The purpose behind this arrangement was to put most of the information for performers on the audio side.

Eventually, of course, the live television production gave way to videotape and film, and the script format changed accordingly. Today, whether television productions are shot on film or videotaped, the script follows the conventional full-page film format. Some television and film producers, however, still prefer the two-column format. An example follows, taken from a film on consumer education produced by Gilbert Altschul Productions. The film is called *Why Do You Buy?*

1. Open on sunrise over the city.	SFX: Alarm clock. Frank getting out of bed, yawning.
2. CUT TO: Frank, as he pulls on a 'camp' looking bathrobe.	NARRATOR: This is Frank Frontlash—he buys things.
Frank looks up as narrator introduces him—nods shyly, scratches his stomach—walks off to bathroom. Camera follows him to door. We hear water turned on . . .	SFX: Water faucet.

SWISH PAN TO:

3. Mildred, through the door of her bathroom, brushing her teeth. She is holding a tube of Close-Up toothpaste in her fist. On the sink counter between her and the camera are a large bottle of mouthwash and a large can of deodorant, plus assorted other cosmetics and toiletries.

   As narrator introduces her, Mildred looks over and smiles hello through a mouthful of toothpaste. As she bends over the sink to rinse out her mouth . . .

4. Low angle, closer in, wide lens. Mildred is bending over the sink; we see her framed by the mouthwash and deodorant; her hand, holding the Close-Up toothpaste, is plainly visible.

   Mildred is taken by surprise. She looks at camera, glances quizzically at the toothpaste in her hand, and begins to slowly straighten up, a thoughtful look on her face. Camera moves up with her . . .

5. FLUTTER CUT: about three cuts of 2, 3, and 5 frames progressively, ECU Mildred and some unidentified guy, exotically backlit, or maybe silhouetted against a sunset; their heads move slowly together as if to kiss.

   . . . by the time she is standing up straight, Mildred has a dreamy look on her face appropriate to her fantasy. She turns to camera with a coy little smile—she's not going to tell us the real reason—shrugs and says . . .

NARRATOR:
This is Mildred Maximum—she buys things too.

NARRATOR:
(Friendly, honestly interested.) Hey Mildred, why do you buy all these things—that toothpaste, for example?

MILDRED (SYNC):
I don't know . . . makes my mouth feel fresh, I guess.

FADE OUT.

   The preceding example was taken from a shooting script, the script from which the film was actually shot. Notice that each shot is carefully described and numbered; that all or nearly all of the camera angles and movements have been worked out; that even the film editor's job is anticipated to some extent (Shot #5, the "flutter cut," would be inserted within Shot #4). Earlier versions of the script might include all of the dialogue and stage business, but not sound effects, detailed descriptions of visuals, or camera directions.

   The more conventional sort of film script format includes approximately the same sort of information as the format just illustrated, but uses the full script page and separates the various production elements in a different fashion. Here is an example, from a script on retirement planning developed by the Mayor's Commission for Senior Citizens, Chicago:

  1. INTERIOR SECTION OF WORK AREA IN PLANT/DAY/CU.

   Close-up of hands that give the impression of capability and experience gently guiding saw or other machine that is out of frame.

SFX: SOUND OF MACHINE.

MUSIC: PICK UP RHYTHM OF WORK

  2. INTERIOR/PLANT/DAY/CU.

   Extreme close-up of face of one of the workers, possibly Walker or Sorenson, as he concentrates deeply and intently on his work.

SFX, MUSIC: CONTINUE.

  3. INTERIOR/PLANT/DAY/CU.

   Extreme close-up of work-piece itself, as blade or knife cuts deliberately.

NARRATOR (OS)

There is a rhythm of work which patterns all of our lives.

SFX, MUSIC: CONTINUE.

  4. INTERIOR/PLANT/DAY/CU.

   Close-up of hands expertly tracing a blueprint modification.

SFX, MUSIC: CONTINUE.

  5. INTERIOR/PLANT/DAY/CU.

   Extreme close-up as hand moves fluorescent desk work light so as to get better view of tracings—as hands move light, CAMERA PANS with light across face of one of the workers.

SFX, MUSIC: CONTINUE.

  6. MONTAGE "A"/PLANT/DAY.

   Three or four additional activities around the plant, keeping the same sense of rhythm and movement.

NARRATOR (OS)

The rhythm of work is subtle and complex. Like music, it creates a

world in which we can forget ourselves . . . a world which demands
skill and concentration. A world which gives satisfaction in return.

SFX, MUSIC: CONTINUE.

7. INTERIOR/PLANT/DAY/INSERT.

Face of plant clock, one that has large sweep second hand.

SFX, MUSIC: CONTINUE.

8. INTERIOR/PLANT/DAY/INSERT.

XCU saw blade as it cuts through wood.

SFX, MUSIC: CONTINUE.

9. INTERIOR/PLANT/DAY/INSERT.

XCU welder's torch moving along metal surface.

SFX, MUSIC: CONTINUE.

10. INTERIOR/PLANT/DAY/INSERT.

XCU clock, sweep second hand moving along.

SFX: RAUCOUS BULL-HORN SIGNALLING BREAK.

CAMERA SWISH-PAN from face of clock to horn.

NARRATOR (OS)

Occasionally the rhythm breaks . . . and underscores our dependence.

11. MONTAGE "B"/PLANT/DAY.

Three or four shots detailing the slowing down and stopping of the work;
machine guards go up on power saws; hand drops pencil and switches off
work light; welder removes safety glasses.

SFX, MUSIC: CONTINUE.

SUPER: TITLES.

It should be clear from the foregoing excerpts that there is a technical jargon
used in film and video production, which the writer must understand and use.
Unlike some kinds of jargon, the language of production does not exist in order
to conceal the mysteries of the trade from the outsider, nor does the ability to
use it confer any special prestige. The language is a pragmatic one; it describes in
economical shorthand the precise effects that should appear in the film.

Directions concerning sound, speech, and music have already been touched
on in our discussion of the audio script, but there are few general observations
to be made concerning visual directions. (A glossary of production terminology
appears at the end of this book.)

Visual directions begin with what, in the theater, would be stage business.
A welder removes his safety glasses, a man yawns and walks off toward the
bathroom, someone picks up a glass from a table. So the scriptwriter's first
task is work out the business of a scene carefully, and to describe it in much
greater detail than a playwright in the theater would. (Traditionally, on the

stage, business is blocked out in detail by the director and actors during rehearsals. But in film and television, most business is carefully preplanned and described in the script.)

The next problem the writer must consider is posed by the camera. What pictures of the stage business does the writer want to appear on screen? For example: a character may back away from another in fear, stumbling a little, his hands reaching behind him. Do we need to see this character from head to toe as he backs off, or will a close-up of his face be more effective? Or can we simply come in on a tight close-up of his hands?

Camera directions have to do with either the position or the movement of the camera. Three general positions are distinguished: the close-up, which refers roughly to a head-and-shoulders image; the medium shot, which shows about half of the body; and a long shot, which shows the full figure. There are many variations on these directions, such as an extreme or tight close-up (ECU or TCU), a medium two shot (a medium shot with two figures in the frame), or an establishing shot (a long shot used at the beginning of a scene, to visually establish the full set). Other directions refer to camera angles; a low angle shot (LAS) means that the camera is below eye level, shooting upward; a high angle shot is just the reverse.

Camera movements are either in-and-out or lateral. A shot may begin as a long shot, then move into the medium shot range, and end as a tight close-up. The camera movement may be described as a *dolly* shot (we dolly in or out), or as a *zoom* shot. The dolly movement is accomplished by actually wheeling the camera closer or back on its dolly; the zoom shot is done with a zoomar lens which, with a change of focus, can bring us from a long shot to a close-up in a flash. The lateral movement of a camera is a pan (for *panoramic*) shot. A pan is generally a rather leisurely movement, the exception being the *swish* pan, which is done so rapidly that the screen image blurs. *Tracking shots* move with the action, usually in a lateral motion.

Besides the vocabulary of camera movement, angle, and position, there is also a vocabulary used to describe transitions between shots. There are three basic terms in this vocabulary: the CUT, the DISSOLVE, and the FADE. The CUT involves an instantaneous change from one shot to the next, and is the most common way of getting from shot to shot. The FADE involves the disappearance of the screen image into black, or the reverse (FADE OUT, FADE IN). The DISSOLVE in its original form meant fading out the image of one scene and blending this with the image of the next scene as it is faded in. Today there are many different and spectacular methods of doing a dissolve. But it must be kept in mind that dissolves vary in cost depending on length. Slow tumbling dissolves run up the processing bill. Dissolves are more costly than cuts; butting two pieces of film together requires no more than a splice and some glue, whereas dissolves must be done in the laboratory.

Each of these transitional devices has a different set of meanings to which audiences have become accustomed. A CUT is ordinarily quite unobtrusive and conveys a sense of continuity within a scene. Except for shock effect, cuts are not used to bridge sequences. A DISSOLVE ordinarily suggests a change of time, setting, or action but maintains the feeling of continuity. A FADE TO BLACK is a definite and unmistakable signal that the sequence is over.

The Slide Film   As we have already noted, the slide film is a medium of its own. It consists of a series of 35mm film slides, run in sequence, and accompanied by a sound track that may include voices, sound effects, and music. The entire process is automatic; the sound track is synchronized with pictures projected on the screen. This permits the filmmaker to determine not only the sequence in which pictures are shown, but the length of time each appears on the screen. The essential difference between a slide film and a 16mm educational film is that the slide film must hold individual pictures for a certain number of seconds, whereas the 16mm film, like any motion picture, is almost completely flexible in this regard. A good slide film, nevertheless, is written, produced, and edited according to the principles of motion pictures. This opening segment of a script from the *Emergency Medical Care* series made by Encyclopedia Britannica will give an accurate idea of how the slide film, or filmstrip, works:

Leader: Flash frame, two START frames, slate frame, warning frame, six black frames.

1. Series title

EMERGENCY MEDICAL CARE
A series of Filmstrips
PARAMEDICS: THE PROFESSIONALS
CARDIOPULMONARY RESUSCITATION
WOUNDS, BLEEDING AND SHOCK
FRACTURES, SPRAINS AND DISLOCATIONS
EMERGENCIES AT HOME
EMERGENCIES OUT-OF-DOORS

2. Record Start Title

START RECORDING NOW

3. EBE Logo Title

(EBE LOGO)
An Encyclopedia Britannica Filmstrip
Encyclopedia Britannica Educational Corporation

4. Night Scene with overlay: ALL ACCI-
DENT SCENES IN THIS FILMSTRIP
ARE AUTHENTIC. PHOTOGRAPHS
WERE OBTAINED IN COOPERATION
WITH EMERGENCY CENTER IN
PASADENA, CALIFORNIA.

5. Same Night Scene:
   Ambulance
   (Repeat Fr. 4)

SFX Code 3 to 9 77T

DISPATCHER: Automobile accident at Grove and Lake.

6. Paramedics treating accident victim.

SFX

7. Same.

SFX

8. Loading woman on stretcher

VO: These men are emergency medical technicians, also known as paramedics.

9. Strapping woman on stretcher.

They are professionally trained to give emergency care and medication . . .

10. Loading in ambulance.

and to transport the sick or injured quickly and safely to a medical facility for treatment by a physician.

11. Taking stretcher into hospital.

If every community had this kind of emergency medical service, highway deaths alone could be reduced an estimated 50-75%.

12. Main Title

PARAMEDICS: THE PROFESSIONALS

13. Ambulance.

SFX: SIREN UNDER

VO: Pasadena, California, has an outstanding emergency medical service. Like police and firefighters, paramedics are available to any citizen in case of emergency.

14. Switchboard, two operators.

This central switchboard receives all calls for help and relays them to the emergency units needed.

15. Third operator at XBD.

OPERATOR: Yes, it is . . . an accident in the 800 block of Euclid . . .

VO: When a call comes in, the operator decides what kind of help is needed, locates the nearest police, fire, or medical teams, and sends them to the scene of the accident.

16. Car crashed against tree.

OPERATOR: Automobile accident at 420 Oak . . . two women and a child injured.

17. PM on radio.

270. En route. Code 3.

18. PM treating victim, police arriving.

VO: The paramedics, reaching the scene of the accident first, begin immediately to examine and treat the injured. The paramedic's first concern is that the victim's heart is beating and that she is able to breathe.

19. SAME.

He works to stop bleeding and to bandage wounds.

20. PM and second victim.

The second woman is also bandaged and prepared as quickly as possible for transportation to the hospital.

21. Policeman and second victim.

POLICE: You were approaching the intersection when you felt the car go out of control . . .

(under)

VO: While the paramedics bring the stretchers, a policeman gets information from the victim about the accident. In some cases police also control crowds and traffic.

This script format seems largely self-explanatory. It is essentially the same as the vertically-divided page format sometimes used for motion pictures, except that here numbered items are single frames rather than shots.

A careful study of the twenty-one-shot sequence shown above (the entire strip includes seventy-four shots) will indicate the procedure used in planning, writing, and producing filmstrips. A fairly detailed treatment for the film comes first to give the photographer a guide concerning the nature of the shots needed. The shooting ratio on filmstrips tends to be high, since shooting individual frames of 35mm film is comparatively inexpensive and not too time-consuming. Successful shots are arranged in a sort of rough-cut sequence, following the outlines of the treatment. From this point on, the process is one of refining the choice of shots and writing the voice portion of the audio track to fit the pictures. Eventually, of course, voices, sound, and music must be recorded and mixed to make up the complete audio track.

chapter 3
Getting the
Assignment

To the beginning writer, getting an assignment to write a film or television program may seem as improbable as breaking the bank at Monte Carlo or pitching a no-hit game to win the World Series. Actually, getting an assignment doesn't require a fairy godmother; just reasonable luck and perseverance. If you have it, past experience may help. But production companies are always looking for fresh talent and new ideas, so your chances for getting work may be as good as the experienced writer's. It helps to know people in the production business, but even that isn't essential. There aren't so many first-rate writers around that producers stop looking for new ones.

New paths to assignments occasionally open up for the beginning writer. For example, the Writers Guild of America has developed an affirmative action program for young writers interested in writing plays for network television. Persons who meet the eligibility requirements and are chosen by the production companies involved are hired to work in collaboration with consultant writers on scripts for ongoing television series.

Except for a month or so in the summer, the month of December, and perhaps a few weeks before and after income tax time, the writing season is continuous. And the ups and downs of the economy make less difference than you might suppose. Even during a period of recession, writing assignments can be found. In fact, if you write advertising and promotional material, bad times may even be good for you, because it is at such times that advertising and promotional money has to be spent to get some consumer money into circulation. And educational and instructional material seems to remain in demand regardless of the state of the economy.

Cutbacks, when they occur, usually take place in the television industry. Television is peculiarly sensitive to changes in the economy, and it responds by laying off personnel, hiring less work done by free-lancers, and relying more on the remaining staff to handle special assignments that come up. This is not the case with production companies; for them, it is less expensive to hire free-lance writers for individual assignments than to maintain a staff who may do nothing during the slow periods of the year.

This is all basic information. As a beginning writer, you will have to learn much more—by experience and by talking to experienced people—about the economic peculiarities of the profession.

In the three biggest markets (Chicago, Los Angeles, and New York), directories listing production houses are available and can be purchased through guilds, labor unions, or other media-related organizations. For example, in Chicago, the directory *Chicago Unlimited,* which lists production companies and talent, is published every year. Other professional directories exist in large cities where there is an active radio, television, and film community.

If you intend to work in television, it is best to start making professional contacts before you graduate. Sometimes you may find an assignment that calls for research and possibly some writing, and if you do it well you will be remembered. You may be offered more small assignments, and possibly full-time employment when you graduate.

A number of colleges and universities that offer courses in broadcasting and film also have arranged internships with television stations (or, in some cases, film production agencies) in their areas. These internships offer you an excellent chance to learn, to earn a modest salary in the process, and to establish contacts that may result in job offers later on.

Some production companies hire college students, usually for the summer. The best thing about this employment, aside from the learning value, is that it, too, can produce later employment possibilities.

Once you have begun to work as a writer, your best reference for more work is past performance. No matter how little your first work may pay, or how mechanical and simple the assignments are, what you write has a way of following you like a shadow. Opinions of you and your work spread quickly. Especially when you are starting out, never regard any assignment as too simple, too dull, or in any way beneath you. Remember: writers are not hired for whimsical reasons. They are hired because somebody needs to have written what they are asked to write.

You can get a writing assignment from a film production company in two ways: they call you, or you call them. In the beginning, you will have to do the calling. If you are a new writer, your first step is to find out about the production house you want to approach. You need to know what they've produced in the past, who their clients are (often this is hard to learn unless you know someone in the company), and what sort of work they do. If you can, look at some of their films that have been produced and distributed.

Usually, if you get past the front door, you will be given samples of past scripts and a screening of past films. Study these carefully.

We said earlier that television stations respond more sensitively to changes in the general economy than do film companies, whose overhead expenses are not usually so high. Nevertheless, in good times or bad, you should not neglect television stations as possible markets for your work. (The same observation applies, in a much more modest way, to radio stations.)

In any television station, there are two departments other than the news that produce documentaries and special programs: the department of programming and the public affairs department. Radio and television stations are required by federal law to justify their licenses to operate by producing a certain number of programs "in the public interest, convenience, or necessity." This usually means that a certain number of hours a week or month must be set aside for public affairs and public service programs.

Part of the required time is usually worked out in public service announcements that run from 15 to 60 seconds each. These announcements are normally produced by advertising agencies and distributed to various stations, where they are logged by the programming departments in time blocks throughout the day. Most of them do not appear in prime time. They may include messages from the National Safety Council, the United Negro College Fund, the Council of Churches, consumer groups, state employment bureaus, and so on.

Aside from these public service spots, stations regularly develop and air public affairs programs. Some of these programs are unsponsored (although sponsorship does not prevent a program from being considered a public service offering), and produced on station budgets. Sponsored or unsponsored, the budgets for these programs tend to be low, and the fees offered to free-lance writers are less than exciting. (It corresponds roughly to the price paid by a medium-circulation magazine for a short article, although the script may require a much greater investment in time and trouble.) Nevertheless, these programs can be important to the writer. They offer a more public sort of credit than educational and industrial films, for example, and they present the possibility of awards and other distinctions that can be extremely valuable to a writer's career.

Another advantage these programs offer to the writer is the nature of the assignments. *Specials* often deal with cultural events of significance. Documentaries tend to examine social problems and injustices, unfortunately abundant in our society. Street crimes increase. Rape ceases to be a taboo topic and becomes an issue for public discussion and action. Senior citizens, especially in difficult economic periods, are disregarded and forced into miserable poverty. Complicated socioeconomic problems that need a public forum, grievances, arbitrations—all these subjects and more can be treated, at least modestly, in documentaries. The research and writing demanded by these programs is a fascinating and valuable experience.

Assuming that you have made contact with all the commercial and public television stations in your area and have left samples of your work (or otherwise convinced someone on a station staff that you are serious and capable), there is a reasonable chance that you will be called upon to work as a writer on a production scheduled for broadcast. Whether the assignment is given by the programming department or the public affairs department, you will be introduced to a producer with whom you will work. He or she will take direction from an executive producer or the director of programming or public affairs. The producer is often the director of the film or videotape presentation as well. You will probably work on one of four kinds of productions: first, a production shot, edited and mixed on film; one shot on 16mm or 35mm film, edited from the original instead of a work print, and then mixed on videotape; third, a videotaped production shot on location and sent back by minicam (a portable videotape unit which both records and transmits back to the studio a live picture); finally, a studio-produced show, recorded in the studio, using some graphics and possibly some film integrated within the body of the script.

You must know what sort of approach the producer has in mind; the nature and degree of development of your script will depend on that factor. Your chance to gain this information will be in one or more story conferences with the producer, depending on the length and complexity of the project. There you will be given all or most of the information that has already been collected on the topic. You will also be told (if you are not, ask!) where you may find more information, what the budget is, who will be the narrator of the film (if one has already been picked), the point of view of the program, the style in terms of dialogue and narration, any locations you must scout, what people you will need to interview, and what television or radio station facilities, if any, will be at your disposal during the period you will be under contract.

We will repeat later on, in the chapter on preparation of treatments, that it's always best in these first meetings to take good notes. It doesn't hurt to have a tape recorder backing you up in case you miss taking down an important point.

You must ask questions. *You must be satisfied, before you finish with these preliminary story conferences, that you know everything the producer can tell you—information, ideas, sources. On such ambiguous and yet important issues as point of view, style of the script, and the general feeling the film should convey, it is often useful to try to state the producer's ideas and feelings back to him or her, until he or she can accept your statement as accurate.*

The next stage in your dealings with the producer will normally involve the preparation of a treatment. This may require one or more drafts. Sometimes successive drafts represent progressive elaborations of the script. *You begin with a very short summary of what the film may be like, then add detail until you have a five- or ten-page document that may describe the production almost shot-for-shot. Or your first treatment may be fully developed, read by the producer and the client, and then revised accordingly.*

If you've taken correct notes during the original story conferences, asked the right questions, and done your research thoroughly, you should get approval on the second or third draft of your treatment. Producers normally find something wrong with the first draft; this may simply be a ritual part of the producer's craft or it may be a necessary procedure to clarify minor misunderstandings between producer and writer. At any rate, you should expect to do two and possibly three drafts of the treatment; more revision than this indicates that either you or the producer must be at fault.

The producer does have final say on what is written. (This is why so many writers try to become writer-producers; they gain control over their own material in the process.) However, in a really good working relationship between writer and producer there is more collaboration and less giving and receiving of orders. The writer is free to suggest approaches to the film not discussed in preliminary conferences. The producer is free to pick up and improvise on the writer's ideas. Together they may develop a more exciting approach, a better line, a more effective scene, than either could have worked out alone.

If the producer and writer have confidence in each other, if each feels secure in his or her own talent and skill, then the two can work together rather than playing the game of one-upmanship. If neither the writer nor the producer feels secure in his or her own identity and professional skill, then each will probably see the other as a threat. The only tactic in this situation is to assure the person you are working with that you are interested only in doing the best possible job, and that you don't care who contributes what as long as the production turns out well.

Actually, a competent producer will always want the writer to excel. Supposedly knowledgeable people often talk about film or television as a "director's medium" or a "producer's medium." It is quite true that directors and producers are exceedingly important to the media, and that they get a lion's share of the credit when a production is a success. *But without a first-rate script, the finest production in the world is nothing but pointless ornamentation.* Good producers know this, and know that they must find good scripts. *The writer holds the key to successful production, especially if the film is to be fully scripted.*

From a purely selfish point of view it is always better to write a fully developed shooting script, since this means that you will have somewhat more control over the final product. (Even experienced writers become angry and discouraged when they see their scripts edited, cut, tinkered with; being human, they naturally feel that the original version of the script—*their* version—would have made a brilliant film, and that the actual shooting script could only produce a visual monstrosity. Sometimes they are right, sometimes wrong; but most writers want all the creative control they can get.) Whether or not you get to write a full shooting script, of course, depends on a number of factors. Some films require that all the scenes and even the camera angles are written in the script before the shooting begins. Other films demand a shooting outline, listing scenes to be shot and the motivation behind each scene. Still other films call for a loose shooting script, giving the director and cinematographer great latitude. The subject, budget, location, availability of people, and other resources will determine just how firmly a script needs to be set before principal photography begins. These decisions will usually be determined by the producer, or in consultation with a senior or executive producer.

Sometimes television or radio station policy will dictate the content of a script. The taking of public editorial positions on issues of community importance has been much debated. For many years the Federal Communication Commission would not allow radio and television stations to broadcast editorials; they were presumed to have no policy whatever. In comparatively recent years, the responsibilities of broadcasters have been turned in the other direction; a station that did not broadcast editorials would be somewhat suspect. This fact complicates the scriptwriter's job. A station might, for example, take a public stand on the desirability of a regional public transportation system. Let us suppose the station argues that a regional transportation authority is necessary to keep public mass transit from financial collapse. At the same time this position is stated, the station has begun producing a documentary that supposes to look objectively at the subject, whether a regional transportation authority representing various counties within a certain geographical area is necessary or desirable, and so on.

Just how objective can the documentary be if the station has already taken an editorial stance? The management will, of course, claim that the station can still be objective and, in fact, will take special pains to allow hearing both sides. A cynic might argue differently to the same conclusion by claiming that many broadcasting stations take editorial positions because they are supposed to take editorial positions; that management commitment to most such positions is less than passionate. Perhaps either of these arguments might be true; perhaps not. In any event, sometimes you are caught in a dilemma in which you are divided between your own observations and values on the one hand, and what you are required to write on the other.

At what point, if ever, should the writer tell the producer: "Sorry, I can't write this. I don't believe it." Our feeling is that taking the position of "either I write it my way, or not at all" should be avoided in nearly every case. To begin with, it is ridiculous to suppose that a writer has a well-considered intellectual/moral position on every conceivable topic that must be defended to the death. Most writing assignments will not run counter to your values, challenge your beliefs, nor upset the even tenor of your ways. What you are likely to discover, when you begin research on a controversial topic (always supposing that you take the position of a researcher and not a partisan), is that there are many ways of looking at the issue, many arguments that seem reasonable, many patterns in which facts might reasonably and honestly be presented. The station's bias—if indeed it has one—may be to all appearances as good as any other.

We are not arguing that the writer should be a pliable hack, willing to sell personal values and professional integrity to the first comer. We simply believe that you should reserve your indignation and courage for situations where your integrity really is in question. These are not many, but when they arrive they must be faced. Courage and anger are valuable commodities—too valuable to be wasted in situations where they are not needed.

Once these preliminaries are over, you begin serious work on the treatment. Most assignments from television stations will allow you little time for anything but getting the script done. Two months from the beginning of a treatment to the actual airing of the program is a generous schedule. Public broadcasting stations seem to enjoy the luxury of taking more time than commercial stations. But time alone doesn't solve production or writing problems; spending more time usually means spending more money, and money is often in short supply. But whether the documentary is produced by a PBS station or a commercial one, you will be surprised at how much can be done with a low budget and not enough time.

Once you have received the assignment and met with the producer for a story conference, you'll be given a deadline to finish the treatment. If the program is to be aired six weeks after the initial story conference, you'll have a week and a half (two weeks at most) for the treatment, and two weeks for the script (which doesn't leave much time for shooting, editing, and mixing before the air date). Deadline dates are usually worked out by back-timing the entire production in this manner: one week to shoot (five full working days); two weeks to edit; two days to mix. This of course leaves slightly less than three weeks for treatment and script. Each production varies, but the producer should be able to give you a reasonable production schedule.

This allotment of time says nothing about inevitable problems of research and writing. The treatment, as we have remarked, will probably go through more than one draft. Scripts, too, require rewriting, and whether you cut and paste or rewrite or both, the process takes time. At the outset of a production, the only person who has all these schedules and possible delays in mind is the producer, who may in consequence give you what you think an unreasonably short period in which to do your work. And you may be quite right. If so, never wait until the last moment to break the bad news to the producer; you should know after three or four days of research whether the deadlines given you are realistic or not. If they are not, say so. Adjustments in schedule can usually be made. But if the producer is locked into an air date, this may automatically make all time problems insoluble, and you will have to do the best you can with the time you have.

Once the first script is completed, the producer will take anywhere from one to four days to read it, note revisions, and then discuss the script with you page by page, describing the changes that he or she wants. *There can be a vast amount of exasperation in the process for the writer, simply because the producer expects the script to grow through revision. You may suppose that a certain change represents what the producer wants in the final version, whereas it may simply be something he or she wants to try. Sometimes you'll be asked to write in a scene—only to be told, after you have written it, that it isn't necessary after all.* Very often while you are polishing a script, lines or scenes that were suggested to you for one rewrite will be cut in the next. Lines taken out of earlier drafts may wind up being put back in.

If you are to maintain your sanity and keep your job, you must believe that this process is necessary. You are not a professional writer until you have learned to rewrite. If you were not only the writer but also the producer of the program, you would certainly rework the first draft of your script—and the second, and the third, if you had time. You would experiment with different effects and discard scenes and lines that didn't work. The writer-producer is one person, so he or she can usually do a job of revision without tears. But it isn't so easy when the writer and the producer are two people, and the producer seems to get all the ideas while the writer does all the work. Working on rewrite with a producer becomes a pleasure when you understand and respect each other, and are both willing to listen.

Unless the film allows for a good deal of pre-production time, your story conferences will probably be entirely with the producer. Where production time is longer, you may also work with the director, and in that case, any questions you have concerning the workability of a particular scene, or the possibility of special visual or sound effects, or anything else within the director's sphere, can be discussed before you write. This saves time, money, and mistakes.

When the documentary is sponsored by an advertiser, you may also have to deal with a representative of the firm and the advertising agency that handles the account. This is not a prospect that lightens the heart of the writer—or the director, or anyone else on the production team. Creating by committee is not the best possible way to write or produce, especially when the committee is internally divided. It is comparatively easy for a writer to work with a production team; the people normally understand each other and have a common goal. When a member of the sponsor's firm comes into the picture, or a team from the advertising agency that represents the sponsor, the situation may become complicated. The sponsor may, very properly, have strong feelings about what he or she wants from the production, without having much experience in the production process. Agency people represent the client and must protect what they take to be the client's interests; this position may or may not favor the production of a good film.

The free-lance writer, in this situation, is an outsider, and consequently must learn to walk softly. As a writer you get your instructions from the producer, not the agency or the sponsor. The producer, however, must deal with the advertising agency and/or sponsor, and if that relationship is not especially good you may find yourself dealing with abrupt and radical changes in the directives concerning the script.

In saying this we do not mean to suggest that every intervention by a sponsor or its representatives is capricious or harmful to the production. In the production of industrial films, for example, the sponsor company, either through its own advertising director or an advertising agency, must have a part in the writing and production of a film. Many industrial films deal with complex technical processes used in producing the company product and are intended to be seen by persons with a great deal of technical expertise. For instance, one such film—made for The Energy Products Group, which manufactures such items as locomotive tires, impellor blades for the 747 jet, and the coolant vessels for the Apollo spacecraft—included this narrative passage:

> In fact, our business has moved us to develop our own brew of alloy steel. We have our 1104.91, 908 and 918. The 908 is the billet material,

the 918 is a plate material. This is a material capable of Y52 and Y60 strength levels with good impact strength. We can apply it to all gas and oil transmission service.

A company that has this to say and is paying for the film in which to say it, certainly has the right to control the content and language of the script. In fact, if they do not, the film could never be made.

Even when a nonfiction industrial film has an institutional message and does not convey company or product information, it still is a statement by the sponsoring client and must do credit to its sponsor. Again, most clients want their visual messages to be consistent with the rest of their promotional material; they may well object to an approach or style in a film that is totally different from everything else they say to the world. There is also the possibility that a change in marketing or product positioning will mean changes all down the line in the company's advertising and promotional materials: logos, signatures, trademarks, styles in radio and television commercials, theme lines (e.g., ". . . a piece of the Rock"), letterheads, and so on. Your film will not be exempt from such change.

In short, a scriptwriter is supposed to be able to take in a range of information, ideas, and attitudes from various sources (not always in apparent agreement) and shape all of this into a unified, intelligible statement that all the the interested parties can accept—and which also will be the basis for a good film. Script writing assignments, fortunately, vary in complexity. At best, you will deal with one or two people who are pretty much in agreement as to what they want, in what form, and when. At worst, you may find yourself reeling from one conference to another, trying to assimilate the last suggestion, which came from a face you had never seen before and might never see again.

The usual staff complement on a documentary made for television is:

Programming or Public Affairs Department

Department Head
Executive Producer
Producer
Writer
Director
Assistant to the Producer
Cameraperson
Assistant Cameraperson
Lighting Director (on projects requiring special lighting effects or interior shots that cannot be handled by simple floods on or near the camera)
Sound
Editor
Sound Mix
Conformer
Technical Director

The staff would be similar if the documentary were produced by the news department, and the parts in this roster are sometimes interchangeable. For example, there may be no executive producer, that title being allotted to the director of programming or public affairs (or the producer may be the person in charge). The producer may also, in some cases, be the director and/or the writer. It is more common for a free-lance writer/producer/director to do an industrial or educational film than it is for such a person to be hired to produce a television documentary. Television stations usually have writer/producer/directors on their staff to handle productions where the budget does not allow for the services of three people. If the television documentary is sponsored, the client may be represented by an advertising director, a creative director, or an account executive, who may be involved in the story conferences, the filming, and possibly even the editing of the program.

Your attitude toward all of these people should be one of cooperation. Productions of the sort we have been discussing are almost always cooperative ventures. Unlike painting, poetry, or musical composition, they are not the end result of a single creative talent. As a writer you must constantly consider how you can use your talent and experience to make a maximum contribution to the joint effort. This is by no means an easy task, but it is a very necessary one.

chapter 4
Before the Script Is
Written: Research

In this chapter we will examine the process of research and writing that produces a story treatment. We shall discuss the process in terms of a documentary script for television or film because the documentary poses more complex problems to the writer than any of the other script types in which we are interested. What we say here will apply in a simpler fashion to filmstrips, audiotapes, and dramatic production. If you have not written for film or television, you may not be familiar with the term, *treatment,* and if your experience is minimal, you may not understand why a treatment should be written.

In the first place, any nonfiction script that uses actuality materials—film footage, still photographs, sound recordings—will only be written in its final form after these materials are gathered and organized into a workable sequence. It is simply not possible for a scriptwriter to anticipate actuality. In the second place, combining actuality materials and scripted materials takes a good deal of meticulous planning, which can best be expressed in a treatment. Even where a nonfiction script is intended for studio production, it must be carefully planned and outlined before it is written. Inspiration may create a gripping dramatic scene but if the purpose of the script is to convey information or persuade, the effects must be calculated.

What is a *treatment*? Actually, the term covers several kinds of documents. A treatment is always a more or less detailed statement on the subject of what the completed script will be like. Some treatments are quite short—perhaps a half-page summary of the ideas and materials to be included in a script, arranged in working order. More often, a treatment is likely to be lengthy and detailed; it will take the reader step by step through the production, describing the pictures or sounds to be used, summarizing the ideas, sometimes even roughing out the narrative and dialogue lines. Treatments are intended (a) to give producers and directors a clear idea of the script, and (b) to serve the writer as a detailed guide or outline when he or she comes to the task of writing the script itself. This applies to fiction treatments as well.

A treatment has special value for a writer. If it is properly and conscientiously worked out, it will include the solutions to practically all of the writing problems you may encounter in actually producing the script. With a treatment, you need never be caught in the terrifying situation of having promised to write a script in a certain way, and suddenly realizing that you simply cannot deliver what you have promised. Treatments, at least in a limited way, are great preventatives of writer's block.

Let us look at an example of the relationship of a treatment to a production script. Some years ago, the National Broadcasting Company agreed, from its Chicago outlet, to do a half-hour color broadcast devoted to a unique exhibit of the works of Paul Gauguin which was then scheduled for showing at the Chicago Art Institute. A writer was engaged to provide a script for the program, and a director was assigned to the project. The director, writer, and executive producer of the program met with representatives of the Art Institute to discuss the nature of the exhibit, and how it might be effectively presented on television.

The broadcast was not to be put on tape or film, but to be done live on the air—a condition that imposed some limitations on the script. For example, certain techniques for "animating" paintings might be quite possible to do on film, and yet be dangerously complicated to attempt on the air. Also, a live broadcast meant that everything had to be done from the NBC studios, and some of the Gauguin works were too valuable to be transported to the studios and set up there. Eventually, however, it proved possible to use some of the original works and some color slides and reproductions for purposes of the broadcast.

It was also decided to approach the Gauguin works through a dramatization of the life of the painter. This was by no means an original idea—the life of Gauguin had provided the basis for Somerset Maugham's well-known novel, *The Moon and Sixpence,* and had otherwise been extensively written about. On the other hand, the story of the middle-aged stockbroker who suddenly abandoned his wife and family to become one of the great modern painters, (eventually to die miserably in the South Pacific) was certainly a dramatic one, and also a convenient and natural framework within which to present the Gauguin paintings and woodcarvings. In addition, the biographical material on Gauguin is unusually rich; his letters and journals survive, as well as many other first-hand accounts of his life.

The writer and the director decided that the visuals in the program would be primarily Gauguin's works. Although actors might do character lines *voice over,* there would be no scenes in which they appeared on screen in the roles of Gauguin, his wife, his friends, and so on.

Research for the script was entirely library research, in which both the director and the writer became involved. Then the treatment was written. In this case, the treatment began in very rough form, as notes on reading, but eventually it was worked out in part as follows:

SO MUCH LIGHT, SO MUCH MYSTERY

(The title is Degas' remark, after seeing some of Gauguin's early works.)

We open on a studio reconstruction of the office of Paul Gauguin in Paris; the cubicle, the desk, the photos of his wife Mette and the children, a Cezanne on the wall, a sign which reads: *Paul Gauguin,* Liquidator. The narrator summarizes his career up to 1883, when he left business to become a painter.

We go from this to the interior of the Marquesas shack in which Gauguin died. Narrator summarizes the end of his life, builds up to the title: *So Much Light, So Much Mystery*!

Go to credits and introduce, *voice over,* Alan McNab of the Art Institute. McNab talks briefly about the exhibit, the fascination of Gauguin's work, the curious drama of his life.

Back to the story of Gauguin when he first began painting seriously. He copies Pissarro, he copies Monet's *Olympia.* This sequence takes us to his painting of the *Study of a Nude,* his first remarkable work. Reactions of other painters, comments of critics on this work. It is his first true success, and probably the work which made him decide to devote his entire life to painting.

In the decision sequence, we use the visual contrast between the *Study of a Nude* and the rather chilly, beautiful bust of his wife, Mette.

This treatment served two purposes. It gave the director a detailed idea of what the script would look like and so permitted specific suggestions for revision. It also gave the writer a comprehensive, detailed outline from which the script itself could be drafted with a minimum of difficulty.

Some of the pages of the script that were developed from this segment of the treatment finally read as follows:

SO MUCH LIGHT, SO MUCH MYSTERY

OPEN ON INTERIOR CUBICLE

CAMERA EXAMINES OBJECTS AS THEY ARE NAMED

PHOTO OF METTE AND CHILDREN

NARRATOR:
This is the office of a French stockbroker in the 1870s. His desk . . . his chair . . . his portfolio . . . his inkwell.

He was a daring and successful speculator, an employee of the firm of Bertin et Cie., a coming man in the business world.

He had married a lovely Danish girl, Mette-

SLOW DISSOLVE TO SIGNATURE ON A
GAUGUIN PAINTING. PULL BACK
QUICKLY TO REVEAL THE INTERIOR
OF GAUGUIN'S MARQUESAS SHACK.
WE LOOK PAST THE PAINTING, WHOSE
SIGNATURE WE HAVE JUST SEEN,
PAST AN EASEL WITH A CANVAS ON
IT, TO A BUNK ON WHICH THE DEAD
GAUGUIN LIES. NOTHING OF HIM IS
VISIBLE EXCEPT AN ARM AND HAND,
HANGING OVER THE EDGE OF THE
BUNK. BENEATH THE OUTSTRETCHED
FINGERS, ON THE FLOOR, IS A
PAINTBRUSH

DISSOLVE TO THE SELF-PORTRAIT TO
BACK CREDITS.

Sophie Gad, and was the father of five fine
children.

Paul Gauguin, painter.

He died in the Marquesas Islands, in May,
1903. Alone, riddled and tortured with disease,
dead of the years of starvation and suffering
and disappointment.

Dead of a hundred paintings, a thousand
sketches, ten thousand bright, strange visions.

The words of the painter Degas might alone
serve as his epitaph, Degas who once said, after
seeing some of Gauguin's paintings, "So much
light! So much mystery"!

MUSIC: CREDITS CUE.
CREDITS. NB: AUDIO CREDITS END WITH
INTRODUCTION OF MR. MCNAB.
MCNAB:
Today the Art Institute of Chicago opens the
Gauguin Exhibit, which I am proud to say is
the largest collection of works by Paul Gauguin
ever assembled.

(*portion omitted*)

First, let us look at the life and works of Paul
Gauguin.

SLOW PAN FROM MCNAB TO A LARGE
DRAWING PAD ON AN EASEL: COME
IN CLOSE ON THE PAD. A HAND
APPEARS IN THE FRAME, BEGINS TO
SKETCH—BUT SLOWLY, WITH SOME
UNCERTAINTY.

NARRATOR:
He was a Sunday painter, an amateur.
But persistent.
He sketched, studied, pondered, sketched
again.
He met Camille Pissarro, the "father of impres-
sionism," listened, watched, studied his work.
He met Monet, whose painting *Olympia* he
much admired.
Again he studied, analyzed, sketched.
When Monet saw one of Gauguin's canvases, he
commented,

SLIDE OF A PISSARRO PAINTING.
BACK TO THE SKETCHING HAND, NOW
IN AN EFFORT TO COPY PISSARRO.
SLIDE OF *OLYMPIA*
THE SKETCHING HAND: A STUDY OF
OLYMPIA

THE HAND DETACHES THE *OLYMPIA*
STUDY FROM THE PAD, LETS IT FALL.
BEGINS AGAIN, WITH HESITATION, A
SKETCH OF A LANDSCAPE.

THE HAND DETACHES THE SKETCH,
CRUMPLES IT, THROWS IT ANGRILY
TO THE FLOOR.

ABRUPT CUT TO FULL SHOT OF
STUDY OF A NUDE.

DISSOLVE TO SLIDES OF ACADEMIC
NUDES OF THE 80s.

BACK TO *STUDY OF A NUDE*

WE MOVE SLOWLY IN TO THE PAINT-
ING, THEN DISSOLVE TO A TIGHT
CLOSE-UP OF THE GIRL'S HEAD.

DISSOLVE TO PHOTO OF THE BUST
OF METTE.

MONET:
Very good!

NARRATOR:
Gauguin protested . . .

GAUGUIN:
Ah, Monsieur Monet, I'm only an amateur.

NARRATOR:
But Monet replied . . .

MONET:
No. The only amateurs are those who make bad
pictures.

NARRATOR:
Still, when Gauguin exhibited his work in 1880,
no one thought it very original or interesting.

The critic Huysmans summed it all up . . .

HUYSMANS:
Monsieur Gauguin is a Sunday painter. A Sunday painter he will remain.

NARRATOR:
The study of a nude!

Gauguin painted it in 1881, using his children's nurse, Justine, as a model.

It is, as you see, a work of great realism, of
visual truth.

It is not the great Gauguin.

Not the savage, not a work of light and
mystery.

But compared to the conventional paintings
of the day . . .

A great picture . . .

And this time Huysmans wrote . . .

HUYSMANS:
I do not hesitate to affirm that among contemporary painters who have worked at the
nude no one has so far struck such a relevant
note of reality. Here is no show, this is a girl of
our own day and one who doesn't pose for the
gallery, who is neither lascivious nor simpering,
who occupies herself usefully by mending her
clothes.

(FADE AUDIO) Up to now Rembrandt alone
has painted the nude.

QUICK CUT TO THE NUDE.

DISSOLVE BACK TO THE BUST.

SLOW DISSOLVE BACK TO THE BUST

NARRATOR:
This is the wife of Paul Gauguin.
A beautiful woman, a Danish woman, a respectable woman.
A woman who despised her husband's painting, and all that it implied.
A woman to whom Gauguin later wrote, in mingled love and exasperation . . .

GAUGUIN:
My poor Mette . . . if only we despised each other!

NARRATOR:
This was the decision . . .
The love which he had for Mette, for his children, then and to the end of his life . . .
Against the drive, the hunger, the compulsion to create beauty where beauty had not been before.

GAUGUIN:
I have resigned from Bertin's. I am going to be a painter. Now . . . I will paint all the time!

BEFORE RESEARCH BEGINS

The first step in writing a script is like the first step in the old recipe for making rabbit stew: first, you catch your assignment. When you discuss the assignment with the producer and/or director, as we have already noted, you will do well to take careful notes on what they say, or to tape the session if you can. You should assume that what you are told about the assignment is *probably* true. Sometimes you will be told quite definitely what is wanted. At other times, especially if the producer has a client who must be pleased by the film, what you are told is more brainstorming than instruction. Very often a producer may understand clearly the general purpose of the film you are to write, along with such matters as length and budget limitations, and yet be quite hazy about details. One writer recently had the experience of discussing a projected film with two members of a production agency, both of whom had been present at a meeting with the client, and each of whom had a different version of what the client wanted.

This sort of vagueness must be taken as one of the hazards of the writing profession. As a rule, it does not present an unsurmountable obstacle to writing a good script. The writer must keep careful account of what is said in the initial meetings, and refer to these notes frequently. Ambiguities of this kind will ordinarily be dissolved as you begin to do your research.

Second, having learned the general conditions and limitations to be imposed on the script, you decide on an approach to the material. Writers may do this on their own, or they may confer with their producers or directors. For example, in the case of the Gauguin special, described above, the director and the writer decided together on how they would approach the problem of showing off the painter's works to the best advantage. Their decision was to present a brief biographical account of Gauguin's adult life, dramatized but using as far as possible actual passages from his letters, journals, and so on. They further decided to use professional actors to speak the lines, but to show only the paintings and carvings of the exhibit as visuals.

Working out an approach to the script does not necessarily involve stating a theme, or even working out in detail the sequence of scenes. It simply narrows down the writer's concerns. It provides, if successful, an interesting and workable pattern that takes into account the available materials, the limitations of budget, time, and equipment, and the nature of the audience.

For example, a film on industrial safety intended to be shown to industrial plant workers with the purpose of increasing their awareness of the dangers of carelessness on the job was to run about 15 minutes. The producer's idea was to do a dramatic, scripted film that could be researched and written within about a month and could be shot, on one or two sets, within a day. The topic of the film was to be the rehabilitation of victims of industrial accidents. Research was to be done by interview at the Rehabilitation Institute of Chicago.

A refinement of the general purpose of the film might be stated in this way: one reason that workers become careless about safety precautions on the job is that they, along with most other people, have no real conception of what the aftermath of a serious accident can be. Thus, the focus on the process of rehabilitation, which is often very long, painful, and uncertain.

The rehabilitation process could not, in a short film, be covered with any pretense of completeness; one dramatically-workable part of it had to be selected. Also, rehabilitation can be looked at from the points of view of many people: the victim of the accident, members of the family, medical and other specialists in rehabilitation, and so on. For a number of reasons, the family viewpoint was the one settled on. As for the actual time of the episode, it seemed likely that the best choice would be a period early in the rehabilitation process, when the victim of the accident was no longer under intensive hospital care, and he and his family had begun to realize the nature of their future lives together.

In preliminary interviewing, one young man who had been tragically mutilated remarked that he had gotten leave from the hospital in December in order to spend a few days with his family. This was the first time that he had visited his home since his accident. Such an episode seemed to fit with the various conditions imposed on the film at this point. The writer had what appeared a workable approach to the script.

When you have settled on an approach to the script, it is often useful to prepare a tentative outline of the script, or to write a statement about it. The operational work here is *tentative,* for at this point your knowledge of the subject is probably very scrappy. However, if you have some previous knowledge of the topic, or if you have conducted some preliminary research, you may be able to write a valuable statement. In a sense such a statement implies the attitude, "I'm being creative now—creatively ignorant," but that attitude may not be as silly as it seems. Too many facts sometimes hide the patterns.

What you write will be, in whole or part, an idealized version of the finished production. The ideal may be totally destroyed by the facts when you get them; but on the other hand, some or all of it may survive in the final version of your script. You write at this stage because it is the one point at which you can dream and create, unhampered by too much information or too keen an awareness of the limitations of your project.

RESEARCHING THE SCRIPT

And now, at last, you begin your systematic research. Begin with a bibliographical search if you have reason to believe that there is useful material in print on your subject. It is a good rule of thumb that reading precedes talking or looking on your own. Any professional interviewer can tell you that when interviewing you do your homework first. See what's in print. Reading can prevent you from asking questions that are already answered, and it can equip you to understand the importance of what you hear and see.

We will not here attempt to give you a full course in print research. You probably know a good deal about it already; and if you don't, a few hours spent in a good library will give you the basics. We will, however, offer a few specific suggestions we have found useful.

No one ever knows enough about library and other print sources. Make a hobby of studying reference books of all kinds, from collections of *Famous Firsts* and *Where Are They Now*?" books to encyclopedias. Find out what special bibliographies are available in your library, and what areas they cover. There are several journals published for scholars that print abstracts of articles and books. Your library may have a clipping file. It probably has a collection of sound recordings and films. Build your own reference files as you accumulate useful information; if you write one successful script on art history, mental health, or manufacturing optical instruments, you are very likely to be asked to write others.

If you start to research a new topic and find that there is an enormous amount of information available in print, don't try to read it all carefully or systematically. In this situation you're going to have to consult an expert who presumably *has* read it all, or at least the significant parts of it. Instead, get together a shelf of books, journals, and pamphlets and spend an afternoon in random reading. Leaf through your books and journals and read whatever strikes you as both interesting and pertinent to your topic. Two or three hours of this sort of study will begin to give you a sense of what the topic is all about. If it gives you the wrong sense, you can correct the impression later; right now, you need to make a beginning.

Learn to scan the written page; there are occasions when scanning can be valuable. It can give you the essence of a page in the length of time it would take a meticulous reader to construe one sentence.

Photocopy the potentially useful material as you go. As far as most library researchers are concerned, the copying machine was an invention of angels. It can reduce your note-taking time to almost nothing and leave you with a sheaf of essential information you can go through at your leisure.

With at least a fragmented background of information gained from reading, you can hope to make intelligent use of resource persons. A film producer who sets out to make an educational or factual film will usually make an arrangement to consult some recognized expert on the topic of the film. Experts are almost always potentially useful to the writer. There are exceptions. An expert who has some professional ax to grind can be a curse and a plague. An expert who feels that his or her function is performed if he or she looks over the finished script and points out errors is an annoyance. On the other hand, an expert who is prepared fairly early in the research process to answer such questions as: "Is this statement correct? Is this view reasonable? What should I read? To whom should I talk?" will almost certainly be invaluable.

It is always a good idea to remember that experts are experts in their fields. They are not professionals in the business of creating films, videotapes, and the like. Their views on writing and producing scripts are probably just as valuable as those of the next ten people you will meet in the street.

Finally, if your research consists in whole or in part of interviews, tape them. Some interviews are done as part of the writer's basic research; others for actual use in the production. If the interviews are recorded for use on the sound track, they must be done on a professional recorder that will give tapes of high quality. If not, the quality of the tape doesn't matter much, as long as it is intelligible.

A documentary called *The Endless Search,* aired on the CBS outlet in Chicago, dealt with the behind-the-scenes work of people at a major museum. There was no printed material relevant to the subject, so the writer's basic source of information was museum personnel: anthropologists, entomologists, paleontologists, the curators, a taxidermist who was actually an artist and sculptor, and members of the art department who developed three-dimensional models and designed exhibition space for public viewing. No narrative track was written for this script; the interview tapes had to be edited so that one scene segued into another, finally telling the complete story.

Occasionally tapes may be edited to make a script rather than a sound track. This was the case with Robert Ford's documentary, *The Corner,* which dealt with a Chicago street gang, the Conservative Vice Lords. Ford began his research by spending about 15 hours in conversation with members of the gang, the conversations being recorded with the full knowledge of the gang members. The conversations turned out to be quite fascinating, and at first Ford thought they could be edited directly into the sound track. Unfortunately, however, the recorded talk—which had been perfectly comprehensible in a "real" situation—turned out to be confusing and even unintelligible when heard out of its original context. As a result, transcripts of the tapes were edited to get a script, which was then performed by professional actors.

Interviewing is a skilled technique you will have to learn. As was the case with library research, we cannot here tell you all you will need to know, but we can suggest ways in which you can begin to teach yourself.

There are as many ways of interviewing as there are situations in which people are interviewed. Techniques and situations range all the way from the highly structured situation in which all questions are carefully worked out and sometimes submitted to the interviewee in advance, to the haphazard, seemingly unprepared conversation. What you do depends on whom you're interviewing and what kinds of information you want.

Structured interviews—those in which you prepare questions in full detail beforehand and ask them just as you have them written down—are effective only if you are talking to a person accustomed to being interviewed, whose answers you can more or less predict. The structured interview simply gives the interviewee a chance to go through a performance with which he or she is perfectly familiar. With any other kind of interviewee you may end by asking the wrong questions and getting pointless answers.

Always prepare for an interview. If there is any way to get background on the people you are to speak to, get it. Even a modest quantity of background information will improve your interview enormously.

If you are doing an *open* rather than a structured interview, there are two basic ways of proceeding. You can probe and question until you find a subject about which the interviewee really wants to talk and then turn yourself into an interested and sympathetic listener. The advantage of this type of interviewing is that it dissolves any possible defenses of the interviewee and sometimes gets him or her to talk more freely than he or she had intended to. The disadvantage is that what the interviewee wants to say may not be what you want to hear, or it may be an elaborate rationalization of beliefs or behavior. The alternative to the sympathetic style is one in which you probe, challenge, and ask questions that may be disturbing. This method may produce useful revelations, or it may simply result in combativeness.

Even in very open interviews, and particularly where you intend to interview several people on the same subject, it is often useful to develop a few stock questions, intended to provoke conversations. In his interviews for the film, *The Corner*, for example, Ford asked members of the gang what their favorite fantasies were; the answers told, by implication, a great deal about the values of the young men, and about their perspectives on their lives.

The Research Process: A Case in Point

Some time ago, Scott Craig was a producer/director for NBC Television in Chicago. His work was producing documentary specials, a profession in which he had achieved considerable distinction. At the time, Craig had just completed one film and was promptly assigned the job of doing another, on crime. As he remarked, "That could mean anything, you know. Safety on the streets. Law and order. Rape. The subject, unfortunately, seemed endless."

Craig's first problem was to narrow his topic. In an effort to do so, he consulted a lawyer friend with considerable experience in criminal practice and law enforcement. The friend directed him to several persons in Chicago with long law enforcement experience. One of them, a federal defender, had for years collected press clipping cases and had them all carefully catalogued and mounted in a book. Craig began to burrow into this huge work.

"The book." he said, "must have been a foot thick. I began to read through it, came upon a section on the victims of crimes, and it became clear that this was an interesting part of crime to deal with. It also became clear that no one was dealing with the victim. Everybody was dealing with the criminal. So the victim emerged as a real possibility."

Researching any topic that involves police work can be difficult, sometimes impossible. The attempt to get cooperation from a police department can turn into a political game between the department and the writer. Craig was able to resolve this problem, only to discover that going through stacks of police files to find suitable cases to investigate would have taken much longer than his allotted time for making the film. The sheer volume of the material was staggering.

Craig went to the Urban League. His reasoning was simple and persuasive. "I said to them that I was dealing with crime. Most crime occurs in black neighborhoods. Can you help me? They said, 'yes.' And right away I had victims to interview."

His research didn't stop at that point. Most large television stations employ couriers whose business it is to receive news footage shot on location and get it back to the station for processing. In this kind of job speed is essential, and the speed is made on motorcycles. Some of these couriers are either off-duty or ex-policemen, and Craig consulted them. "They're extremely helpful," he said, "because if you ask them 'Who do you know?' they can tell you about people they know and cases they've investigated. Their information was very useful to me."

At this point, Craig faced the problem of how to do his interviews and what to do with them once they were completed. Some films use *talking heads*—close-ups of people talking about what they do, think, propose, hate, or love. The interview thus becomes part of the film rather than research information. Other films use passages from interviews *voice over*. That is, the voice appears on the sound track while the screen shows a place, an action, or a process that relates to what the voice is saying.

Craig doesn't believe in filmed interviews. "I believe," he remarked, "that we're dealing with a visual medium and that if you treat a documentary subject visually, you should do so without bastardizing the subject. I think that interviewing should be done without a camera, while you are still in the research stage. I think that a great many documentaries, from network on down, show their research. The filmmaker goes out and interviews someone that he or she has hardly met. Talk, talk, talk on film, and then the writer goes back, cuts up the research, and calls it a film."

What Craig managed to do in his film, *Victims,* was not to have people in the film talk about the crimes committed against them, but to show them functioning after the fact. For example, a woman who had owned thirteen cleaning shops was shown working in one of them. The point of the sequence was to show how she had carried on in spite of what she had gone through, how she kept the shop open even after many robberies, in one of which her son had been murdered. A sequence of this sort takes time and trouble to research, understand, and create on film. The effect cannot be achieved through a quick, superficial interview with the victim.

The Research Process: Time and the End Product

How much time should you devote to research? Obviously the answer varies. There is no formula that will tell you how much time you should or can spend preparing to write a script. There are, however, three factors that may be considered in working out a rough estimate: the demands of the film itself, the budget of the film, and the nature of your own investment in the film. Ideally, the answer should depend on the first factor alone. Some topics are familiar, some are not. Some topics are controversial, others are not. Some topics can be presented simply, others require a complex film statement. The result is that some films could be researched in a few days while others might require months.

To say this, of course, is to assume that every film you write will have an unlimited budget and that the producer is producing for generations to come, rather than for here-and-now. This assumption is never true. There is no such thing as an unlimited budget, and the audience for the mass media is always today's audience. Thus, films produced for local broadcasting stations and those aired as public affairs or public service documentaries are slotted for no longer than three months in production from research to air date. Other documentaries or news specials may be allowed even less time, some as little as three weeks from research to air date. In addition, your own financial interests in writing the film must be considered. You are paid a flat fee for writing a script, which includes research. Even if the producer would allow you unlimited time to work in, you would still have to decide how much time you could afford to spend on the project.

We might add at this point a cynical (but in our experience accurate) generalization. There is never enough time for research, just as there is never enough time for writing. Deadlines always occur yesterday.

What does research tell us, if it is adequate?

1. You begin with an idea or a topic. The first thing you find out is whether the idea can be made into a film. Or perhaps more to the point, whether it can be made into a good film. Some ideas work best when they are read, others when they are listened to. A good film is a communication that is seen.

2. What will be the difficulties in producing the film, and how may they be overcome?

3. What are the best sources of information on the subject? Are they books, things and places, or people? What can you hope to learn from them?

4. How many locations will be necessary to shoot? Sometimes the location is surveyed by members of the technical crew: soundperson, cameraperson, lighting director. They can be helped considerably if the writer has already walked through the locations, made some notes, and perhaps taken some photographs.

5. What are the possible approaches to the topic? What points of view could the film take? Always, while doing your research, you need to keep in mind the necessity for getting a grasp of the subject, a sense of its structure, a way of presenting it.

6. What is a likely date for script completion? This is a delicate sort of projection for a writer to make. Enthusiastic writers almost always minimize the problems they will face in doing the script and the amount of time it will take to deal with them. Enthusiasts almost always have to struggle against unrealistic deadlines. Perhaps that is simply the price they pay for the invaluable quality of excitement.

The business of researching and writing teleplays and screenplays is far more complex than the procedure we have outlined above. Partly because of agreements between the Writers Guild and producing organizations, the process of producing a script is fragmented into a half-dozen parts. If you are working on assignment—as is usually the case—you may be asked to write a first treatment, revise someone else's treatment, take a story outline and "fill in" the dialogue, write a script, revise someone else's script, or so on. Of course any of these fragmented assignments *is* an assignment in itself, contracted for and paid for by the producer.

There are really only two situations in which a writer sits down and writes something for network television or film production that he or she hopes to sell later: a screenplay, usually for a "made for TV" film, or the pilot script for a new series. Screenplays are saleable, even for unknown writers. A number of new writers make such sales every year. But trying to sell a pilot film and a series idea can become extremely complicated.

Here is one example of these complexities. A writer developed an idea for a new television series, wrote a script for a pilot, and interested a backer in his project. The script was then submitted to a large literary agency for an opinion and, possibly, an expression of the agent's willingness to try to sell the idea to the networks. The writer, his backer, and the agent met. Also in the room was a *senior writer*—a person of considerable reputation and current success—whose function was to endorse the script and its value and, in effect, to guarantee its success. The institution of the senior writer is peculiar to television and film production; where a relatively unknown person has produced a piece of work, the senior writer functions almost like the co-signer of a bank loan. He or she is there to insure than an industry insider will oversee the script's development and be available for consultation or rewriting.

In this case, the agent said that he had read the script but refused to commit himself on it until he had heard from the senior writer. The senior writer replied that although she knew the person who had written the script, she had not read the script for fear of prejudicing herself. She added that she was involved in many other projects and could hardly take on one more in any case. At this, the agent refused to state his opinion of the script and the project collapsed. The writer and his backer then had to face the necessity of going from one agent to another until they found someone who would read the script and voice an opinion of it. We include this one case as an example; it would be possible to fill a book with others. The ways of film and television production are as complex as astrophysics, as tricky as summit diplomacy.

Up until a few years ago there was a method of film financing that enabled a number of astute lawyers and accountants to greatly reduce their clients' tax liabilities. They formed film investment syndications by buying into film properties in production, near completion, but not as yet in distribution. It worked this way: Group A wants to buy studio X's film for a million dollars but only wants to put up $250,000, and take a note on the remaining $750,000. In effect they are buying into a film valued at a million dollars without putting up all the money and willing to payoff the remaining $750,000 on proceeds from the sale of the film. What they are doing, however, is taking all the deductions entitled to them on a million dollar investment. In addition, they estimate the life of the film, as say, 18 months. And the group takes whatever depreciation they can based over the film's life value so that in the end the books show a loss.

The IRS saw it a different way and eventually Congress wrote new legislation eliminating this tax loophole. The net result was less "independent" money pumped into films. There are still ways of financing films: outright loans repayable at a future date. Here the investor is entitled to a legitimate deduction, which decreases his or her tax liability, and, hopefully, when the film makes a profit, the taxable monies reduced by the loan, plus the profit, puts the investor ahead.

Fortunately, as we have said, most writers of televison and film drama work on assignment and function in collaboration with associate producers, story editors, story consultants, producers, and executive producers. Few scripts bear much resemblance to their beginning forms, and writers occasionally may be genuinely puzzled to recognize their brain-children.

chapter *5*

Before the Script
Is Written:
The Treatment

So far in our discussion of media writing, we have spoken very little about writing in the traditional sense. We examined the special social/business/creative world in which screenplays, slide film scripts, and audio documentaries are produced. Only after these preliminaries do we come to a procedure that hints at a kinship between the media writer and the essayist or novelist: writing the treatment. And even at this point, the media world is different. A novelist or playwright may do something similar to a treatment before turning out a first draft; a media writer *must* do it.

FACT AS DRAMA

People not involved in some facet of media production often assume that there is a sharp and easily recognizable difference between fiction and nonfiction. Fiction is storytelling, it is dramatic, it involves human beings and their problems, it tells of dramatic crises and great decisions. Nonfiction, on the other hand, simply deals in information—information that may be interesting and useful, but is seldom exciting and rarely presented in a dramatic style.

As far as present-day writing goes, neither part of this assumption is true. Modern fiction and drama, especially the most popular works, tend to be heavily factual; a detective story, an historical novel, a play about modern politics are likely to be all the more interesting if based on extensive research. But more to our purpose, almost all nonfiction is presented in a dramatic framework. Consider some of the documentaries and other productions we have already referred to:

A presentation of the works of Paul Gauguin becomes a dramatized biography of the painter, from which we gain some appreciation of his genius.

A documentary on a Regional Transit Authority is seen as an aspect of the continuing political struggle between city and smaller communities.

A feature on crime looks at the struggles of the victims of criminals to reorganize and continue their lives after the brutal shocks of robbery, destruction, even murder.

A slide film on paramedics deals in human crisis and tragedy and the efforts of paramedic teams to cope with disaster.

The fact that there are strong dramatic elements in all of these productions is no accident. The tendency to convey fact through drama does not represent a traditional preference of scriptwriters. Rather it seems to be an essential feature of human communication and understanding. There are few situations in which information is presented "straight," without reference to human values and problems, or any hint of drama. Even the highly technical script done for the G&W Energy Products Group (referred to earlier) is not totally without its dramatic human reference; the script is entitled *Points of Pride,* and its theme is the pride and satisfaction the Group and its employees have in doing a difficult and complex set of jobs better than anyone else.

If you want "straight" factual information about anything, where do you go? To the dictionary. To scientific reports. To computers. If you read encyclopedia articles, you will as often as not find them conceived and written in dramatic terms. If you consult an almanac, you will find lists of various records, first accomplishments, most popular films and books—all of which suggest struggle, competition, victory and defeat. If you examine a school textbook on any subject, you will find that it offers you some sort of drama—if indeed it is readable at all.

And that qualification, "if indeed it is readable at all," tells the story. Facts seen out of their human/dramatic context may truly be almost unreadable, unhearable, incomprehensible. Many years ago, Rudolph Flesch, in *The Art of Plain Talk,* set forth a "readability" formula for the use of writers. Using the Flesch formula, it is possible to determine whether a given piece of prose is easily comprehensible at, say, the fourth grade level, or the eighth, or whether it is inaccessible to anyone but college graduates. Flesch used three criteria in his formula, two of which were certainly not surprising; he said in effect that if a writer uses short words and short sentences what he or she writes is likely to be understood quite easily by almost any literate person. But his third factor was surprising; he said that readability improves in proportion to the number of *personal references* in the text. What this apparently means is that we absorb information most easily when we see it in the perspectives of human life, human experience, and human problems.

But there is additional support for the idea that we communicate fact most effectively when we do it in dramatic terms (*drama* being thought of in the Aristotelian sense as "an imitation of the actions of men"). Kenneth Burke, a brilliant contemporary social philosopher and critic, tells us that all human social organizations have a class structure through which we allot the various duties and rewards of social cooperation. Politically, the United States is a republic, which means that we have special ways of choosing leaders, changing leaders, allotting power, making decisions, and so on. In the same way, families, business enterprises, religious groups, and community organizations all have their structures which serve the same general purposes. The great bulk of human communications, Burke believes, have to do with these social structures: maintaining them, modifying them, trying to destroy them, understanding their meaning, working out the relationships of individuals to other individuals and to the social order. Since these communications have to do with human fears, hopes, satisfactions, and frustrations, they naturally are expressed in dramatic forms. A rebellion within a family is drama, as is heresy within a religion. The choosing of political leaders is dramatic ritual. A great deal of what we often take to be simple entertainment—television plays, popular novels, and so on—actually dramatize and test the values of our society, show us typical situations, describe right and wrong behavior. We can draw a parallel to this fact by stating that news stories in the press and on television fall into dramatic forms; could we really understand a war, an economic crisis, or a political scandal without seeing it in terms of a dramatic struggle between the forces of good and evil?

Nonfiction scripts, whether they are intended to educate, persuade, stimulate discussion, or anything else, must exploit the dramatic elements in their subjects. Some informational and persuasive scripts are done quite literally as dramas with fictitious characters and story lines, even though they may be based on carefully researched facts. But drama is not only involved in the finished product. Scriptwriters do their research, select their material, and develop their themes as dramatists. We will try to show just how this process works in later sections of this and the following chapters.

ORGANIZING THE MATERIAL: LOGIC AND DRAMA

The structure of drama, and of all fiction, is not really a very complicated affair. It comes to us as an ancient tradition—so old and universal that it has become embedded in human thought. We know the world through the logic of story-telling. A story, whether acted out or told, concerns the behavior of human beings—"the actions of men." A story concentrates on the situation of one human being at a particular time, a person with a problem, a need, a conflict, who acts to resolve the problem, to satisfy the need, to resolve the conflict. He encounters obstacles, whether created by a human opponent, presented by nature, or imposed by a social system. He makes a countermove. In the end, he fulfills his need or resolves his problem, or he is defeated and destroyed. With some variations, this simple formula will serve to describe what happens in fictitious works ranging from *Hamlet* to *Star Wars*, or in documented works from *Nanook of the North* to Sandburg's biography of Abraham Lincoln.

Following is a brief but complete treatment for a film dealing with the problems of the Sioux Indians in South Dakota.

Native Americans have been living the past hundred years virtually ignored by the white man. Ignored up until a few years ago when they decided to call back a few of the "promises" made to them. Like land taken from them by treaties that even the most biased white man might consider suspect.

But restitution alone can't bring back self-esteem. Take, for example, the plight of the Sioux living in South Dakota. They live in two worlds—that of their own traditional culture, and the white society of Rapid City. The discrimination, the double life, the search for identity are the concerns of our film essay.

We see the documentary as, first, a film story about a young, dedicated guidance counsellor, a Sioux woman who single-handedly takes on the whole white school system and at the moment represents the only force for successfully integrating the public high schools in Rapid City. Her contributions toward easing the situation of the Sioux students consist of helping them to adjust to the school situation; attending to their basic needs by finding homes, clothing, and transportation to school; acting as a role model (virtually the only one the Indian students see in their school) and thus motivating them to continue their education; conducting sensitivity sessions for white teachers. She has the patience of a revolution that has taken thousands of years to effect. But her position is funded through Title IV and those funds will run out at the end of this school year. Her loss would be a great one to the student body at the high school.

We next see a young Sioux boy whose idea of living in harmony with nature is imprinted into his living pattern. What happens when the boy is stuck in a large public high school and bombarded with sounds: lockers clanging, the rush of feet running up and down the stairs, and the bells ringing at frequent intervals? The youngster who has lived in tune with his own inner clock is now shoved into a pinball world. His isolation is created by others as well as self-imposed. When the boy goes to the lunchroom no white students will join him, and so he sits alone; if he does not see another Sioux student, he may not eat at all—the loneliness and isolation are too much to bear. This Sioux boy finds it easy to simply drift away from school back to a life lived at a more comprehensible pace, supported by the love of a large family.

We also see a talent show in rehearsal at the high school—not a Sioux in the crowd, though they comprise 15% of the student body. We intercut quick shots of Sioux students who walk through the corridors and sit alone in classrooms in silence and with heads down. Cut back to the all-white rehearsal with a match dissolve if we can or a match cut to the reservation at Pine Ridge where there is a rehearsal for a traditional festival. We see that the Sioux faces that were sullen at the high school are now alive and excited.

Any narration used in our film essays will be provided by the Sioux students talking with the guidance counsellor—she's the best choice to interview them, not us. And we will hear the Sioux "Elders" who will explain their heritage that our students can barely articulate but know in their hearts to be true.

Let us assume that the above represents an early stage in the development of a film treatment. The statement does establish several basic ideas about the film. It will deal with the psychological and social problems of the young Sioux in a white school. It will tell the story of a young Sioux woman who is a high school guidance counsellor. It will use footage filmed at the reservation at Pine Ridge, but will presumably concentrate on life at a high school in South Dakota. Narration will be largely voice-over, edited from tapes of interviews between the guidance counsellor and students, and from statements by elders of the Sioux tribe. The theme of the film is described as "the discrimination, the double life, the search for identity."

At this point, we might raise two questions about our material. First, what is the most effective way to arrange these materials in a film? Second, do we need to add to or amplify the materials listed above?

Let us begin with one of those things that "everybody knows." Everybody knows that the first few seconds of a film, an educational program, or a story are the most important. *Why?* In a television program, that is when a viewer is likely to decide whether to stay with you or switch channels. Even in the case of a classroom film, when the audience has no such choice, the first few seconds may make the difference between attention and inattention. And in any situation—reading, viewing, listening—the audience gets a series of cues from this first segment that set up expectations—expectations which, if they are properly met, make understanding possible and interest high. So how shall we begin our film on the young Sioux?

Probably the most dramatic, interesting idea suggested in our treatment is that of the contrast between the Sioux life of the reservation and the white life of the school. This contrast bears directly on the Native American problem and in addition has excellent possibilities for a dramatic use of visuals and sound. Let us say, then, that we open with an intercut sequence showing the differences between morning on the reservation and morning at the school; the same Sioux boy would be shown in each sequence. On the reservation the country is open and uncrowded, the sounds of nature and friendly voices, the homes are human in size and feeling. The boy walks on the land, not concrete, and he does not feel threatened. In the school he is alone; not only alone amid a crowd of white students who ignore him, but also alone away from the natural world he understands. The school is physically too big and too hard; he is bombarded with harsh, booming sounds. The sounds, the hardness and coldness close in on him.

These sequences could be cut and arranged so that we intellectually understand the contrast, or they could be edited with such precision that we would feel trapped and bombarded along with the boy. In either case they would make a powerful segment in the film. Would this be the best opening?

There is another possibility. Our treatment, as far as it has been developed, says that the film will be primarily the story of the guidance counsellor, so perhaps it should begin with her and show the problems of the Indian students in relation to her efforts. This approach to the film would have at least one advantage: she is a specific person, not a general type, and the realness of her personality and life would have dramatic impact. On the other hand, a dramatic view of her activities might be hard to find. She evidently has the patience and the stamina to work long, routine days in order to get what she wants.

Which opening should we choose? Actually, aside from the necessity of getting an interesting and compelling opening sequence, the answer to this question depends on the nature of the theme, or central idea, of the film, and on the materials available to use in developing the theme. In short, while working out the order in which materials are used you must consider the overall structure of your film. Following are these basic structural elements; you will probably find the organizational plan familiar, for it is commonly used to work out structure in all kinds of informational, instructive, and persuasive works. Don't disregard the plan because it is familiar; almost everyone recognizes it, but even professional writers sometimes forget to use it.

1. *The lead.*   There are, in general, two modes of statement possible for a nonfiction script: the rhetorical and the dramatic. The rhetorical mode gives you a statement like that of a speech—organized around a progression of ideas and arguments, using anecdotal material, statistics, and so forth to illustrate or prove the ideas. The dramatic mode produces a specialized kind of play, existing to prove a point or leading to a conclusion. If the rhetorical nonfiction script is like a speech, the dramatic nonfiction script is like a fable with an attached moral. Between speech and fable there are of course infinite variations and combinations.

If your script is essentially a play with a moral, the *lead* is the first episode. If the script is mainly in the rhetorical mode, it may be a short, striking anecdote, or a set of facts or ideas expressed in visual and sound terms. In either case it must do two things: involve the audience in what you have to say and lead directly and smoothly into a statement of the theme.

Leads must be highly economical statements. Avoid explanation and exposition when you are writing them. Concentrate on making a forceful, accurate statement. One of the mistakes beginning writers often make is explaining too much, too early. If a character is introduced they give his entire life story before permitting him to act. If they are showing Native Americans in an urban environment, they write in history and urban sociology rather than letting the appearance and actions of the people themselves speak.

Crime stories on television often use *teaser* openings in which the viewer sees the crime committed even before the series credits are shown. These teasers could be confusing, by the beginner's standards: the people are unidentified, the setting isn't named, often it's impossible to tell clearly what is happening, and above all, we have no idea of the motivations involved in these actions. Of course what the viewer does get is an atmosphere of suspense, danger, and violent action, which is enough. It is sometimes surprising how much explanation people can do without.

Note, however, that the lead must lead directly into a statement of . . .

2. *The theme,* or *central idea.*   This is the most difficult part of the treatment to state correctly, and it is by all odds the most important. Perhaps the main reason for the difficulty is that the theme must be expressed in one simple sentence, no more or less. If you must use more than one subject and one verb to state your theme, you have two themes and perhaps you should do two films. If when you are asked "What is this film about?" you have to say something like "It's about the troubles young Indians have in going to white schools" or "It's about the Indians' loss of identity," the chances are that you haven't done enough research or thought about your material enough. At any rate, you haven't come to the point where you can state a theme.

Journal Films is a Chicago concern that distributes educational films. Among its offerings is a series of short films on consumer education. One recent addition to the list dealt with the various recourses that consumers have when they buy unsatisfactory products. The film touched on such matters as conditions of sale, conditions under which goods can be returned, guarantees and warranties, consumer protective organizations, and so on—a considerable range of factual information. The theme of the film, however, was succinctly expressed in the title, *If It Doesn't Work, Complain!*

Why is stating the theme so important? Because everything else in the treatment relates directly to it. As we have noted, if you don't have a clear notion of your theme you cannot make an intelligent decision about your lead. In the same way, the main body of the film must grow out of a preliminary statement of the theme and the conclusion must restate it.

We repeat: the statement of the theme is the most important sentence in your treatment.

3. *The body of the treatment.*   In a dramatic script this will include the action from the end of the opening episode to the beginning of the final sequence which resolves the story conflict. The structure thus runs: *lead*—establishes the basic problem of the script in terms of dramatic conflict; *body*—states the theme and develops and builds the conflict to its highest tension; *conclusion*—resolves the conflict and restates the theme.

In a rhetorical script the *body* will pick up on the statement of theme, separate and clarify its various aspects or develop arguments to show its validity, and offer specific anecdotal material to illustrate and demonstrate all generalizations. If this sounds as though a good treatment might read like an outline for a term paper or thesis, we do not mean in the least to convey any such impression. Indeed, the art of writing a good treatment (and eventually a good script) for a nonfiction film consists in developing a strong purposeful intellectual structure and then carefully concealing it under layers of story-telling and drama. A good treatment should be a gripping and engaging statement; it should be, but never seem to be, a cool arrangement of ideas.

4. *The conclusion.* As we have noted above, the conclusion to a treatment or film restates the theme and, if the script is dramatic, resolves the conflict. Doing this may require a few lines, a separate scene, or even a short sequence of scenes. If the script is rhetorical, the conclusion may consist of only one or two sentences or visual images, already identified with the theme.

Planning or writing a conclusion involves one problem every writer faces and deals with more or less effectively, but which is nearly impossible to describe. This is the problem of devising the film, television, or audio equivalent of the *curtain.* In the theater the *curtain* is a line or combination of line and action that expresses perfectly the climactic moment of an act, or the resolution of an entire play. In the musical *1776* the entire play builds to the eventual signing of the Declaration of Independence. At the end of the play the delegates have at last resolved or ignored their differences, overcome their fears, and decided to sign the document. They come slowly forward to affix their signatures, one and then another and then the next. Suddenly the action freezes, and the onlookers realize that they are looking at a *tableau vivant* of the famous painting of the signing of the Declaration, which every American has seen a thousand times in the course of his or her life. The tableau is held; this is the *curtain,* the ultimate meaning and effect of the entire evening.

In an audio script, the equivalent of a *curtain* must of course be expressed in sound: sometimes in a spoken line but often more effectively in a sound effect or a phrase of music. Television is rather like the theater; the curtain is likely to be a combination of a spoken line and an action. Film is first and foremost visual, so that some great film curtains are powerful visual images. None of these guidelines are absolute rules; the curtain of *1776* is really a freeze frame that would normally occur in a film rather than on the stage. The one essential fact about the curtain, as we have remarked, is that it must at once conclude and summarize the meaning of your script.

POINT OF VIEW

This is both important and rather ambiguous. Important, because your choice of a point of view will affect the whole tone of your script. Ambiguous, because the term does mean several things, all of them important for you to consider in doing a treatment. Let us begin with a relatively simple problem, the meaning of point of view in narrative prose.

Every piece of narrative prose is written from the viewpoint of the reader, a character in the story, or the author (the omniscient viewpoint). The action of the story comes to the reader through the chosen viewpoint—the story is what the "first person" sees, feels, understands. Thus, quite obviously, a story told from four different viewpoints is not one story, but four. This fact always comes as a surprise to people who somehow feel that there is a single reality out there somewhere, which should be the same for everyone who experiences it.

Viewpoint in narrative prose can be a deceptive stratagem for the writer; viewpoint characters can be useful for what they do not notice, for what they misinterpret, or for the false conclusions that they draw. That's why Conan Doyle's mystery stories are nearly all told from the point of view of Dr. Watson. If Watson is easily puzzled, mystified, confused, so are we who read the stories. But more important is the fact that without Watson's warmth, loyalty, simple honesty, and common-sense view of life, the stories would lose most of their force and charm.

Viewpoint in a play is a very different matter. Playwrights ordinarily stand outside their characters; they show them acting, reacting, speaking, doing, and we in the audience must deduce from these exterior cues what the inner worlds of the characters are like. Nevertheless, point of view is a very real thing in any play. The characters connect with each other through their roles in the set of incidents that makes up the play. *Macbeth,* for example, includes the witches and their prophecies, Macbeth and his relationship with his wife, the life and death of King Duncan, the family life of Macduff, the madness of Lady Macbeth, the drunken existence of the porter, the flight of the young princes, even the bumbling ineffectiveness of the court doctor who fails so tragically in treating Lady Macbeth. It is easy enough to see that Macbeth is the protagonist and the viewpoint character of Shakespeare's play, but consider what a play called *Lady Macbeth* would be like. It would certainly show her as a beautiful, vital, and power-hungry woman, easily dominating her rather reluctant and stupid husband. It would show her contemptuously thrusting Macbeth aside to kill with her own hand when he could not. It would of necessity detail the mounting strains and fears that finally break her. Would the witches appear in *Lady Macbeth?* Quite possibly not. And certainly the final battle and Macbeth's bloody end would not figure in her story at all.

As an exercise in working out viewpoint, you might consider what *Macbeth* would be like if the story were told from the perspective of Duncan's sons, the rightful heirs to the Scottish throne.

Viewpoint considered in this way plays a part in any dramatic treatment of human experience. One problem in working out the treatment of the documentary on the Sioux Indians, which we discussed earlier, could be phrased in terms of viewpoint. Who should be the viewpoint character in the film? The guidance counsellor? A young Sioux trying to get through high school? One of the elders of the tribe? Could you possibly tell the story from the point of view of a white person living in Sioux City? Or might it be desirable—this is always a possibility in documentary—to tell the story from several different points of view?

Very often you will not have to search for a point of view in preparing your treatment. Educational and industrial scripts are usually intended to accomplish very specific ends in very specific ways, and in such cases the point of view may simply be given to you as part of your assignment. Documentaries are not quite so specialized, however. In the case of Scott Craig's *Victims*, his assignment from NBC was to produce a film about crime. The assignment could have meant almost anything—safety on the streets, law and order, rape, the family life of policemen. One of Craig's immediate problems was in choosing a manageable part of this material—and with it, a point of view. He chose to concentrate on the victim of crime, and when he decided to show the victims of violent crime as they tried to recover from the experience, he had his point of view.

There is one more way in which point of view in the nonfiction script can be understood, and perhaps it is the most important way of all. We mentioned the possibility of using an omniscient point of view in writing prose narrative. The author, having created the universe of his or her story, presumably can take a god's-eye view of the people and events in it. This may not be the most natural or effective point of view to adopt where fiction is concerned, but it becomes much more natural in writing nonfiction. An essay describes the author's feelings and perceptions in relation to a particular topic. A report is inevitably written from the reporter's point of view.

Often enough, we do not think of the uses of viewpoint where a statement is supposed to be objective. We somehow persist in the illusion that it is possible to catch and preserve whole a moment of reality, like a butterfly upon a pin. "Actuality" recorded on film or tape is "reality," is "the truth," and not a product of skill and bias. Such notions are of course nonsense. A representation of events in words, on a stage, on film or tape, or paper is always artificial. There is no report that cancels out the bias of the reporter. It is far better to recognize the artificiality of art and understand the nature of our biases than deny they exist.

Even a robot reporter would be biased in favor of its own programming. Writers are not robots and might as well recognize it. They cannot make themselves, for example, so callous to human suffering that they avoid even the slightest touch of sympathy, fellow-feeling, or outrage in its presence. They cannot divorce themselves from anger or hostility or sadness or humor or any number of other feelings that move us as we look at the endless spectacle of human experience. When you have realized that your emotions are as much a part of your equipment as your typewriter or tape recorder, emotions peculiar to your personal view of life, you will have discovered a great and valuable truth about your profession.

Once you have come to this realization, of course, you must go further. You must learn to look coldly at your own biases and regard your feelings with deep suspicion. The two attitudes—"Everyone is biased, so my biases are as good as anyone's," and "I have the most marvelous feelings about everything"—can produce some of the world's most irresponsible and dreadful writing. Feeling can be an embarrassingly bad substitute for understanding. An individual's biases, all too often, are devices designed to protect him or her from seeing what things are really like. Ernest Hemingway, in the course of his writing career, spoke again and again about the necessity to see things "truly," to understand the "true" nature of feeling. His stress was wise and accurate. The most difficult thing in the world is to understand the nature of your own perceptions and reactions. If you are to develop your writing talent you must learn how to do this.

INDUSTRIAL, EDUCATIONAL, AND DOCUMENTARY SCRIPTS: DIFFERENCES IN PROCEDURE AND STYLE

The research and preparation of industrial, educational, and documentary films differ from each other in significant ways, for instance, in style.

Industrial films are primarily public relations ventures. They are produced for clients who wish to say something positive about what they do. The film may show the client's product; it may introduce a new line of products to salesmen or distributors. It may present, or at least talk about, a public service with which the client wishes to be identified—in the field of ecology, for instance.

Industrial films may be produced for government agencies such as the Department of Health, Education, and Welfare, and by public service organizations such as the Red Cross or the National Safety Council, as well as by business and industrial concerns. Such films often differ very little from educational films and in fact are used for purposes of instruction. The distinction between industrial films of this sort and educational films is intent. The source of the educational film doesn't matter much as long as it is authoritative. But when a corporation produces a film about public health, say, or ecology, the film always bears the trademark of the corporation and is intended to have a definite public relations value.

The educational film is produced to inform, to present controversy, to break down barriers to understanding; in short, educational films convey information, pose questions, offer solutions. Some educational films are traditional classroom teaching tools; they substitute for a printed text. Others are open-ended films intended to introduce class discussion or student projects. Still others are presentations of values, also to provide a basis for student discussions.

Documentary films deal always in information and analysis and only occasionally suggest courses of action. Industrial and educational films, however, are always intended to motivate.

The experience of researching and writing an industrial film differs considerably from that of writing educational or documentary films. The client has a great deal to say about how you go about developing and researching an industrial film. You may find yourself working closely with the client's own advertising director, or with a creative director and account executive if the client uses an outside advertising agency.

Decision-making starts with the client, sifts down through the advertising director or the creative director, and finally reaches the writer. Any ideas you have about the script must be channeled up this chain of command; you must reconcile yourself to a situation in which you never make decisions concerning the script, or the film. You may suggest ideas, but they are always accepted or rejected by others. Because clients exercise creative control, they will want to see a detailed statement of the idea before approving a final script. This is where the pre-scripting process begins to differ sharply from the procedures followed in making a documentary.

First, unless the industrial film runs longer than 15 minutes, the client will often want to see a storyboard. *Storyboards* are a series of panels like small television screens, with rectangular spaces below them to type in the copy lines that go with the panel visual. In the panels will appear simple drawings to illustrate in uncomplicated terms how the film will make its points (they cannot, of course, show complete visual techniques such as dissolves, slow fades, matts, or wipes). Storyboards are also employed for all videotaped and filmed commercials, and some educational films. They are seldom if ever used in documentaries. But all motion pictures for theatrical release have storyboards, a step that follows the final revised script.

In storyboarding, the writer works with an art director in developing the visuals that go along with the copy points. In this situation you should have some idea of the kind of visuals you think should be in the film, but the art director is there to make the necessary refinements and to develop alternative concepts.

You normally meet with the advertising director or the creative director once the storyboard is finished to discuss the storyboard, perhaps revise some of your ideas, change the visuals, and rework copy. When approval is given after these changes the storyboard is colored for final presentation. (First-draft storyboards are generally done in black-and-white sketch and the final ones are fully colored.)

The next meeting is the difficult one with the client. Clients are not media professionals, and some have almost no idea of what is involved in producing the effects they want. But you must remember that some of them have acquired a great deal of knowledge about media writing and production. A great many clients are impressed by effects they have seen in other industrial films, in commercials, even in feature films. One person may remember the use of a floating dissolve, or a lyric he's liked, or even a story line. The success of the film *Love Story* produced a flood of other Love Stories, many of them condensed into 30-second commercials. Sometimes you can identify and adapt the technique or the feeling the client wants but sometimes you cannot. If you cannot you must substitute tact for the client's ideal film footage.

The final, completed script can either be clipped to the storyboard or held separately to be passed out during the last meeting with the client, which usually is held fairly close to production time. Several months can pass from the time of the first storyboard presentation to the client to the final approval and beginning of principal photography.

Industrial films that are not storyboarded are researched and treated much the same as a documentary. The treatment takes the place of the storyboard. But unlike the documentary treatment, the treatment for an industrial film is a strategic more than a factual exposition. Treatments for industrial films "position" the client's product or message. An industrial film treatment begins by stating the purpose of the film in the opening paragraph. Then, if the film is intended to deal with specific problems, these problems are identified. There will be a statement of how the film proposes to attack them. If the film does not deal with problems, the next step will be a statement of the points the film will cover. If the film techniques being used are unusual, they should be briefly introduced—for instance, "We'll cut to a split screen showing the four features of the product framed in upper left, upper right, lower left, lower right." Finally, the treatment should explain how the film will be resolved. It may also include a brief summary, outlining the main points of the treatment for quick reference.

*The End Of
Preparation*

After all these preliminaries of research, decision, conference, and creation, you may find yourself in possession of a treatment that reads as follows:

> 1. "Something began me and it has no beginning. Something will end me and it has no end." *Carl Sandberg.* The quote begins the film as we SLOWLY PULL IN on the COLORED PHOTOGRAPH OF THE WORLD in the 75th Anniversary exhibit.
>
> 2. We stay on this shot as the NARRATOR CONTINUES. "We are all part of beginnings in the middle of other beginnings." The CAMERA continues to MOVE IN until the WORLD TURNS OUT OF FOCUS and we slowly DISSOLVE to Hall #5 and the EARLY FARMER DIORAMA. We're TIGHT on the SUN in the BACKGROUND and then we slowly PULL BACK to reveal MAN (2000 B.C.) looking to the sun for "his answer." His hands are raised, one carrying a branch bearing leaves, the other hand beckoning hope. The NARRATOR CONTINUES: "It may be that in man's quest for knowledge, the only discovery he finds is the . . . *ENDLESS SEARCH.*"
>
> 3. ROLL OPENING CREDITS as we start building CONVERSATION which begins to be audible but is not yet distinguishable. Slowly we MOVE BACK and DISSOLVE INTO A SERIES OF MONTAGE CUTS tracing the history of the *Endless Search.*
>
> 4. INTERCUT WITH THESE SCENES the SUBJECTIVE CAMERA moves down a hall taking us closer to the conversation; the last visual DISSOLVES to the ASSISTANT DIRECTOR OF THE MUSEUM in the middle of a conversation he is having with a GUEST in his office whom we don't identify or see. The GUEST is US. The Assistant Director explains that the Museum is involved with people and that "we do two things mainly, we generate basic and new information and we transmit that information in several ways and on several levels."

Of course the treatment before you may not read quite that way.

It may be somewhat differently phrased and set up in a slightly different typographical style.

It may read rather like a plot summary for a play or a short story.

It may appear to be essentially an analysis of a problem in communication.

It may even be a series of stick-figure sketches with patches of narrative and dialogue under each of them.

Treatments and storyboards vary as much as the requirements of their films and tapes. It would be impossible to describe all their variations. One of the things you must learn from experience is to find out, when you get an assignment, what sort of research and planning is expected of you and how to go about it. Each of your first half-dozen or so writing assignments will be a learning experience; after that the patterns will begin to repeat themselves.

For the time being, we hope that you will remember and use a great deal of the information that has been set forth in this chapter. One fact, we feel, is absolutely essential for you to keep in mind. *Two-thirds of the work of writing a nonfiction script must be done before you begin to write the script.*

TREATMENTS FOR SCREENPLAYS AND TELEPLAYS: FICTION

When you write a treatment for a screenplay or teleplay you are telling a story in the simplest form possible. The story has to have a narrative line, it must have a beginning, middle, and end, and ordinarily it is told in the historical present tense (that is, "We find ourselves in front of a dingy building on South Wabash Street in downtown Chicago. A man walks into the frame—he stops and peers into a dusty window . . . "). The length of a treatment is variable. It may run to five or ten pages for a half-hour teleplay, twenty or thirty pages for a two-hour television movie, or thirty to forty-five pages for a theatrical motion picture. The difference between a treatment and a short story or short novel is simple but important; a treatment is not a complete work in itself; its episodes are intended to film well, and read well.

Here is an example of the opening of a feature film treatment, written by Herbert F. Margolis and Paul M. Rubenstein for Universal Pictures.

Inside a military hospital ward, NO NAME, a soldier in his early 20s with the face of an Eagle Scout, is pleading with a sympathetic Army doctor, MAJOR TRILLING.

"All the guys here who can walk are going someplace," he says. "Why not me?"

No Name isn't going anywhere because he has no place to go. Two medics found him wandering in a battlefield bleeding from a head wound two months ago, and since then his memory has been missing in action. No dog tags, no papers.

Everything about him is lost. If he had lost an arm or a leg the Army would have sent him to a military hospital for treatment. But amnesiacs are troublesome. Front line doctors have little time to restore memories.

"He'll have to be patient." That's what Major Trilling has dropped by to tell him again . . .

When a character is first introduced, as No Name is in the first paragraph, his name appears in caps and is followed by a one- or two-line description.

No Name's problem is given in the second paragraph: "All the guys here who can walk are going somewhere. Why not me?" The explanation of his situation follows in paragraph three, and we learn that Major Trilling has no answers for him.

Shortly after this we meet LIEUTENANT HOWARD BOLT and CORPORAL FREDDIE GIBBONS. Bolt and Gibbons are two military confidence men. Bolt faces an investigation of some of his shady deals with possible courtmartial to follow. Gibbons is his friend and faithful assistant. Overhearing the conversation between Major Trilling and No Name, Bolt decides to provide No Name with his own identity as Lieutenant Howard Bolt, complete with a set of orders that will take the new lieutenant far away.

Later, after the treatment was sold and revised, the whole idea of an amnesiac character No Name was changed. The writers also concentrated on telling a story about an experimental university set up by the Army, through the point of view of the revised character.

Stories told in treatment, with minimal characterization and heavy stress on story line, often seem simple. But they must be. You treat one character, one problem at a time. They become more complicated and more interesting in script form, when characters have been developed and dialogue and visual statement added. A charming and successful 1978 film, *Heaven Can Wait,* is the story of a professional football player who has a motorcycle accident. His soul is prematurely taken off to the hereafter by an inexperienced heavenly messenger. When the football player protests, it is discovered that he was not destined to die for another twenty years or so, and the authorities must find him another suitable body. The story line is simple, easy to follow, and the *reader* is immediately hooked into the story.

This reader is not just a casual friend checking what you have written. Most stories submitted to studios wind up first in the editorial or story departments, where people are paid to read material to synopsize for their bosses. The reader also fills out a form which rates many other things including structure, dialogue, plot, setting, and characterization, on a scale from poor to excellent. This filtering process starts even sooner, at the agent's door. Hundreds of stories are submitted to agents each week; only the ones that pass their reading are sent on to the readers at the studios. It's a winnowing effect. We mention this to illustrate just how important it is to write a successful treatment. It's the difference between a business deal and depression, perhaps.

Treatment writing, especially for comedy, requires simplicity. *If in doubt cut it out.* Keep paragraphs limited to building a single action, rather than a clutter of several. In general, following these rules in writing treatments for screenplays and teleplays will make the job much easier, and hopefully rewarding:

1. *Stress story line.* Treatments sell or do not sell depending on whether they present an interesting, straightforward story from the first sentence. Most readers scan the pages. Unless they see the story quickly they won't see it all.

2. *Write your treatment in short, economical paragraphs.* Try to break your story into the smallest units of action (and sometimes explanation) and devote one paragraph to each.

3. In each paragraph, especially those dealing with action, *check the three elements: action, fact,* and *feeling.* Always tell the reader what happens in this brief segment of the story, add the necessary facts concerning characters and setting, and be sure always to suggest how the viewpoint character feels about what is happening to him or her.

4. *Include dialogue lines* when they effectively summarize an action, a feeling, or a character, or when they are important to the structure of a scene. For example, the climax of a scene may be expressed in a line of dialogue, a tag-line. Such a line should probably be in your treatment.

5. Remember that a treatment is a kind of diagram for a script, which in turn is a plan for a film or television program. *Never forget the end product, the completed work.*

In the following fiction treatment (which was marketed for a Television Movie of the Week), you'll note, among other things unique to fiction treatments, that each new character is set in CAPS, that each new location is also set in CAPS, that a few lines of description (sometimes also referred to as *back story*) are included just after each character is introduced, and that each character must have a problem that is resolved along about the last third of the story.

Although simple enough in form, the fiction treatment may pose problems, especially for the beginning writer. A common flaw seen in many treatments is setting the story in dialogue rather than in narrative because the writer feels more comfortable in handling emotion in dialogue, rather than in third person, present tense narration. To overcome this initial block, think of the treatment as something similar to a novella, short story, or feature article, where the paragraphs must have fact *and* feeling.

We think the example given here, *Uncle Chet and Uncle Joe,* incorporates most, if not all, that writing good fiction treatment requires. It is an original story by one of the authors.

CHET GOLDKAUPF, 40's, still holds the record for the most points scored in a basketball game at FENKER HIGH SCHOOL, on CHICAGO'S north side. No one has ever come close, 40 points against nearby Roosevelt. In between classes in P.E. that he teaches, when it's an unusually rough day, he's also breaking up a few fistfights or a crap game going on in the back of the gym. And to remind him who he used to be, Chet stops off at the gold plaque hanging in the corner of the gym teachers' worn out office that stinks from chlorine escaping from the swimming pool along with the sour smell of gym shoes, sweat socks, and perspired, oily bodies. This locker room perfume has one place to travel—through the vent and into the coaches' office. And there, in the middle of the plaque, a name, Chet Goldkaupf, and an inscription: *40 points against Roosevelt High School, February 14, 1930.*

On the gym floor in front of a bunch of oddball, oddsized students, he screams at them "Laps! Ten laps across the floor. Now, move. One, two, three, four . . . keep your legs up. Kaponitz, you run like a sissy, Kaponitz."

For 20 years, he has stood in the same spot, in the middle of the gym, with the same yardstick banging cadence on the gym floor, molding the future accountants, doctors, lawyers, engineers, and felons into physically fit young adults.

He also coaches the basketball team. Never once taken it to the city playoffs. Goes home at night, tired, grumbly to a muted childless apartment four blocks from the school, to sit down to dinner and adore his food more than he has ever adored his wife, MARION, 40's, whose only words it seems now are, "Chet, the last time you looked at me I was 28 years old. Aren't you curious?" And when that doesn't work it's usually, "Your mother called last night. She told me she died in her sleep. She went to Heaven and met Stella Dallas, and Ma Perkins. Then a miracle happened. She heard the theme song they played on Lorenzo Jones. She woke up. It was the middle of the afternoon and the radio had been going all night. Her hearing aid was shorting out. Chet will you think about taking your mother to Belltone and getting that damn thing fixed? Chet??"

As usual, he's lost in the sports page, and the classified, and a girlfriend his wife suspects him of having.

Three desks away from Chet Goldkaupf's in that same smelly coaches' office is the desk of JOE RAPPAN, also in his 40's, but with no records or gold plaques. For twenty years he's stood naked or sat naked in Fenker High's swimming pool inspecting how seriously his students consider hygiene before they line up on three sides of the pool to be given a 30-minute lecture on pool safety, and about ten minutes actually in the tank swimming or screaming if they've dived in the wrong way and felt the slap of water taking vengeance on their scrotums.

For 20 years he's sat on that folding chair, blocking the entrance to the pool like an unmovable watchdog, warden, guard, flesh in stone, eyeing pores like a hawk. Looking for rashes, itches, bumps, blebs, ring worm, dirt, ordering those shivering students who haven't used enough soap back into the showers again, until their bodies are squeaky clean and not a crack, crevice, or crease line has registered impurities.

Joe Rappan and his wife, ROCHELLE, 30's, live in a small six room bungalow on ST. LOUIS near BRYN MAWR also shared by two beautiful kids, DANNY, 16, and DEBBIE, 14, plus a mongrel named Douglas, a hamster named Hairy, a goldfish named Walter and a mother-in-law named NETTIE who hates germs, turns her head within fifteen feet of seeing any of the children, washes her hands fifty times a day, keeps a separate drawer for her own silverware, uses hand napkins to wipe her face, keeps a separate cupboard for her dishes, cups, and sees her doctor once a week who has gone to such madness as now keeping a a list of all the new diseases she has made up so he can keep the complaints straight. He has now even asked her to keep a diary which occupies most of her life.

"How do you spell leptospirosis?"

"Dogs get leptospirosis."

"I know but so do people. I think I've got leptospirosis from Douglas. That dog should be put to sleep."

And in his fitful nights staying up and tossing and turning, Joe, perish the thought, wishes in the most private recesses of his consciousness that it's not Douglas who should be put to sleep, but his mother-in-law.

What Joe possesses, though, is an undying optimism. Partly brought on by the fact that when he was serving in the infantry during World War Two, he accomplished something rather unusual by forward spotters in time of war, he survived. It wasn't so easy for a little young man who measured 5'5" and weighed a hefty 190 pounds, to run like hell for cover when his CO yelled, "duck."

And after the war, working as a lifeguard at FARWELL BEACH in CHICAGO, scrambling up his guard tower, that wasn't easy either because now he had ballooned to over 200 pounds. Once, for a bet, he attached himself to a yacht moored in MONTROSE HARBOR and made the late afternoon editions of all the newspapers, as a human buoy. He won a hundred buck bet floating and bobbing, without sinking, and after getting off on a misdemeanor, later the charges were dropped, he used that money to enroll in Loop College and eventually received a degree in education.

When Fenker High needed a swimming coach, Joe persisted, and got the job. He also put Fenker into the record books by coaching ten consecutive winning teams.

Unlike Chet whose eyes roamed farther than a stray dog's, Joe's faithfulness to Rochelle could never be challenged.

Joe, rotund, lovable, and a joker, finds his opposite in Chet, tall, trim, even at 45. From the back, when they walked down the school hallways, if they had put branches on their arms they would have been mistaken for a tree and a bush.

Fenker High students nicknamed them Mutt and Jeff.

And, in the summer of 1948, after talking about it all year, Joe and Chet opened up a DAY CAMP. From money Joe received from mortgaging his house, and money Chet won on the horses, football games, and baseball games, they bought a used Pontiac station wagon and a used Chevy wagon to transport baseball bats, gloves, balls, tennis shoes, blankets, kool-aid, bandages, pillows, sheets, and twenty kids who would start spending the summer with "Uncle Chet" and "Uncle Joe."

For six years, business picked up but in 1955 they hit a bad season and when the camp opens in 1956, so many other day camps are in competition with them, better staffed, better equipped, that they stand to lose their shirts and in Joe's case his house, unless they turn a profit.

At the end of each summer all the day camps compete in a JUNIOR OLYMPICS sponsored by the city of Chicago. Everybody shows up for this one. The Mayor. The Governor and the parents.

So far, they have placed last in every event for the past two years. Word gets around. Parents send their kids to winners not to losers.

When they open up the summer camp season in 1956, they have registered fifteen kids. Among this army of aliens one is a thumbsucker. One is a bed wetter. One is non-verbal. One is just out of the juvenile home. Another one is allergic to trees, grass, pollens, and chlorine in the swimming pool, it makes his eyes burn so he can't see where he swims, gets his directions mixed up and is often seen circling underwater, thinking he's really swimming from one end to another. If they can just open up his eyes, he may turn out to be the best swimmer they've ever had and win one of the events at the Junior Olympics.

Then there's the "OX," so nicknamed because he is as strong as an ox with about the same kind of brains to match. Until one day Joe happens to see him brooding under a tree, away from the others during lunch. Sitting in the shade writing something down on a piece of paper and crumpling up the paper and hiding it when he sees Joe has noticed.

By the time he's grabbed the paper out of the kid's pockets Joe's convinced he's going to read obscenities heaped at him but instead reads lyrical poetry, so beautiful, that Joe picks another tree to hide and cry.

Everybody has given up on the "Ox" and he has put his despair to rhyme. Now if Joe and Chet can just get the "Ox" to be as facile with weights as he is with words, then ALL AMERICAN DAYCAMP has a chance at winning first prize in the "clean and jerk."

Each morning the two station wagons are piled with kids. First stop the PARK RECREATION HOUSE where the toilets overflow on a regular basis.

For a nominal fee they've paid the Park District for the use of a room upstairs for lunches and arts and crafts, the small gym downstairs and a cramped locker room.

Twice a week the kids go to BERNIE'S, a deli on Lawrence Avenue. They are treated to hot cornbeef sandwiches, cole slaw, and pickles and Chet is treated to a few hidden moments with COOKIE, whose brother ITSIG owns the place.

Cookie, 20's, raven black hair, a walk that sets off a mad dash to be first at the counter among the luncheon patrons, isn't your normal nine to five counter girl.

She fills in for her brother the Mondays and Sundays the RIALTO THEATER is closed and she walks across the boarded floors in her brother's place with the same electricity she uses to dance across the Rialto's stage. You see Cookie is a stripper. Has been for five years. She's the headliner. In fact, Itsig, who is really very quiet and soft spoken, even honors his sister by naming a speciality of the house after her. COOKIE'S CHILI.

While Joe watches over the disheveled campers and makes sure no one starts a pickle fight or squirts catsup all over the place, Chet is in the back room with Cookie, smooching, hugging, and watching her try out new routines for his opinon.

It may not be as exotic and erotic watching Cookie bump and grind among the cases of soda pop, barrels of pickles, and slabs of meat but it sure as hell beats monitoring fifteen screaming kids in the front room.

Cookie has always imagined herself another Ginger Rogers. Looks upon the five year engagement at the Rialto as a step ladder to success and looks upon Chet with sympathetic eyes—in love with a guy who scored 40 points at Fenker High eons ago, and has scored a big goose egg when it has come to marriage.

One day, she keeps telling herself, Chet will give up his football bets, baseball bets, basketball bets, the bookie, his wife, and the daycamp, and finally settle down to a "normal" life with her. But then Cinderella is also a fairy tale.

Through the closed door, she can hear her brother's usually timid voice stretching far beyond it's limits because going on outside the back room is one helluva catsup fight among five of the campers and a soda pop squirting contest among the other ten.

When Chet runs out to see what the noise is, Joe has picked up the metal lid of a garbage can and is using it as a shield to charge into the fracas.

Within a week, six parents have withdrawn their kids from any further camp activities and are demanding full refunds or threatening legal action.

Chet's all for telling the parents to take a flying leap. But the stakes are a little bit higher for Joe. With his home mortgaged and camp overhead much higher than anticipated, his youngest girl in braces, his mother-in-law refusing to sign her social security payments because the office is always misspelling her last name, she's become the latest free loader.

And after a particularly brutal argument between Chet and Marion, the coach who still holds the record for most points scored, is seen by his gawking neighbors being tossed out of his apartment and shielding his head from a barrage of old baseball gloves, basketballs, gym shoes, scrapbooks, and every other well-used item representing the sum of his existence, by his wife, who has a pretty good throwing arm.

Late that night, Joe is shaken from his sleep by Douglas barking at some mysterious figure lurking in the shadows of the front porch light.

A lost soul, badly in need of a shave, a cigarette dangling between his lips and a pencil figuring out the latest point spread for the Phillies-Cubs baseball game.

When Joe opens the door, still squinting from sleep, after peeking out the front window first, to see who the slumped body belongs to, the first thing he hears out of Chet's mouth is, "What do you think, Phillies and four or Cubs and six?"

From then on, the Rappans have a new house guest and Aunt Nettie has a ripe target for every prejudice, idiosyncracy, malady, imagined and real, that 40 years of hypochondria can do to a widow who was married at 15, passed herself off as a diminutive innocent but who, in fact, was a foxy lady.

"Joe, I swear. That woman is out to destroy me. Can't I sleep with the dog downstairs in the basement. She sneaks into my room at night. Makes funny faces at me. And those dirty gestures, my God, Joe, where did she learn them all from. She thinks I'm sleeping. But my eyes are really opened. I know she's going through my drawers, too."

"C'mon, Chet."

"I swear she is. I saw her wearing one of my socks yesterday when she was complaining that the circulation had stopped in her feet. Why can't it just work the other way. Then she could put a sock over her head and I wouldn't have to ever look at that *face,* again!"

No one in the history of ALBANY PARK has ever heard of or recorded a miracle. No miracles on Ainslee Avenue or on Bernard or Catalpa or the street the Rappans live on, Saint Louis. Yet, in spite of this hard evidence, each night, after Joe goes over the books and sees the cash flow running out faster than the camp's cash coming, he prays for one to happen.

Somehow God, in his infinite wisdom, decided that MAURY, 12, was to be a bed wetter, RALPH, a thumbsucker, DAVID, allergic to trees, grass, and pollens, NORTON, an ox and a poet, BOOTZIE, 10, non-verbal, and God, who is also supposed to be ever wise and just, must be getting a little senile.

All American Daycamp is a misnomer. Give me your tired, your weary, your downtrodden is what it should have been called.

The days never end for Joe. He pours through books from the library on bedwetting, thumbsucking, allergies, non-verbal behavior. More psychology books than he ever read just to get his degree.

He has to nearly tie Chet to a chair to read over the same material. Something on these pages may work.

If Bootzie, the non-verbal one, can't hit a ball even if it were the size of a watermelon, at least, at the end of the summer he can say, "Pitch it to me a little higher."

Perhaps if David wouldn't be afraid that he's going to die every time he sneezes, or choke to death every time he eats a piece of food he thinks he's allergic to then maybe his fears would diminish and his allergic reactions lessen in scale.

If Joe is going to lose his house, his small savings, his sanity, then at least when he goes down these kids will have a little more self-esteem and dignity.

Chet's answer to it all is roaming the south and west sides of Chicago where kids have always been considered tougher and better at sports, offering them "scholarships" to the daycamp, a few bucks under the table for winning in the Junior Olympics and a promise that college recruiters will be out the week of the Olympics with contracts in one pocket and "incentives" in the other.

The camp which has always prided itself as being exclusively for "northsiders" takes on a peculiar geographical look. All American Daycamp kids have crewcuts. So how come "greasers" are now wearing daycamp sweatshirts?

Names like, SWENSON, MCCALAUGH, CALHOON are in the intercamp baseball lineups with names with LIPSHULTZ, SHAPIRO, and KAPLIN.

During a hot meeting of campowners, All American is accused of bringing in ringers who are probably high school dropouts and the Association threatens to revoke All American's license even though All American now sounds All American.

Joe pleads with Chet to stop his recruiting policies. They're running out of gas chasing all over the city, picking up these kids who are way over the age limit of 13, anyway.

Three more parents withdraw their sons from the camp after they all report their boys have learned how to jump-start cars, break into homes, and shakedown summer school children out of their bus money.

On top of that, two counselors quit on them in the middle of the season.

Now where are they going to find replacements???

Joe's wife quits her job.

And Itsig's sister takes a temporary leave of absence and shows up one day in a sweatshirt and gym shorts that no camp counselor has ever filled like that before.

"Chet??? We'll be arrested."

"Will you relax for a minute. She can teach these kids how to run?"

"Are you crazy?"

"What young red blooded All American Daycamp boy in his right mind won't want to run after her in a game of tag. *Believe* me Joe, they'll learn how to run!"

And, swim, in a game called Catch the Dolphin. David, the one allergic to chlorine, opens up his eyes for the first time when he sees who's in the water. Cookie, the mermaid, wearing a costume she dragged out of moth balls, once worn by SIZZLING SUSIE, in the 20's, she's found buried in a footlocker in the basement of the Rialto.

Bootzie who hasn't alked in months, sidles up to Cookie one day, who's sitting on the tailgate of the Pontiac station wagon, eating lunch and when she puts her sandwich down and begins paying attention to him, he squints up to her in the sunlight and says, "You're a n . . . nice lady, you k . . . know that. I w w . . wish everybody was a . . . as nice as y . . . you. Ca . . . can I marry you when I gr . . . grow up?"

Joe hears it first then Chet, then the rest of the campers. "Bootzie's talking. Do you hear him?" "Bootzie's talking???? He's got a nice voice. It doesn't squeak like mine!" The whole camp buzzes . . .

Once he talks, Bootzie displays another rare gift. A fantastic throwing arm. He can toss a league ball half a block. A softball 35 yards and a javelin 30 yards.

Bootzie can do something!

Cookie's got a cure for Ralph, the thumbsucker, too. A whistle the Rialto's stage manager has used on occasion when the place is being raided.

The thumb goes out and the whistle goes in.

Then in a few days, he gets so tired of blowing the whistle that he spits that out too. Now with his right hand free, he can hold onto a pole.

To begin with Ralph is pretty tall for his age, and his legs are long and gangly. Chet notices the kid's got great spring in his legs and within a week, he's got him pole vaulting.

That leaves Maury, the bedwetter. Maury has the habit of stopping in the middle of doing something and having to do something else.

In the middle of a baseball game, Maury can hit a fly out to left field, good for at least three bases, but stop midway between first and second and then run rather peculiarly after that.

Joe's wife remembers when their son had the same problem. She told him he would turn out to be just like his Aunt Nettie if he kept on doing it.

Aunt Nettie???

The next day, the oldest camp counselor in history gets off the bus and shuffles up to the baseball diamond wearing an umbrella to shield the sun, a black overcoat so her arms won't sun burn, a pair of boots to keep her feet clean, a can of aerosol spray so that all the germs of All American Daycamp won't infect her and while she's walking up to her daughter, Rochelle, Joe has taken Maury aside and whispers, "See that woman?"

"Uh huh, Uncle Joe."

"Look at her carefully."

"I am."

"What does she remind you of?"

"Isn't that your mother-in-law, Uncle Joe?"

"That's okay. I promise I won't get insulted."

"A wierdo."

"That's right. And you know why she's like that way?"

"No, Uncle Joe."

"Because when she was about your age, she had a problem and nobody helped her."

"What kind of problem, Uncle Joe."

"The same kind of 'problem' you have."

"And she walks around looking like that now?"

"Always has and always will."

Maury's eyes follow Aunt Nettie as she waddles over to a park bench along the first base-line, sprays the bench with the aerosol can before sitting down. Pulls her coat collar tightly across her chest even though it is already 75 degrees outside and hides her face in the umbrella.

Three days later little Maury Rothstein hits a long fly ball to right field and runs from first to third base without stopping . . .

The camp roster depleted by half is running in the red, thanks to the rumors and faithless parents who keep pulling their kids out.

Uncle Chet is falling behind in his payments to the bookie and Joe is falling behind in his payments on the house.

To pick up extra money, Joe starts selling used cars for his cousin who has a lot squeezed between a hot dog and custard stand on one side which he also owns and a bowling alley on the other.

He uses Joe as his shill. Lovable chubby Joe, a cuddly teddy bear in the middle of a thief's market who has to keep the prospective buyer from walking off the lot and steer them, instead, in the direction of the mobile house trailer which his cousin MOE uses as a sales office and loan department.

One thing Joe can do is tell stories. A fantastic story teller who needs only look at his parents and aunts and uncles for his material.

From selling cars he knows nothing. From telling stories he knows everything. So to make his cousin Moe, who keeps looking out the trailer window, think he's pitching hard selling cars, Joe tells the customers stories.

They laugh. They stay. And then they walk in the direction of the trailer.

Moe hasn't seen business this good in years. The fact that Moe looks like a crook, talks like a crook, and is a crook may have something to do with it.

But now with Joe there, even a crook can be excused for selling cars.

With the commission he's picking up from his moonlight job, Joe is paying off daycamp bills and loaning Chuck money to keep from getting his fingers smashed by a private "consultant" hired by the bookie to collect on bad debts from dead beats.

The City's Junior Olympics is now two weeks off. Maury hasn't wet his pants or bed in weeks. Does the 100 yard dash in respectable time.

Ralph can jump ten feet in the pole vault.

David hasn't closed his eyes in the chlorine pool and has been clocked doing the 440 in competitive time. Not so good. But it could be a lot worse.

Bootzie's throwing a javilin almost 35 yards now.

Cookie's only working three nights at the Rialto and has sewn sequins on her All American Daycamp counselor's polo shirt and gym shorts.

Already Chet is placing bets with the other daycamp owners on the outcome of the Junior Olympics . . . but sometimes, at night, he drives by his old apartment, parks a few houses away, and just stares up at the second floor window to see Marion's silhouette through the closed bedroom shades.

A few times he's about to open the car door, about to take the steps up the courtyard or the back porch and maybe just stop in for a few minutes and say hello but his intentions only get as far as his car's door handle and then he looks down and drives away.

The week before the Olympics, Joe tells his cousin he's had it and when Moe protests, Joe thanks him first and when Moe grabs onto Joe's shoulder and won't let him go, Joe tells him where he can drive that clunker convertible that has gone from white, yellow to red in order to sell it.

"Moe, you can take that piece of junk you call a classic, put it in reverse and park it up your . . . " as a motorcycle that passes by with a bad muffler drowns out the "exact location" he had in mind for Moe.

In the 20 years he's been married, Joe never once has gotten drunk. Really stewed. Yeah, maybe a little tipsy, but nothing like what happens to him a few hours later.

First, he stops at a bar a few doors down from the Rialto. Something he's never done before and gets smashed.

Then with his embarrassed eyes closed, he pays the cashier at the window and walks into the Rialto Theatre, something else he's never done before.

Then he staggers down to the first row, plops on a seat, and yawns through the comedy act until finally he gets up and announces to the other fifty patrons, one of them Chet who's burying his face in the back row, flabbergasted at the roly-poly body making its way up on the stage and telling the equally startled comedians, "I don't think you're funny. You know who's really funny? My Aunt Nettie is really funny. I call her my Aunt but she's really my mother-in-law. So that doesn't make her my Aunt, it makes her my enemy. She's so afraid of catching someone else's germs that she cooks all her meals with penicillin.

"Last week my doctor told her she was in perfect health, and when she heard that she thought she was going to die.

"She married my Uncle Sidney when she was 16 years old. It was a very religious ceremony. All my relatives prayed to God it wouldn't last.

"My Uncle Sidney had a junk yard. She wouldn't let him near the dinner table until he took a bath.

"The bathtub was outside the house in the front yard. Every night at 6 o'clock, my Uncle Sidney would drive up, get out of his car, take all his clothes off, and jump in the tub. All the neighbors would run to the front window. This was years before television.

"The one thing cleaner than my Uncle Sidney were the neighbors' windows. But the only channel they could get was my Uncle's nightly bath.

"The day my Uncle Sidney died, all the neighbors went into mourning and filed past the bathtub to pay their last respects. I don't know who they were grieving for more—my Uncle Sidney or what they would be doing at 6 o'clock from now on.

"My Uncle Sidney made a living from dirt in his nails and was buried in dirt up to his nails.

"He . . . he never worried about dying. So it didn't come as a surprise to him when he did.

"You know who goes to the cemetery every other day to make sure he has fresh flowers? Me!

"Do you know who pulls the weeds around the grave once a week so you can still see his name on the stone? Me!

"Do you know who thinks she has two weeks to live? My Aunt Nettie!

"Do you know when she came to that conclusion? Forty-two years ago!

"Excuse me . . . I think I'm going to throw up."

Joe races from the stage and falls into the arms of Chet who holds him like a child while he sobs forty-six years of frustration out of his system and Cookie runs to get him a cup of coffee and a cold compress.

All the way home in Chet's car with Cookie rubbing his head, he babbles apologies until he's carried into his house, past his horrified wife, and stops long enough in front of Aunt Nettie to cough in her face . . .

Now, it's the day before the City's Junior Olympics. Of course, the newspapers are playing up the favorites, like Jack Armstrong Daycamp, which has won in seven out of the ten divisions for the past two years. Camp Kwama is considered a tough competitor. But nowhere in the list is even a mention of All American Daycamp. Until Joe sees that particular sports page is next to the obituaries, and by some printer's error the words All American Daycamp and a few lines saying they have placed last in every division three consecutive years are on the obit side.

The MORNING OF THE OLYMPICS, in the best tradition of "let's win one for the gipper," Chet has mounted the Pontiac's roof, charging the campers up while A and D Gas Station charges the Pontiac up with jumper cables, and Joe, inside the front seat, nods at the attendant who tells him to start the car.

"It's all in the mind. Losing is an attitude. Tell yourselves you're the best," Chet blares. He rolls his eyes skyward.

"You can do it. Because if you don't you little ba . . . Joe and I are going to lose our shirts. Now don't let the other campers intimidate you. Stare 'em straight in the eyes, except you, David. I know your eyes cross when you're too close to people."

"Get out in that field. Think like a champion. Give it the best you've got. Just stay on your feet."

Suddenly the car lurches forward and Chet falls off.

WINNAMAC PARK, a few hours later. First of all, every city politician is out pumping hands and personally taking credit for the "Games."

One of them bends down close to Joe who's stooping tying Bootzie's gym shoes. "Hi. I'm Martin Oberhauser, running for Alderman in the 42nd ward?"

"Yeah, so what. You want me to tie your shoes, too."

Cookie, to the chagrin of the awfully embarrassed politicians who are shrinking behind their wives' backs, recognizes some of her more faithful and regular Rialto customers, nuzzles right up to them on a first name basis.

Chet, looking over his brood of "rejects," sizes up their chances, peeks at his wallet, catches the attention of two camp owners, and within a few moments is wagering a few more bets.

And on the other side of the field, another transaction is taking place. Aunt Nettie, wrapped in her worn winter cloth coat, is huddling with a slick cigar smoking Ward Committeeman she's known for years.

"Nettie, you're crazy. It's like taking candy from a baby. Save your money."

"What kind of point spread will you give me, Manny." Her eyes, once you can see them hidden under the umbrella shielding her from the sun, have taken on the peculiar squint of a riverboat gambler.

"On your son-in-law's campers??? A point spread? You want odds? I'll give you odds. Seven to one that none of 'em will even make it up to the starting line. The kid with the pole. I'll bet you his pole will go higher than he will."

"Not him. The other one over there," Nettie demurs.

"The Ox??? Nettie, there's no division for feeding pigeons and squirrels. Look at that kid. He's on his hands and knees with those squirrels. I know all about him."

"Every camp in town refused him. His parents even wanted to give me a little extra under the table if I could talk to Cothran who owns Happy Trails and get him in. Nettie, Nettie, in a game of friendly Kalookie, I'm glad to take your money, but on him???! Forget it."

"My five against your twenty-five says he'll place third in the cross-country."

"What country?"

"You're chicken, Manny."

"Nettie, I think this time you really have a genuine illness. Okay. My twenty-five says he can't. Not only he can't but this country will celebrate its next centennial before he finishes the cross country. You're on."

A few moments later, Nettie has taken the "Ox" aside and is whispering something in his ears while she shields the side of her face closest to his mouth from catching anything.

"A bear?" the Ox replies in bewilderment.

"A bear, Norton. Do a bear."

His bear imitation is as good as his squirrel imitation or his pigeon or the other thirty animals he can imitate.

He does it so perfectly that even Nettie jumps forgetting for a moment, the bear is Norton.

"Do a bear every time you pass a tree or a building. And when the runners start turning around, tell 'em about the bear that escaped from the zoo this morning."

In the 100 meter free style, Cookie, who's coaching David, stays at the end of the pool. What a sight. David turns the first lap in record time. The second a little slower. The third, trailing a swimmer from Happy Trails, the fourth hearing Cookie shout that she promises to get him into the Rialto the day he turns 16, and the fifth and final lap, David heads for the finish like a torpedo, breaking the old city record.

In the pole vault, Bootzie has reached nine feet. His first try at ten feet falls short and so do his gym shorts which drop just as he readies his spring.

The ridicule among the other campers is brutal. He stands there for a moment looking like he's not setting for a second attempt but another 10 years of being non-verbal all over again.

"No Bootzie," Jack is yelling. "Talk! Talk back to them. They're no better than you. Pull your pants up first and then give it back to them like they're giving it to you. Please Bootzie. Talk. Talk???"

For a few moments, muted breathless seconds, Bootzie just stares at his tormentors. Then he raises his shorts up and stammers, "d . . . did that j . . . just to get y . . . your atten . . . attention."

He jogs back to the starting line. Rubs some rosin on his hands and the pole. Sucks in a deep breath. Flexes his knees, and starts his run again . . .

Up . . . over . . . and down, clearing the bar at ten feet.

While Bootzie's setting up for 10'5", Norton, the "Ox," is panting a mile away trying to keep up with the rest of the cross-country runners.

He's taunted by the faster runners. Far enough away from the starter not to be noticed he growls like a bear.

Two of the runners ahead of him turn and look at each other not wanting to hear what they've just heard.

The bear growls grow louder, as the "Ox" gains on them.

When he's alongside, he pants, "Bear. Big one. Saw it. Escaped from the zoo."

A half mile later he growls again. A couple of more runners pull back when news of the escaped bear hits them.

But Norton's conscience is bothering him when he nears a few more runners. He can't do a bear any more. That's cheating. He wants to run the race on his own terms. So he does a squirrel. Who's going to be afraid of a squirrel? Or a pigeon? Or a frog?

"Did you hear that guy who just passed me? He's rebeeping like a frog."

And the "Ox" starts gaining momentum and carrying on a conversation with his imaginary friends. And that kind of concentration begins working because it's getting his mind off his cramped legs.

While the "Ox" keeps up the pace, Ralph, the reformed thumbsucker, is getting last minute pomposities from Chet. "Now remember, you don't flick your wrist, see? Gotta be all in the arm. Arm motion like this. Let me show you."

Chet lamely throws the javelin a few yards. "Slipped," he excuses. "All in the arms." He tries again and this attempt is about as feeble as the last.

"Uncle Chet?"

"What is it," Chet snaps.

"I know what to do. Let me throw it my way, okay?"

Before he can confuse Ralph any more, Joe grabs him away by the arm, admonishing, "What are you trying to do to him, Goldkaupf? Make him lose?! You probably got half our money bet against us."

"Joey, don't get excited. You're right about half of the money but you're wrong about how I'm betting it. Okay, I placed a couple a few weeks ago, but I swear the bets I've been making since then are for us to win."

"It's a good thing I got my hands on the rest, Chester Goldkaupf. Somebody in this organization has got to exercise some money management." He squints cautiously. "How much you got bet? You know, I mean, the odds. What kind of odds they been giving you?"

"I don't know. Six to one. Seven to one. Ten to one."

"Chet, I am really disappointed in you."

"Joe, I promise. If we win, I swear I'll never bet on anything again."

"You wanta make a bet on it?"

"Believe me."

"Good. Because I'm taking the same oath. The other half of the money, *my half* . . . "

"Yeah, so what about *your half,* partner. You going to buy me out. Push me out, right partner?! My high school buddy. I *bet* you figured it was going to be really easier taking over."

"You just said you wouldn't bet after today."

"I know you. You've been waiting. Just waiting for the right moment to tell me I've screwed up so much, you're running the camp from now on!"

"Why don't you let me finish a sentence. The other half of the money, *my half,* that half has been invested in a certain way whose yield, *partner,* may be twice as much as yours . . . "

Chet shakes his head wildly. "No . . . "

"Whaddaya mean, 'no.' Yeah! Twenty to one with Krantz who owns Big Foot, let's see, O'Ryan of Blazers I have down for twenty-five to one on three events, all third place. So far we have won two and that means . . . "

"I love you . . . you hot air balloon."

"Five hundred bucks, so far, and my crazy Aunt Nettie, I just found out she's got one going with Dorf, the committeemen of the 40th ward."

"On who?"

"Norton, she's got him doing crazy animal calls." Then Joe adds coyly, "He's got half the field running the other way out of fright."

"Nettie, the hypochondriac who belongs to the disease-of-the-month club???"

"Same Aunt Nettie."

WINNAMAC PARK is in a state of shock by mid-afternoon. An angry bunch of camp owners approach Joe and Chet accusing them of everything including spiking the soda pop. So far, All American Daycamp has placed no worse than third in three events and the owners have misplaced the true meaning of sportsmanship. How can they set an example for their campers if they stomp around acting like sore losers.

A bet is a bet.

Angry dollars exchange hands, not to mention the menacing looks.

Chet appeals to the owners' sense of reconciliation. "Our kids are just better. Let's say they are *gifted.*"

"Your kids," Krantz, of Big Foot, bellows, "aren't supposed to win. They're setting a poor example. We tell our campers if they don't behave and mind and listen to us, they'll wind up like those rejects at All American. Now, how are we going to explain all this to 'em."

"Don't," Joe reasons. "Have them just come by tomorrow. We're accepting applications for next season."

"You guys don't have a ghost of a chance opening up next year."

Chet, who's waving the money back in their faces, simply smiles and says, "Boo!"

Minutes before the awards presentation begins, the first of the cross-country entrants wheezes in.

To the astonishment of everyone there, Norton, the "Ox," is pumping his legs like crazy, then falls across the finish line, in a dead faint.

Joe, the first over, starts fanning him.

Chet bends over waving his hands.

Aunt Nettie holds her umbrella over him.

"Say something, Ox, anything. Do a pigeon. A squirrel."

"Have him do a giraffe."

"I don't think he knows how."

Suddenly Ox stirs and does himself. "I did it Uncle Joe. I did it. I finished. I did it on my own."

"You and that zoo you carry in your mouth," Chet cracks.

"No, Uncle Chet. No funny noises. I ran the last two hours with my mouth shut. I only opened it to breathe. No animals. No bears. No pigeons. No squirrels. Just me."

Even the newspapers carry the upset in the morning editions. CAMP CARRIES FOUR EVENTS. BIGGEST UPSET SINCE TRUMAN BEAT DEWEY IN '48.

By the afternoon, the phone at Joe's home is ringing off the hook. They're besieged by parents who want to make sure their kids have a spot in next year's roster.

In three hours, they've filled next year's season and have a waiting list.

That night, Cookie performs at the Rialto, breaking in a new act. It has an Olympic setting. What she does with a torchlight, a hurdle, and a see-through swimming tank with a small diving board attached is absolutely breathtaking. Every eye in the house is riveted to her events.

When it's all over, Chet is waiting backstage to throw a robe over her shoulders. "You were fantastic."

"Was I really, dahling," she gestures dramatically, like Tallulah Bankhead. "Simply mahvelous that you think *so,* Broderick."

"What's this Broderick. I'm Chet."

"Would you be a dear and tell my admirers I'm too tired to see them tonight."

She sweeps past him. Closes the door to her dressing room, locks it, and then begins to cry.

Chet is dumbfounded, pounding on the door. It's futile to pound any more. She's not going to open it up. He stands there like a piece of stone until he feels someone touching him.

"Hi."

His wife, looking very uncomfortable, anxious, unsure, yet hoping, just like when they first met. She asks first, "I didn't mean those things I said about her. She's a very nice person. I couldn't ever be like her. But once, at the lake, remember when they were telling everybody to stay away because they were expecting a seiche to come in and the waves could have washed everyone into the harbor—we were standing like everybody else, tempting fate and you said to me, 'What are we doing standing around here waiting to drown . . . I love you . . . ' remember?"

Chet looks down at his feet.

"Guess what the weather forecaster said might happen tonight? We might even see some of the same people . . . although it was a long time ago."

"It wasn't that long ago, was it . . . ?"

SEPTEMBER . . . the first week of school at Fenker High. In the middle of the gym floor, in front of a bunch of oddball, oddsized students, Chet Goldkaupf screams at them, "Laps! Ten laps across the floor. Now move, ah one . . . two . . . three . . . four . . . keep your legs up. Kaponitz, you run like a Sis . . . like someone who's been practicing all summer, Kaponitz. I'm proud of you . . ."

And between the east and west sections of the huge building, in the swimming pool that reeks of chlorine, Joe Rappan, covered in a beach towel wrapped around his waist, extolls the virtues of cleanliness and his grading policy.

"Two cuts and you get an automatic 'F.' "

The same mock wrath he's used countless times in past semesters seems to be working again as twenty shivering freshman listen like raw recruits the first day of basic training.

" . . . and when I mean wash, I mean wash. I don't want to see a spot of dirt. No one gets by me unless he's clean—all over. You understand?"

Then he raises his hand and shows them . . . "a bar of soap. See? In case any of you don't know what a bar of soap looks like, I'm going to pass it down. I want you to touch it. Smell it. And—use it!

"Now . . . line in two's. Aaronson, Agie, Arkin and Bauman . . . in the showers . . . Becker, Bradkowskie . . . Cooper and Creighton, next . . . Derwinski?? Who's going to hold Derwinski up? Don't worry Derwinski, there's nothing wrong in being short. As long as you know how to swim . . . Short people are the last to get hit by rain—and the first to drown . . . next, Diremus, Douglas, Dobofsky and Dummas . . . next Epstein, Espenshade, Eubank and Fabbrinni . . . next . . ."

FADE OUT . . .

chapter 6
Writing the Script: Format

No matter what anyone may tell you, there *is* a right way to write any script. It's not enough to have content, a fine idea, excellent research. Without proper format, the content will never reach an audience. Format means the way a script is set up on a page, the ways in which sound, music, narrative, dialogue, and visuals are used or not used, the ways in which scenes and sequences in the script are developed, and other related matters.

Format is important. If there is a producer somewhere waiting impatiently for your script for an educational film and you lay on his desk something that looks like the script for a radio documentary, he will be annoyed. And it will be your fault. And the annoyance might have been avoided if you had understood that there is a difference between radio and television, between an educational film and a documentary, and had written your script accordingly.

What we propose to deal with in this and succeeding chapters is *format,* the special styles or types of media script—documentary, industrial, educational, institutional advertisements, products advertisements, television news copy, teleplay, and screenplay. Each of these categories has its own format to follow. Learning these formats intellectually isn't especially difficult; learning how to write them effectively takes much more trouble.

You can expect these formats to change, and as a professional writer you must be aware of the changes as they take place. In fact, if you are an exceptionally talented and capable writer, you may be able to anticipate them on occasion. Changes come about largely through the technology of communication. Audiotape was a revolutionary device when it first appeared, twenty-five years ago. So was videotape, and so currently are the new portable video cameras. Such inventions create whole new languages of sound and vision; or rather, they make necessary such new languages, which writers, directors, and editors are then left to invent.

The basic observations we make in this book will, we believe, remain true for a long time. Many of the specific comments and observations on format will probably remain true for the next several years. But never forget that you, as a writer, will be working with media that have been, throughout their short history, in constant change. You are responsible for updating your own knowledge.

FORMAT: THE AUDIO SCRIPT

Any audio production, whether for recording or broadcast, deals wholly in a language of sound. An audio script must therefore make provision for the use of voice (narration and dialogue), sound effects, music, and some special devices for distorting sound. The following is a sample page from an audio script, in which the narrator is talking about and dramatizing his childhood fantasies.

HENRY:	Why, I remember when I was a boy, not more than eight or ten years old. I got a copy of an old story for my birthday, a French story, *The Song of Roland.* (BEGIN FADE) I read that book, and re-read it, until it finally fell apart . . .
MUSIC	*A FANFARE OF TRUMPETS, FOLLOWED BY TRANSITION MUSIC UNDER . . .*
VOICE 3:	Now marvellous and weighty is the combat.
	Right well they strike, Roland and Oliver;
	A thousand blows come from the Archbishop's hand;
	The dozen peers are nothing short of that;
	With one accord now all the Franks do battle.
	Pagans are slain by hundreds, by thousands;
	Who flies not then, from death has no warrant.
	The Franks have lost the foremost of their band,
	They'll see no more their father or their clans,
	Yet they strike on; their hearts are good and stout.
MUSIC	*UP, THEN FADE UNDER AND OUT. . .*
HENRY:	Yes, the old times, the old battles: to live in a bright world of flashing armor and strong colors and flashing words. I had no good old times to remember, so I created a world. For a long time, I used to ask my mother . . .
BOY HENRY:	Mom, can I have the sickle? I want to cut the weeds in the back lot.
MOTHER:	Henry, you were just out there yesterday! Whatever has gotten into you?
BOY HENRY:	Aw . . . I just want to cut the weeds. Can I, Mom?

MOTHER:	Well, I suppose you can. But I'm really a little worried about you, Henry.
HENRY:	(AS AN ADULT) You understand that the Saracens wore green. Green was their color. And they were tall, thin men with brown faces like seed pods at the top of a stalk. And when they rode down in the long, terrible sweep of a charge, they rode by hundreds and thousands. And great Roland stood alone against them, with the sharp sword in his hand.
MUSIC	*TRUMPET FANFARE, SEGUE INTO . . .*
SOUND	*CLATTER OF MANY HORSES AT A GALLOP.*
VOICE 3:	(EXULTANTLY) With Durendal my sword I'll lay on thick and stout! Felon pagans to the pass shall not come down!
SOUND	*FADE HORSES INTO . . .*
MUSIC	*TRUMPETS UP, DISTANT.*
HENRY:	Yes, I liked to cut the weeds, and nobody ever knew why.

Many features of this typographical format will appear in modified form in scripts for video and film production. Notice that all designations—*character names, sound, music* appear in CAPS in the left-hand margin. Directions that affect performance—*begin fade, exultantly*—are set in caps and parentheses, and inserted into the text of speeches at the appropriate points. The same would be true of directions for sound distortion—usually either *on echo* or *filter.*

Sound and music cues are distinguished typographically from the rest of the script. Each cue has one or more lines to itself and is set entirely in caps and underlined (italicized). Speeches, whether dialogue or narrative, are typed in ordinary lower-case style.

It is extremely important for the writer to understand and use this or some similar workable format in writing audio script. These typographical rules are not merely conventions designed to produce an attractive page; they are most important in the reading and production of the script itself. What the audio script does is to separate visually all of the essential production elements. Actors must not, by accident, read sound cues as if they were lines of dialogue. A music director must be able to tell at a glance what his cues are and precisely where they are placed in the production. The director of the production must be constantly aware of the several sound elements being blended into a single effect.

We shall discuss problems and techniques in writing dialogue and narration in later chapters; meanwhile, a few notes on the other elements in the sound script will not be amiss.

In writing a scene for audio production, the writer must always be aware of the relative volumes of sounds, since he will manipulate these to give the listener an illusion of perspective. When you listen to a dramatic scene done in sound, you visualize the high volume sounds as being nearest you. The actors who are *on mike* are close, those who fade off are moving away. The same thing is true of sound effects and of music used to suggest action as well as feeling. A writer can create rather elaborate perspectives in a scene by taking a little trouble. For example, suppose a scene takes place at an outdoor party on a spring night. Three characters are having a quiet conversation in the foreground, on mike. At some distance, slightly off mike, we hear the sound of passing traffic. The whole nature of the listener's imagined image of this scene could be radically changed simply by changing the relative volume levels of these sound elements.

Sound effects are a language of action and feeling. Most effects when used in the simplest way suggest action: footsteps, a door closing, a plane taking off. When used in a special acoustical setting, an element of feeling is added. Thus, echoing footsteps do not convey precisely the same thing as simple footsteps, and a creaking door does not have the same quality as an ordinary one when it opens.

In writing sound cues, be sure, first, that what you are describing is really a sound. Amateur writers often make the mistake of writing stage directions as if they were sound effects: "John moves on tiptoe to the table." Second, be sure that sound is identifiable in context. Sounds are not as simple to decipher as we sometimes think. Gunshots are mistaken for backfires. Rain on a tin roof sounds much like a light machine shop in full operation. Always make sure that the context of the scene prepares the listener to "read" sound cues correctly. If it is clear that your characters are running from a house to escape a desperate situation, the footsteps, door slams, motor sounds, and so on are likely to be read correctly.

Music, in contrast to sound, is always a language of feeling. It is used to provide transitions between scenes, to back speeches for added emotional effect, sometimes even to create an exclamatory effect (as when an important line is followed by a sharp "sting" of music). A good music cue must always show where the music comes in, changes volume, and goes out. Thus, in the example given above, the battle passage from the *Song of Roland* is preceded by the cue: a fanfare of trumpets, followed by transition music under . . . (the passage from the poem). At the end of the passage, the script calls for the transition music to be brought up in volume, then faded under the next scene and finally out.

Music cues may, but need not, specify the kind of music to be used. A cue may simply call for a musical transition. Or it may call for a "light, gay" effect or a "mysterioso" effect. Sometimes the writer will wish even to specify a particular part of a particular composition; in the documentaries of the World War II period, the opening chords of Beethoven's Fifth Symphony, which signified *V for victory,* became extremely familiar to radio listeners.

Occasionally a music cue may be used almost as if it were a sound effect. The sounds of a Fourth of July parade must certainly include marching bands. The trumpets in the *Song of Roland* script, above, function in this way and are segued, or blended, into the actual sounds of charging horsemen.

A final technique available to the audio writer is the use of some special devices for distorting sound, the principal ones being the filter and the echo chamber. We have already discussed the mechanics of these effects, so we will just note that the filter is used to suggest distance (both physical and psychological) and the echo chamber to give an impression of great size or spaciousness.

These various audio languages, when blended with the spoken word, make up the language of a sound script—a language with great possibilities for conveying human feeling and flights of the imagination.

FORMATS: FILM AND VIDEO

With few exceptions, scripts written for film and videotape are similar in appearance, with video instructions on the left-hand side of the page and audio instructions on the right. The page itself is divided down the middle. Except for such matters of stage business as it may be necessary to insert into an actor's speeches, all statements about visuals belong on the left-hand side; this includes statements about camera angles and positions, moods that are reflected in the visuals, scene locations, lighting conditions whether natural or indoors. If the assignment calls for a full shooting script, the video instructions must be detailed.

There is not much room for detailed descriptions on the script page, so you must learn to *headline* and to use appropriate abbreviations. For example:

VIDEO	*AUDIO*
INT: NURSING STATION.	
INT: DOCTOR USING HOUSE PHONE, CALLING INTENSIVE CARE FLOOR. CAMERA DOLLIES IN AS DOCTOR ANNOUNCES ARRIVAL OF PATIENT BY AMBULANCE.	NATURAL SOUND THROUGHOUT.

Or the video instructions can be much shorter:

VIDEO

EXT: MASSIVE TRAFFIC JAM
ON X-WAY. USE LONG LENS.

The abbreviation *EXT:* stands for exterior, *X-WAY* for expressway, and the instruction *USE LONG LENS* means use a telephoto lens, which gives a visual effect of things almost rolling on top of each other because depth of field is nonexistent. You've perhaps seen a film shot of someone running toward the camera but never seeming to gain ground. This nightmarish effect is created by the use of the telephoto lens.

We shall talk about *technical effects* and how they can be used to orchestrate and dramatize actuality later, but for the moment it is enough for you to understand that whatever feelings, directions, ideas, or moods you may have that affect the visual quality of your script should be expressed on the left-hand side of the script in simple film or video terms, written in economical headline form, and always evaluated in terms of advancing your story.

With a few exceptions, the left-hand side of the page is typed in caps and single spaced. Occasionally a production house may prefer that you type all *body copy* in lower case. If so, comply. The best thing to do is to ask for a sample script to see the style they prefer and use it as your guide until you have memorized it.

We have already discussed the ways of writing a treatment. The shooting script is the logical extension of a treatment. All treatments, as we said, are written in third person present tense and summarize or capsulize what action will take place in the script. Since this is the case, the script translates treatment ideas into their full form. For instance, the opening paragraph of the treatment written for *You Bet Your Sweet Life,* a documentary film about a major university-affiliated hospital in Chicago, was designed to visually express the relationships among the hospital, the university, and the city:

> We'll open the film with a series of quick dissolves which will establish the lakefront campus, moving in on three buildings with indigenous sound. We'll hear what's going on inside but we'll see the buildings' exterior in a mosaic. The last shot will be a dissolve showing the downtown Chicago skyline, then we'll dissolve to the health science director's office explaining the hospital, staff, and needs.

This part of the treatment is so specific and detailed that it could be, and was, expanded into a series of specific shot descriptions in the script itself.

Treatments should always be thought of as the means of telling a visual story. How long they are depends on how much visual instruction the reader needs. For example, most documentaries have fairly detailed treatments or shooting outlines, especially since some scripts are written after the film is shot. If this is the case, then all the director has is the film outline or treatment to tell what scenes are needed, and what the attitude and mood of the piece are to be.

Now we shall move over to the audio side of the page and offer a few suggestions about writing narration and dialogue. Later in the book we will discuss this aspect of scriptwriting in detail. Unless the script you are writing is strictly *cinema verite,* using natural and spontaneous conversation as recorded on the scene, it will include lines of dialogue and narration. These items are always placed at the right-hand side of the script page, under *AUDIO,* double-spaced and in lower case. The name of the speaker (character or narrator) is put in caps. Instructions on how lines should be read, or on essential business that must be cued in with lines, appear in caps and parentheses. Here is an example from an educational script on consumer education:

AUDIO

ADELLA:
That's right. Look what happened to me and my panty hose. (THIS IS A CONVERSATION STOPPER. THEY ALL STARE AT HER.)
JENNIE:
Adella, I'd love to know what happened to you and your panty hose—that is, if you can tell the story in mixed company.
ADELLA:
(QUITE SERIOUS) Oh, no, it's nothing like that! See, I bought three pairs of panty hose at this discount place, because they were only 89 cents apiece.
JENNIE:
And they didn't last.

All sound effects are described on the right-hand side of the page; use the abbreviation *SFX* (sound effects) and then describe the effects desired.

For example:

AUDIO

SFX: STACCATO SOUND OF AN IBM PUNCH CARD MACHINE.

Music cues also appear on the right-hand side of the page, and are written in the same general style as sound cues. Not all documentaries need music, nor do industrial and educational films. Music, generally speaking, provides emotional support for visual sequences and spoken words; it is not to be used arbitrarily, but only where the support, the extra emotional depth, is useful. If you're writing a documentary on ghetto life, you may not need music to express the feeling of a ravaged neighborhood block that looks like part of a bombed-out city. The neighborhood turned junkyard—the remains of buildings, twisted wire, steel, half a wall, furniture so worthless that nobody has bothered to steal it, maybe a child kicking an old rusted-out door to a stove—won't need a bass viol moaning in the background to underscore their meaning.

Most documentaries today don't use music, but there are other kinds of scripts that do: most commercials, many industrial films, some educational films. In all cases, music should reinforce the visual images, never compete.

In fact, you as a writer may have to deal with the problems of music in your film or video scripts only on occasion. Take, for example, the case of filmstrips or slide films. A filmstrip, by its nature, cannot give the same feeling of movement, of rhythm, as a motion picture. As a result, shot sequences for a slide film have to be planned, shot, and edited with great care and skill; and even then, music is often thought essential to compensate for the lack of visual mobility. But, though considered important, music cues may not be stressed because of the way in which the strip is made. First, the pictures are shot, selected, and edited into a proper sequence. Second, the narrative and dialogue sections of the sound track are recorded and edited. (Some of this material may be *natural sound* recorded at the scene of the shooting; some may come from taped interviews and other pre-recorded material; some may be written narration or dialogue that has been recorded by actors in a studio.) Finally, the production is *scored* for music. (With a filmstrip, this usually means selecting passages from pre-recorded music and editing them together.) Finally, the whole production is brought together; sound and music keyed in with speech, and everything coordinated with the visuals.

The writer's part in determining the use of music in such a production is likely, at most, to consist of indicating points in the script where music may be required, with an occasional suggestion of the sort of "feel" the music should provide.

Regardless of the shifting responsibilities of writers as they go from filmstrip to audio script to documentary, the fact remains that they—you—must cultivate a sensitive ear and eye. How a script reads is important only because it must convey your ideas clearly to those who need to understand them. But how it "works" is everything. Can you *see* it? See the people, the movements, the scenes, the light qualities? Can you *hear* it? Hear it as exposition, yes; but also hear it as drama, and as poetry? These are the critical questions.

We have noted that the script page is divided into an audio side and a video side. Perhaps that typographical convention is unfortunate, for it may lead you to suppose that sound and visuals should in fact work separately. That is not the case. The audio and video aspects of a script make up a totality; they should always be thought of as mutually reinforcing. Don't yield to the temptation to underrate either. If you happen to be good at writing dialogue and narration, and not so good at visualizing, don't write what is essentially a sound script on the theory that, after all, it's the producer's or director's job to invent the pictures anyway. As a case in point, let us look in some detail at the mechanics of the filmstrip.

FORMAT: THE FILMSTRIP

A filmstrip assignment may seem to you to be comparatively easy—much easier, for instance, than writing a script for a 16mm film. You would be quite wrong in this assumption. In a filmstrip you are not dealing with a motion picture, but with something that ought to work rather like a motion picture. What you have is a series of still frames that, along with narration, dialogue, sound, and music, must tell a story. In essence, you must solve two problems in writing a filmstrip. The first is to give the strip a feeling of flow and movement, working in the two- to six-second time segments for which the individual frames are shown in automated sequence. The second is to plan and write your sound track so that it keys in exactly with the frames.

There is a third problem, very real and practical but unacknowledged. This is created by the fact that many people who write and produce filmstrips would much rather be making films. Making films is prestigious; film is, after all, an art. Making filmstrips is, in comparison, pedestrian and dull. The quality of filmstrips would improve enormously once the people making them were convinced they were practicing a difficult, highly skilled craft, working in a medium that has its own special usefulness.

Here is a fairly typical case. A filmstrip is commissioned on housekeeping at an auto truck-stop. It is to be directed at employees of these truck-stop operations. The client, a major oil firm, wants a set of lessons in how to keep these mammoth truck stops as clean and attractive as possible. It would be easier for the writer in many ways if the client had ordered the script done for 16mm sound film. But the client would certainly have spent much more money on the 16mm film and might well have gotten a less effective statement.

Writers are asked, first, to come up with treatments that have the characteristics of good film scripts even though the element of motion and action photography is lacking. The script must have structure and flow from a beginning to a middle, and end. The ability to fulfill this request requires that writers have a functional knowledge of the characteristics of filmstrips, so that they can exploit the medium to the full while working within its limits.

All filmstrips are similar in certain superficial respects. The average ten-minute filmstrip runs approximately thirty pages and has roughly 112 frames. The frames are numbered consecutively and appear with a brief description typed in uppercase and single-spaced on the left-hand (video) side of the page. All sound effects and music, as well as narration and dialogue, appear on the right-hand side of the page, typed in lowercase, double-spaced. Any directions to characters or the narrator appear in parentheses just after the character name or narrator, and they too are typed in uppercase.

An example:

VIDEO	*AUDIO*
1. CU. GRILL OF TRUCK.	SFX: DIESEL ENGINE SOUND AS TRUCK STARTS.
	NARRATOR (V.O.):
	Truckers move most of the commerce of this country.

VIDEO	AUDIO
2. MS. TRUCK PULLING ONTO HIGHWAY.	The men and women who drive them help link up one end of the country with the other.
3. WS. TRUCK ON HIGHWAY.	Without them we have nothing.
	MUSIC: UP TO ESTABLISH THEN FADE TO B.G.
4. AERIAL SHOT. TRUCKSTOP.	NARRATOR (V.O.): What can we do to keep progress and commerce moving ahead? We can provide a support service for the trucks and the goods they haul.

Several points are worth noticing in this brief example. First, on the video side of the page, camera angles are included and abbreviated: *CU* for close up; *MS* for medium shot; *WS* for wide shot or wide angle. Each frame is explained clearly but briefly, almost in a form of headline writing: *TRUCK PULLING ONTO HIGHWAY*. Finally, each new frame is numbered.

On the audio side of the page, the term *sound effects* is abbreviated *(SFX)* and the kind of sound desired is explained in uppercase: *DIESEL ENGINE SOUNDS AS TRUCK STARTS*. The term *NARRATOR* is typed in uppercase and the symbol *V.O.* is used to indicate *voice over*. The copy is clear and to the point. Most training films are most effective when they tell a simple story simply. In a sense, filmstrip training films (the same is true of didactic films of any sort) are most effective when they are least "creative." If the script calls for too many unusual visual effects, or gets lost in poetic narration, the message may vanish.

We do not mean that complex visual effects are never used in filmstrips. We have seen such techniques as *gel downs* (reducing the contrast or richness of a color transparency), *dropping down colors* (allowing printed overlays to be clearly readable), *overlays* (art work), *split screens* or *quadrant screens* (showing two or four different visual actions in the same frame), and other such devices used in filmstrips. It's much more interesting to write scripts that use such techniques because they do expand the possibilities of the medium. However, they may be unnecessary or even a liability to your actual purpose; at best they are much more expensive to produce. When you are tempted to use any but the simplest and most direct ways of communicating your ideas in a filmstrip, be skeptical of your motives, and always consult your producer. You are the guardian of your professional judgment, and he or she controls the budget.

Filmstrips are widely used as teaching tools in elementary and secondary schools, and sometimes in colleges. They may be intended for the students, to be used in classroom settings, or for the indoctrination of instructors who are to be involved in new teaching and counseling situations. Very often it is the filmstrip that introduces the instructor to new possibilities in education—and these strips are accompanied by print collateral such as teaching guides, study guides, evaluation sheets, and so on.

One filmstrip series, *A Guide to Growing,* was developed for a secondary school program in student contract advising, in which the young person contracts with an advisor on what he or she will take in the course of a semester. The strips dealt with the advisor's role in this relationship. The strip featured an advisor and four students, each with specific needs. The following examples taken from the strip show how the narration and dialogue, music and natural sound weave together to (1) advance the story, (2) provide as much realism as possible, and (3) allow an intimacy with the viewer.

19. CU. FAVORING THE STUDENT AS HE CONTINUES EXPRESSING HIS FEELINGS.

We've all gone through the process of growing up. It *can* become rather confusing at times, and it does help to have a friend you can turn to.

20. CU. FAVORING DAVE.

Well, I think of myself as a friend to my advisees as well as a counselor and teacher.

21. DIFFERENT ANGLE, DAVE AND STUDENT.

Because if I'm really going to help my kids, I've got to know them as individuals. And each of them *is* different . . .

Take Jean Jansen for example . . .

22. PSYCHEDELIC FRAME

MUSIC: UP BEAT ROCK.
STRONG DRUM RHYTHM.

23. CU. JEAN JANSEN

MUSIC: CONTINUES

24. MS. JEAN WITH A BOYFRIEND TOGETHER AT SCHOOL.

MUSIC: CONTINUES

25. MWS. JEAN SPRAWLED ON THE FLOOR IN THE PRIVACY OF HER BEDROOM TALKING TO SOMEONE ON THE PHONE.

MUSIC: CONTINUES

26. MLS. (FULL LENGTH) JEAN MODELING SOME MOD CLOTHES IN FRONT OF HER MIRROR.

MUSIC: CONTINUES

27. LS. JEAN IN A SCHOOL SITUATION

MUSIC: CONTINUES

28. SPLIT FRAME. MASK SHOTS #23 THRU #27 IN SQUARES

MUSIC: FADE UNDER FOR BACKGROUND.

DAVE MARX (V.O.):

That's Jeanny . . . fourteen years old, bright, attractive . . . and not terribly interested in academics. (CLIPPING THE LIST OFF) She likes boys, clothes, movies, and rock music. My problem . . . how to take all that energy and direct it toward learning. Jean's parents know she does enough work to get by . . . but they also feel she can do much better . . . and so do I.

29. LS. ALVIN SPARKS, HANDS IN POCKETS, WALKING ALONE DOWN A STREET. HIS HEAD BENT DOWN LOOKING ABSORBED IN HIS OWN TROUBLES.

MUSIC: MOOD—GUITAR, SULLEN, DISTRAUGHT SOUNDS

30. CU. HIS EYES SOMEWHERE ELSE. LOST IN THOUGHT AND HIS OWN CONFUSION.

MUSIC: CONTINUES

31. WS. ALVIN, STANDING NEAR A CONSTRUCTION SITE, THE WORKERS TOWERING ON SCAFFOLDS ABOVE HIM.

MUSIC: CONTINUES

32. MCU. ALVIN IN CLASS. LACK OF INTEREST EVIDENT.

MUSIC: FADES UNDER AND BACKGROUND

33. SPLIT FRAME. MASK SHOTS #29 THROUGH #33.

DAVE MARX (V.O.):

Alvin Sparks . . . sixteen years old . . . not much of an achiever in traditional academics. He's thinking about dropping out of school and getting a job in the building trades.

Education is a bummer to Alvin because up until now school has been one big bore and not relevant to his goals . . .

34. CU. TED BRODY HOLDING A CHEMISTRY MEASURING GLASS TO HIS EYES.

FADE MUSIC BACKGROUND AND THEN UP WITH NEW MUSIC I.D. TO ESTABLISH TED BRODY.

35. MS. TED ENGROSSED IN BOOK IN THE LIBRARY.

MUSIC: CONTINUES

36. WS. TED SITTING ALONE, OUTSIDE SOMEWHERE NEAR LCS BUILDING, THINKING . . . DEEP IN HIS OWN THOUGHTS.

MUSIC: CONTINUES

37. SPLIT FRAME. MASK SHOTS #34 THROUGH #36 IN SQUARES.

MUSIC: FADE THEN BACKGROUND

DAVE MARX (V.O.):

Ted Brody . . . fifteen years old. He's an excellent student. A boy Ted's age would have three years—even longer—to decide about his future, what he wants to do. But not Ted. He knows what he wants to do.

37. CONTINUED

Medicine. He's already decided. A doctor . . . and going on to specialize in orthopedic surgery.

Ted's got it all figured out at the age of fifteen. Trouble is, Ted's so wrapped up in himself and the future, he's missing out on the present. And not only that—Ted isn't relating to his peers and other people.

He can understand the scientific side of life—but he doesn't see the human side. That's going to hurt him as a doctor and though he doesn't realize it, it's hurting him now.

38. SPLIT FRAME. MASKED IN OVALS: JEAN, ALVIN AND TED.

As teacher/advisors, I'm sure you've probably met the Teds, the Jeans, and the Alvins—and others, so you know how important it is to really get to know them, so you *can* help them.

The above excerpt is long enough to show something about the internal structure of the script: namely, that it is dramatic in form; the basic element that advances the plot is conflict. This fact is, of course, easy to see in *A Time for Growing,* which on the face of the matter deals with human beings, their problems, and possible resolutions to these problems. Later in the script, the students talk to Dave Marx, the narrator/advisor. Alvin Sparks is struggling to make it in high school. Right now everything in his life seems unsettled. He doesn't know if school is right for him or not. Getting advice from his parents hasn't helped because they seem as confused about Alvin's future as he himself is. Conflict is the principle that makes this story move. Conflict advances the story, helps to determine the plot, helps to shape character, tells the writer something about mood.

Notice how all these things happen in the next excerpt from *A Guide to Growing:*

In these goal-setting meetings we establish relevant goals and effective action to accomplish them; and then periodically I review these goals to make sure they're still relevant to the student's needs.

FADE OUT.

SFX: OUTDOORS

60. LS. ALVIN SPARKS, OUTSIDE OF LCS BUILDING. HIS MOOD—ANXIOUS

DAVE (V.O.): Alvin Sparks is going through a trying period in his life.

FADE SFX.

61. ALVIN ENTERING DAVE'S OFFICE.

A couple of days ago he walked into my office . . . he had had it with school . . . with everything. He was planning to quit and get a job.

62. CU. ALVIN.

ALVIN:
I just can't take it any more. I'm not interested in school.

63. MCU. DAVE.

DAVE:
What are you interested in? Do you know what you want to do?

64. M2S. FAVORING ALVIN.

ALVIN:
I really think I want to become a welder . . . my uncle's a welder and he says he could get me into the union when I'm eighteen.

65. CU. DAVE.

DAVE:
What about your folks?

66. ANGLE FAVORING ALVIN.

ALVIN:
You know how they are . . . my dad keeps saying, ''Gotta get a college degree . . .''

SFX: CONVERSATION IN BACKGROUND

67. DIFFERENT ANGLE AS
ALVIN CONTINUES.

DAVE (V.O.):
I felt that since he couldn't get into the union until he was eighteen, it seemed right that he stay in school, receive as much training as we could offer him here, before he left . . .

68. ANGLE FAVORING DAVE
TALKING WITH ALVIN.

SEGUE SFX INTO—

DAVE:
If you stay in school we could design some program which would give you a good background for your apprenticeship—

69. ANGLE FAVORING ALVIN.

ALVIN:
Does that mean I could do some welding?

70. ANGLE FAVORING DAVE.

DAVE:
Possibly—we'll talk to the Industrial Arts instructor and see what he has to say . . .

BRING UP SFX.

71. M2S. DAVE AND ALVIN
CONTINUING.

DAVE (V.O.):
Alvin agreed that we ought to talk to his folks about the whole situation before we change anything . . . If there's any way you can help a student, you want to try . . . and yet each student is different and that makes my job all the more challenging and worthwhile . . .

Like Ted Brody . . .

72. ANGLE MCU. TED BRODY
IN A SCIENCE LAB—INTENT.

73. DIFFERENT ANGLE ON TED.

His parents had called me earlier on the phone. They were concerned that Ted was so wrapped

up in his books that he just didn't have time for a social life. But his parents only hit half of the problem. I suppose Ted's whole approach to life is if it doesn't relate to science and medicine, it isn't important.
FADE.

Once the script had set up the problem, and had dramatized some of the obstacles to its solution, the next step was to show at least the beginnings of a resolution:

81. MCU. TEACHER, CLASSROOM.

... Also the fact that since advisors have been in on the planning from the very beginning, we can more easily identify CPU opportunities that might tie in with the short courses for our students.

82. WS. OF PLANNING GROUP.

So group planning is another aspect of my job— and a good way to check with the other teachers on what they can do for my students and what I can do for theirs.

83. MS. DAVE AND ALVIN GOING OVER PLANS.

Alvin has decided to stay in school—providing we can change his program and focus in on his interests in welding. I've talked to a few teachers already about it and I feel it's possible.

84. ANOTHER ANGLE. ALVIN AND DAVE GOING OVER PLANS.

Before the parent conference we checked the proposed schedule to make sure that we could make the changes and that Alvin would be ready to explain his feelings to his folks.
SFX: BRING IN CONVERSATION IN BACKGROUND.

85. MS. GROUP MEETING. ALVIN, HIS FOLKS, AND DAVE.

That parent conference was really critical for both Alvin and his folks. He didn't know how they would react—and quite frankly, neither did I ...
FADE IN

86. ANGLE FAVORING FATHER.

MR. SPARKS:
I don't know ... Alvin never talked to us like this before.

87. ANGLE FAVORING MRS. SPARKS.

MRS. SPARKS:
Your uncle ... he's making a living ... but Alvin don't you want something more? Your friends ... they're going on to college. Your

88. ANGLE FAVORING ALVIN.

father and I . . . we've saved some money . . . if that's what you're worrying about . . .

ALVIN:

That's not what I'm worrying about, Mother! It's not a crime if you don't want to go on to college . . . I like working with my hands.

89. ANGLE FAVORING MR. SPARKS.

MR. SPARKS:

Tell me something, Mr. Marx. If Alvin goes along with this interest, could he still get into college if he changes his mind?

90. ANGLE FAVORING DAVE.

DAVE:

We've worked out a program that will give him a solid background in welding and mechanics, but it's flexible enough to still keep him eligible for college.

Alvin, why don't you explain the idea?

91. MCU ON ALVIN.

ALVIN:

With this new program I can take courses in Physical Science . . . working with metals . . .

FADE UNDER TO BACKGROUND OF LEARNING COMMUNITY CENTER.

92. WS. IN THE LEARNING COMMUNITY —ALVIN AND DAVE OFF IN A CORNER WHILE TED, JEAN AND OTHER STUDENTS RAPPING.

DAVE (V.O.):

The day after the conference, we went through his new schedule . . . and we both feel that school makes a lot more sense for Alvin now. Scheduling is one of my advising responsibilities, so I make sure that included in the schedule is a regular once-a-week meeting with each of my advisees. Sometimes we'll meet individually . . .

No one has ever won a Pulitzer prize, an Emmy, or a Peabody Award for a filmstrip, but that is only a reflection of the fact that useful work is seldom glamorous. Writing good filmstrips that do what they're supposed to do is a skilled and difficult job, as many writers have discovered on accepting filmstrip assignments because they looked easy. The writer new to this medium usually winds up complaining bitterly that a filmstrip should not take so much time and skill and trouble, or require so many rewrites. Perhaps it shouldn't, but it does.

TELEPLAY AND SCREENPLAY

In selecting a screenplay writer as a good example, William Goldman came to mind as one of the top five or ten screenwriters in the country. His film credits include such motion pictures as the Academy Award winning *Butch Cassidy and the Sundance Kid* and *All the President's Men*, as well as *Magic, Hud,* and *Waldo Pepper.* Goldman's novels, too, are legendary: *Boys and Girls Together, Soldier in the Rain, Temple of Gold, Your Turn to Curtsy My Turn to Bow, Marathon Man* (also a screenplay), and the already-mentioned *Magic.*

Goldman possesses a talent for knowing when to turn a feeling, often at the moment his audience least expects it. He has the art of sophistry down to a science. And his characters are so rich in life you can't help but feel with them, unless you happen to read with your hands covering the words or see his movies with muffs over your ears. For instance, consider this page in *Boys and Girls Together.*[1]

The old man took two steps toward them and started to speak, his voice kind, explaining. When he spoke his nostrils dilated. Sid watched them. "My daughter is the local lure. Granted she is ripe, she is also, believe me please, sour."

"I am helpless before her charms," Sid said.

"I assure you, you have no chance. Is your suit cashmere? If not, strike three goodbye."

"Persistency is my middle name," Sid said.

"Then I weep for you and also wish you joy." Old Turk gestured softly and retired.

"Nice man," Sid said.

"He's word happy. A frustrated philosopher." She handed him the sandwich. "Two bits you owe me."

"You can have my heart."

"A quarter is preferable."

Sid held the change in his hand. She reached out and took it. Even her fingers, soft and pink and round, aroused his passion. "We touched," Sid said. "Your hand and mine. Now I can die."

"Outside, not here." She moved down the counter, disappearing behind a barrel of pickles. . . .

This sophistry that hooks the reader or viewer is also seen in a section of dialogue from Goldman's screenplay, *Butch Cassidy and the Sundance Kid.*[2]

CUT TO:

Butch and Sundance riding on. The shadows are deeper now. So is their strain.

CUT TO:

Butch and Sundance. Abruptly they halt.

[1] Reprinted by permission. Copyright © 1970 by William Goldman.

[2] Reprinted by permission of International Creative Management. Copyright © 1969 by William Goldman.

BUTCH

I think we lost 'em. Do you think we lost 'em?

SUNDANCE

No.

BUTCH

Neither do I.
(and they are off again, riding flat out)

Formating a screenplay is not just adhering to a model physical or mechanical appearance on the page. True, before starting a line of dialogue in a new scene you must first introduce the scene by setting it up in *body copy*, those lines written in third person present tense that run from left-hand margin to right-hand margin. Some call this *master scene technique*, but the term *body copy* is normally used among screenwriters. These few lines of description set the tone and tension and also assist in advancing the action of the story.

More than likely you will either DISSOLVE TO or CUT TO a new scene (we detail this later in the book) and FADE OUT and FADE IN if you want to express a big jump in time. Within a scene you will CUT TO to identify a shift in angle or POINT OR VIEW (POV) by writing NEW ANGLE FAVORING or ANOTHER ANGLE FAVORING. All these camera terms are placed either flush left or flush right. The following selection from a screenplay, *The Michigan Avenue Boys*, illustrates how a new scene is introduced, how the body copy helps advance the action, and how new angles, cuts, and dissolves are treated to get us from one scene to the next.

SMALL FADE IN:

INT.—LILLIAN'S BEDROOM—THAT NIGHT

Preacher is propped up on Lillian's bed, underneath a make shift canopy.

CUT TO:

Dalloway and Carole Sue, properly garbed, march down the aisle, as the Victrola in a corner plays, "Oh Promise Me" sung by Laurence Eddy.

CUT TO:

NEW ANGLE

They pause in front of the bed—waiting.

CUT TO:

NEW ANGLE

Lillian, dressed angelically, and Boulanger, sporting the best suit Lillian has in her "private collection" follow in tow.

CUT TO:

Preacher, coughing up painfully, looks at the pair, gathers up his waning strength and speaks up loud and clear.

PREACHER HARGITAY

By the authority of no one . . . since I've never taken authority that well, I, Preacher Hargitay, in accordance with our own laws, since we seem to break everyone else's conduct this ceremony bringing the fair, young Carole Sue—and the fairly young Ryan Q. Boulanger in holy matrimony—of sorts.

(beat)

In witness thereof is Timothy J. Dalloway, the brilliant inspector and questionable crook, and Lillian Randolph, who makes the best turnovers anyone's ever ea . . . forget it.

(beat)

Ryan Q. Boulanger and Carole Sue, do you take each other to be unlawfully wedded . . . to love, honor, and obey . . . until either death or a conviction do you part . . .

BOULANGER and CAROLE SUE

(in unison)

I do . . .

PREACHER HARGITAY

Good, then in accordance with the state of any state you want, I, Preacher Hargitay, ordained by the somewhat crappy but profound life I've led, pronounce you Ryan Q. Boulanger, and you Carole Sue Caldwell—husband and wife—in a manner of speaking . . .

CUT TO:

Boulanger and Carole Sue kissing. Dalloway hugging Lillian, and Preacher lying back on his pillows exhausted, yet exhiliarated.

PREACHER HARGITAY

(beginning to cough up some blood)

Oh, Lord, thank you for seeing fit to let me serve you as an unrepented sinner.

(beat)

I bequeath my wordly bounties to these . . .

(the coughs are more severe and the breathing more laboring)

to these other lost souls . . . who . . . who have joined me in our chicanery . . .

(beat)

One other thing . . . it hurts like hell so please make it fast . . .

Preacher closes his eyes, his face stiffens, then when life leaves it, his face relaxes . . .

CUT TO:

Chief Postal Inspector Timothy J. Dalloway, touches his cold hands, and then closes his lids . . .

DALLOWAY

(quietly)

God bless, Preach . . .

Notice that you don't number scenes in a screenplay or teleplay the way you do a nonfiction script—or burden the body copy with an overkill of technical camera terms. ANOTHER ANGLE FAVORING MICHELLE suffices, or a MEDIUM 2-SHOT OF MICHELLE. The reason is simple enough. The screenplay goes through a series of revisions, at least the first three usually done by the initial screenwriter. But the script may go through more revisions by another screenwriter called in to take a crack at it or do a polish, by the producers, possibly by the major actors, and always by the director. The script may have gone through several generations by the time it gets to the director, and only then, when the director agrees on the shots, is the script given to a script typist and the scenes numbered in accordance with a production board (that has pockets to hold scene descriptions in the order they are going to be shot).

Something else worth noting: it isn't unusual for a script to be changed during the shooting and lines improvised on the spot. Film director Robert Altman allows his actors that latitude. Films like *Nashville, The Wedding,* and *California Split* are examples. However, even Altman keeps intact the "frame" of the script, the direction the story is going.

Another myth is that each page of script equals approximately one minute of story. Not true. Most screenplays are 135 pages in length, so that's the number you shoot for. The same holds true for a teleplay. A half-hour sitcom does not run thirty pages, but more like thirty-eight and sometimes as many as forty-two.

A complete half-hour sitcom pilot has been placed in the Appendices, as well as examples of nonfiction and fiction treatments, and a nonfiction script. In some instances, production companies prefer writing all dialogue in upper case, whereas other companies prefer the dialogue in lower case, with either single or double spacing between lines. The same holds true for body copy. In screenplays, however, dialogue and body copy are always single spaced and in lower case. So the best advice we can give is always ask the production staff for sample copies of their scripts to see what style they use and to make sure yours is consistent with theirs.

But reading screenplays written by people like William Goldman teaches you something else about format. You should attack the scene at the moment of conflict. Some writers call it "coming in high at the action." The concept of attacking the scene at the moment of conflict in screenplays and teleplays (we use the term here interchangeably) forces the writer to focus. In a novel you may have four or five hundred pages in which to build character conflict and advance the action of the story, but the nature of the screenplay is quite the opposite. You must compress the story into 135 pages, which if transposed to regular novel form would mean much less than a hundred pages. Yet the reasons for weaknesses in character and story in both scripts and novels run parallel. The fault usually lies in poor motivation.

Since there may be seventy scenes in a screenplay, that's a heck of a lot to compress and still keep a story intact. Of course the visual can move the action along and take the place of a lot of words, but relying too much on the visual for this may preempt the story and play hide and seek with the audience. Most of you, maybe all of you, have walked out of a movie theater muttering, "I could have done better than that." Chances are you could. The fact that a screenplay is produced doesn't guarantee that it works.

Think of the screenplay as a piece of canvas that is stretched out on a huge frame. Each scene is a fastening point. Eventually all the scenes adhere to the frame, and the canvas is complete. If there are any ripples or bubbles in the canvas between the first and last point, a piece isn't fitting properly, and consequently there is an uneven story.

This is what format should really tell you. It means nothing to be able to identify the parts of a script much like the parts of speech unless you understand the essence of it all.

Writing is not knowing that your first tab goes . . .
Here (body copy)
       your second tab goes here (dialogue)
              your third tab goes here (parenthetical)
                     your fourth tab here (CHARACTER'S NAME).
Writing is using the format to make something like this happen:

INT. KITCHEN—NIGHT
MORRIS, 40's, is rummaging through the refrigerator looking for something to eat when he hears a familiar voice scolding . . .

                         ETHEL'S VOICE (O.S.)
       Don't touch a thing in there, you know what the doctor said about
       late snacks.

                              MORRIS
                         (caught in his tracks)
       I'm not touching, I'm just smelling.
                         (beat)
       He said nothing about smelling a late snack.

Knowing where to set your tabs won't make the story happen, won't make the characters come alive, and if we, as authors, were to just show you a script and say "here's what screenplay format looks like," we would be grievously wrong. Format *is* much more than a mechanical device. It's what makes the brief scene above work. MORRIS has a problem, he's overweight. He also has a conscience, his wife ETHEL. She has just caught him in the act without being in the same room. Ethel's ears are like police dogs. Morris' hands are like a steam shovel. The scene is attacked at the moment of conflict and builds from there.

When we speak of conflict we're not necessarily referring to the kind that makes you tell someone off or want to punch someone in the mouth. The conflict we're talking about is more internal and takes longer to present itself. For example: a three-year-old child loves to eat cookies. The toddler knows the cookies are kept in a jar out of reach, stuffed way back in the cupboard. His desire is the cookie. His problem is how to get the cookie. For days, perhaps even weeks, he watches his parents take cookies out of the jar. They give a few to him. It's easy for them, all they do is open the cupboard, reach in, and grab some. But it's so difficult for him, virtually impossible because of the jar's inaccessibility. In a corner of the kitchen he notices a small step ladder his mother uses to reach for things beyond her grasp. With the precision and memory of a computer the toddler works out in his own mind the steps needed to get at those cookies. One morning, while his parents are still asleep, he tiptoes out of his room, sneaks into the kitchen like a commando during a dawn raid, and quietly scoots the step ladder close to a butcher block table placed near the cupboard. He waddles up the ladder, steps on top of the table, and gleefully reaches the cookie jar before he's discovered.

This is a classic example of conflict: the thesis or statement of the problem(s) (the premise), an antithesis, the struggle with the problem(s) in search of a solution, acting on the decision(s), and finally, the synthesis or resolution of the problem(s). This is given more detail in chapter seven.

As we grow older the cookie syndrome stays with us and takes on new forms. The "cookie" may be *power, money, love, position, comfort, contest,* etc., but the thrust remains the same: *object, need, conquest.*

When we say, "attack the scene at the moment of conflict," we are calling upon a concept to act within the boundaries of a frame that we identify as format. The format demands that you attack the scene at the moment of conflict because of the time constraints of the script. Movies are usually two-hour rather than all-day affairs. So the format forces you to think of scriptwriting as painting; anything less doesn't fill the frame, anything more spills over it.

The mechanics of format tell you where to place your margins and set your tabs, but they also tell you more, to write no more than seven words of dialogue per average line and to hold scenes to a few pages (with some exceptions). This compression is a necessary evil. Gratuitous dialogue, like the example below, just doesn't belong:

JOE

Let's go to Frank's party.

SYBIL

Good, I want to go to Frank's party.

JOE

I'm glad you do so now we're off to Frank's party.

Visual images should be substituted whenever spoken lines become embarrassing to the ear.

Scriptwriting happens to be measured in time as well as esthetics. Its worth is what it can do for an audience in a half-hour, an hour, or more. To the purist it may be an unconscionable sin to view the art this way. However, there are very few purists in the *business* of writing. Format, like breathing, is an absolute necessity. Screenplay writing and teleplay writing must have boundaries, and so it follows that mass media writing is linear to a degree.

Media writing also implies an audience; always present is this idea of *transmitter* and *receiver*. You are the transmitter, the audience is your receiver. If magnetic or electrical waves are broken up during transmission rather than sent in a particular *format,* the signal diffuses, weakens, and breaks up. This holds true with words, and a parallel can be made for writing. In essence the format is like the shell of a building, seen as the amount of floors, the number of walls or partitions, and their resilient quality. All things considered, a strong format amounts to structural soundness.

chapter 7

Conflict
and Movement
in the Script

The filmstrip *A Guide to Growing* that we discussed in the last chapter may seem light-years removed in form, purpose, and technique from a successful contemporary novel or a distinguished work of modern historical journalism. It is our purpose in this chapter to show the ways in which these works are very similar.

A student had asked a film writing instructor what books he might read to learn more about writing. The instructor thought for a moment and recommended that the student study several then-popular works, including Charles Webb's novel, *The Graduate,* and Bernstein and Woodward's account of the Watergate scandal, *All the President's Men.* At the level of technique and structure, fiction and nonfiction come together. The transcending principle that makes them more alike than different is that most ancient of literary forms, drama.

STRUCTURE IN THE GRADUATE

A few years ago a gifted young writer, Charles Webb, wrote *The Graduate.* The book became moderately popular and eventually was sold as a screenplay. In paperback the book became a best seller. The film that resulted was a spectacular success, setting a style that was widely imitated in other films.

One reason for the success of *The Graduate* was the simplicity of its premise and the straightforward, uncomplicated nature of the story line. A young college graduate, back in his parents' home for the summer, is pressured to identify with his parents' confused and corrupt world. He yields to the pressure when he is seduced by the mother of the girl he is dating. In the end, he breaks with the mother and carries off the girl just as she is about to marry someone else.

The timing of *The Graduate,* especially in the film version, was fortunate. The book and film said precisely what young people, disturbed by the confusion and amorality of the adult world, wished to hear. Some adults, regarding the premise as juvenile nonsense, were enraged. The majority of people, young and old, willing to consider the issue with open minds, were stimulated and interested. None of these reactions would have been possible had Webb and the film-makers not been quite clear about the nature of the story they had to tell.

The Graduate, like all good writing, can provide some useful lessons in the writer's craft: the similarities between instruction and entertainment, between fact and fiction; the differences in media, and the similarities in structure and flow of story that bring them together. We can make these lessons pointed by looking at the story line of *The Graduate* as it might appear in several formats:[3]

Novel

The trip lasted less than three weeks. It was late one night when Benjamin returned and both his parents were asleep. He tried the front door and found it locked. Then he tried the kitchen door at the side of the house and the door at the rear but both were locked. He attempted opening several windows but most of them were covered with screens and the ones without screens were locked. Finally he walked back around to the front porch and banged on the door until a light was turned on in the front hall. Then his father, wearing a bathrobe, pulled open the door.

. . . "Dad, I haven't slept in several days. I haven't eaten since yesterday and I'm about to drop over."

"You haven't eaten?" his mother said.

"No."

(Some lines later)

"Well, tell me where you stayed."

"Hotels."

Mr Braddock nodded. "Maybe this trip wasn't such a bad idea after all," he said. "Did you have any other jobs besides fighting fires?"

"Yes."

"Well, what were they?"

"Dad, I washed dishes. I cleaned along the road. Now I am so tired I'm going to be sick."

"Talk to a lot of interesting people, did you?"

"No."

"You didn't?"

"Dad, I talked to a lot of people. None of them were particularly interesting."

In the exposition that sets up the following dialogue and opens up chapter three of *The Graduate*, Webb establishes a quite visual scene very simply.

Now what if these lines, or some of them, were transposed to a documentary film script?

VIDEO	*AUDIO*
WS: BEN TRIES FRONT DOOR BUT FINDS IT LOCKED.	
CUT TO:	
KITCHEN DOOR, LOCKED.	
CUT TO:	
DIFFERENT ANGLE FRONT DOOR LOCKED. BEN POUNDS ON DOOR. AS WE PULL OUT, WE SEE LIGHTS GOING ON INSIDE HOUSE. A FEW MOMENTS LATER, DOOR OPENS, BEN'S FATHER.	
DISSOLVE TO:	
KITCHEN. MR. BRADDOCK, BEN, HIS MOTHER SIT AT THE KITCHEN TABLE. BEN DOESN'T WANT TO TALK. HE'S TIRED AND WANTS TO GO TO BED.	
VARIOUS ANGLES IN KITCHEN	MR. BRADDOCK: Did you have any other jobs besides fighting fires?
	BEN: Yes.
	MR. BRADDOCK: What were they?
	BEN: Dad, I washed dishes. I cleaned along the road. Now I am so tired I am going to be sick.
	MR. BRADDOCK: Talk to a lot of interesting people, did you?
	BEN: No.
	MR. BRADDOCK: You didn't?
	BEN: Dad, I talked to a lot of people. None of them were particularly interesting.

Now let us try the format for a *dramatization*, which is used for fiction scripts, screenplays, and teleplays.

INT: KITCHEN—NIGHT

Mr. Braddock, his wife, sit patiently at the table, even though it's in the middle of the night, waiting for their son to tell them what he's been doing for the past three weeks on the road. But Ben's tired. He'd rather sleep.

                          BEN
                  (grimly)
          Dad, I washed dishes. I cleaned along the road.
                  (beat)
          Now I am so tired I am going to be sick.
                     MR. BRADDOCK
                  (trying to make conversation)
          Talk to a lot of interesting people, did you?
                          BEN
          No.
                     MR. BRADDOCK
          You didn't?
                          BEN
          Dad, I talked to a lot of people. None of them were particularly
          interesting.

Obviously there is a difference between the book by Charles Webb and a filmstrip on a new concept in secondary school learning. But is there really that much of a difference between Ben's:

                          BEN
          Dad, I talked to a lot of people. None of them were particularly
          interesting.

and the line where Alvin turns to his parents:

                     ALVIN:
          That's not what I'm worrying about, mother!
          It's not a crime if you don't want to go on to
          college . . . I like working with my hands.

In each instance the lines advance the action. They press the conflict forward, moving it bit by bit to new levels, always working through the viewpoints of the characters within the scene. This is the essence of structure and flow in a scene.

In the next chapter, we shall discuss in detail the writing of narration and dialogue. Here we wish to make a single important point about dialogue as it relates to scene structure. Skilled writers developing a scene, whether they are writing fiction, drama, nonfiction prose, or documentary, seldom advance their story line in a direct and simple way. Like a climber working up a steep incline they are inclined to zigzag—turning, moving against their own logic, but always going up. In this sort of dialogue fact and fiction come together, as well as drama and prose narrative. Carl Bernstein and Bob Woodward's *All the President's Men* could readily be adapted to film because, although nonfiction, the book reads like a novel. For example, consider a passage in which a man named Clawson discovers that an associate, Marilyn Berger, has told reporters that she and Clawson discussed a document in the Watergate case in her apartment, over a drink.[4]

Clawson protests,

> ". . . Are you serious? No. Christ? You going to tell them that?"
> "I told them already."
> "You told them that?"
> "Well, you did come over for a drink."
> "Well, for Christ's sake."
> "What's so wrong with coming over for a drink?"
> "Are you kidding?"
> "No," she said.
> "You and me in your apartment."
> "Well . . ."
> "You have already told them that?" Clawson said. "Jesus Christ. Well, you have just shot me down. If it appears in the paper that I am over at your house having a drink . . . do you know what that does?"
> "I don't see why."
> "You don't?"
> "No. I have a clear conscience."
> "Jesus Christ. Who did you tell?"
> "I told the guys."
> "That's incredible. Just incredible," he repeated.
> "I don't see what so wrong about that."
> "Marilyn, I have a wife and a family and a dog and a cat."
> "Well, I have lots of people come over to my house for a drink."
> "Oh, boy. That's the worst blow."
> "There's nothing bad about it."
> "[It] should not look bad," Berger insisted.
> "Incredible. Just incredible."

[4]Copyright © 1974 by Carl Bernstein and Bob Woodward. Reprinted by permission of Simon & Schuster, a division of Gulf & Western Corporation.

"It's incredible that you [are so upset] about that when the other thing is really substantive," Berger told him.

There was a long silence. "Okay. Amazing."

"I have nothing to be embarrassed about," Berger said.

"That's the most embarrassing thing of all." He hung up.

We repeat that this exchange of dialogue is not between two characters in a work of fiction. The passage is presented as factual reporting of a real conversation.

A scene in an industrial documentary film about a large metropolitan hospital shows a department chief and a resident physician leaving a room occupied by a woman hospitalized for what may be a terminal illness. The department chief and the physician are talking about the woman's case.

"She hasn't understood how sick she is. She delayed treatment for too long."

"I know. But she also wants to go home."

"Well, at this point there's nothing much more we can do for her here. I think she can go home. But with the idea that she will be coming back."

"I agree. She does want to go home badly." The resident swallowed as if the lump were in his throat and not hers.

"We have to treat the patient's disease but we also have to treat her as a person. It's her emotional needs we should be concerned about now."

"She'll be happy to hear that she can go."

"Just keep an eye on her. And we'll see what happens."

"Okay."

This scene was not scripted; it was shot in *cinema verite* style. The writer and editor, from this footage, constructed a scene that ran approximately a minute and a half. The scene was mounted with the above dialogue, exhibiting the same structure we have seen in a novel and a passage of nonfiction prose.

As another example, here is a dialogue sequence from a film on retirement planning. The man, Tom Walker, has been forced to realize that he is near retirement age. He and his wife, Georgia, have just returned from a neighbor's birthday party. She comes into the living room from the kitchen and Walker says,

"Any chores left?"

"Another day, another dollar. Did you enjoy the party?"

"Uh-huh."

"I thought you were worried about something. You were awfully quiet."

"No, it was a busy day but I enjoyed the party. . . . It was a *funny* day."

"Why?"

"I don't know. . . . Did I tell you Mr. Burling came over to the shop?"

"No, you didn't."

"I'd forgotten, but it was twenty years ago this morning that he hired me. . . . I guess I get a pin and a dinner in a few days, but he wanted to announce it today."

"He's nice."

"Then Bill West had a meeting on retirement planning this afternoon."

"Oh. . . . Well, I suppose all that *and* Steve's birthday shouldn't happen on the same day."

"You always know what I'm thinking, don't you?"

Structurally, all scripts have their beginning, middle, and end. But that in itself is not enough for the writer to know. Within each scene there are mini-beginnings, middles, and ends, rising actions, climaxes, carrying the story further along, developing the conflict on different levels. Even in *cinema verite,* where you shoot actuality, recording the natural presence of an event, you still edit the film in a literary style.

It's in this weaving of plot and subplot, action and subaction, where we can best see the parallels between good filmmaking and strong literary writing. Unfortunately, too few new writers see this similarity and its importance. If there is a secret to writing non-fiction scripts it is the revelation that film structure and literary structure are very similar. The more you experience this structural similarity, the more you will understand how excellent nonfiction scripts are put together.

Even open-ended films, which raise questions to be explored later in classrooms or discussion groups, employ the same sort of structure to make certain issues available for discussion and debate. Open-ended films are usually educational in nature; they force a writer to explore an issue visually, orally, and in depth, leaving the way clear for a discussion of solutions.

What all these films share with each other—in fact with all writing, nonfiction and fiction—is the notion that without conflict, either internalized or externalized, and without the other elements of good writing *(plotting, character growth, rising conflict, unity of opposites, movement, point of attack, transition, crisis, climax, resolution),* the script will lack the dimensions it needs to make the ideas, and characters who are the spokesmen of these ideas, come alive. That's why writing is so fascinating. No matter what the assignment, you have a power to create and move to action, a power to motivate character growth, a power really to do anything that a good writer can do.

DIALECTIC AND SCENE STRUCTURE

Lajos Egri has written a remarkable book on playwriting called *The Art of Dramatic Writing.* One of the key words in his approach is *dialectic.* This term comes from ancient Greece and was used to mean conversation and dialogue.

According to Egri, the Greeks, especially the citizens of Athens, regarded conversation as "the supreme art" and "the art of discovering truth." In his book, Egri discusses a *dialectic principle* that applies not only to the writing of dialogue, but to every other element in the play script as well.

The technique of dialectic, as it is demonstrated in the Platonic dialogues, works this way: (1) the speaker assumes that some statement is correct; (2) he searches for and states reasons why it is not correct; and (3) he modifies the original statement in the light of the contradiction. After that, of course, it is possible to find a contradiction of the corrected statement, and so to proceed again indefinitely.

The first statement in this sequence is called the thesis. The contradiction is called the antithesis; it is the opposite of the original proposition. Finally, as Egri says, "Resolution of this contradiction necessitates correction of the original proposition and formulation of a third proposition, the synthesis, being the combination of the original proposition and the contradiction to it." Egri calls these three steps—thesis, antithesis, and synthesis—the law of movement.

In a television documentary about the work of Pierre Auguste Renoir (see appendix G), Vincent Price, who served as host of the program, said:

DISSOLVE TO: SHOT 67 PAINTING #18 THE BRIDGE AT CHATOU SLOW PANS MOVE IN AND OUT MOVING DISSOLVES TO PULLOUTS, PULLINS. ALWAYS A VISUAL SENSE OF FLUIDITY.	VINCENT PRICE: (V.O.) Renoir believed that the only real way of experiencing a painting was to live with it. To live with the moment, the feeling. He kept a notebook of his thoughts and every once in a while entered them on paper. "Artists do exist," he wrote. "But one doesn't know where to find them. An artist can do nothing if the person who asks him to produce the work is blind." "It is the eye of the sensualist that I wish to open."

In narration like this it is possible to locate something of the dialectic in the structure. Renoir states his premise: "Artists do exist." Next comes the antithesis, "But one doesn't know where to find them. An artist can do nothing if the person who asks him to produce the work is blind." And finally the synthesis: "It is the eye of the sensualist that I wish to open."

There is nothing in writing that does not move. Within movement is countermovement. And within that countermovement there is an opposed current. Forces work on forces, and so the course of communication changes constantly. In film, these changes occur not simply in the written word, but in terms of sounds and visuals.

There are various ways in which to create a visual dialectic in films; for example, through *juxtapositions of shots*. We might see a group of doctors—relaxed, talking together. There is a telephone call. An emergency. Heart victim. Then the sudden change of these men into a team of skilled practitioners, now working under tension, with training and experience, and full of adrenalin. This series of positioned shots, edited as we have outlined above, would be an example of a dialectical treatment of visuals.

In a documentary film produced for the Chicago Group (a communications firm specializing in marketing problems) we see a marketing seminar taking place at a resort motor inn. A group of executives from all over the country have come together to learn concepts of effective marketing previously unfamiliar to them. These men and women, unknown to each other before, have been broken into teams of three to develop strategy and solve hypothetical marketing problems. Although the companies the teams represent are fictitious, the executives nevertheless take the assignments seriously. The moods and actions of these teams constantly change, as they would in real situations. Thus, when their performance is filmed in *cinema verite* style, it already has a dialectic structure.

At the end of the first day of the seminar, for example, cocktails and hors d'oeuvres were served the executives in a "hospitality suite." The cocktail hour was filmed so skillfully and smoothly that the executives apparently did not know when camera and sound were rolling. What was captured on film is thus perfectly spontaneous. The conversation is mixed; some pertains to the seminar, some to a random range of other topics, from film directors to the fact that one man's father had been a famous magician.

This curious blend of dialogue and visuals was edited almost in sequence; what is shown in the party scene follows almost exactly the order in which the crew crisscrossed the room picking up bits of sound on film. The film's director was able to position himself in such a way as to be able to hear and see almost everything that was going on, and then through a series of hand signals "lead" his camera and sound persons to the action. In effect, the film was being edited inside the camera, before it even got to the editor's bench.

What this juxtaposition was all about is a visual example of dialectics. If you are going to grasp the best element of film writing, you must begin to comprehend the visual dialectic. As we've said before, writers must *see* as well as *state*. Without these perceptions, a writer uses only a fraction of the senses necessary to create. To put into play all these senses, you are called upon to push your awareness into areas you may have never thought about.

Just as there is a grammar in English that writers must understand in order to write, so there is a grammar in film. Such terms as *close-up, long shot, wildtrack sound* are grammatical terms, analagous to *noun, verb,* and *adjective. Close-up* can make an exclamatory visual statement; *long-shot* may be like a short paragraph to introduce a scene. But there is more to film grammar than parts of speech and definitions. The essence of a grammar is the relationship between elements, adjective to noun, and so on; in film grammar some of these relationships are expressed in *structure, pacing,* and *orchestration.* It is this language of film that heightens your awareness, your sense of people and things around you; this tells you what to look for in developing structure, rising conflict, character growth, point of attack, orchestration, character conflict.

People are individuals. Some are talkers, others are listeners. Some are aggressive, others more passive. Some are troubled, others relaxed. Out of this melange of contradictions and changes, the writer can create a script that not only shows the dynamics of the event in which they are involved, but something about the nature of their life experience.

Event and character are intricately interwoven in nonfiction, fiction, and drama, as in life. In writing we sometimes suppose that conflict and story are aspects of events—that they are part of the *plot. Characters* then simply become ways of making tangible, of externalizing, the plot line. This is not true, as you must have concluded from our discussion of the dialectic principle in writing. Conflict and resolution—the center and essence of all kinds of writings about human beings—run through actions, spoken words, moods, motives, and so on to the larger concepts of theme and story. Since this is the case, we need to pay a little special attention at this point to some aspects of characterization.

chapter 8
Characterization and Dramatic Structure

Most people tend to think and talk as if there were a sharp and easily made distinction between drama/fiction and documentary/reporting. Reporters deal in actual events; dramatists in events that are the product of their own imagination. Documentary is about actual, living people; fiction is about fantasy people who look real but never existed on land or sea. Our view of the matter is different. *We observe that fiction and drama, especially as they exist in the media today, require heavy infusions of fact if they are to work.* Stories must relate to the experiences, either first-hand or acquired through media news and other sources of "fact," of their audiences. On the other hand, "factual" histories and news reporting of such events as the Cuban Missile Crisis, the Watergate scandals, or the signing of the Declaration of Independence apparently must be put in dramatic form if they are to be understood. John F. Kennedy, for example, was a real person who has become a character in fiction and drama.

A writer of scripts, fiction or nonfiction, has to understand and use the methods of the dramatist. At the most basic level this knowledge involves a usable concept of human character both real and fictitious and how character relates to story structure. Let us try to describe such a concept briefly and generally.

CHARACTERIZATION

The central feature of character is *motive*—a catch-all term that lumps together all the psychological and biological factors impelling human beings to action. We say that a person in real life acts out of love of humanity, love of another human

125

being, a desire for revenge, to improve status position in the eyes of others, or simply due to starvation, illness, or fear of death. No matter that these reasons are not of the same order and even imply different concepts of human psychology; human beings generally see motive as the most essential fact about themselves and other human beings. Why? Not simply because we use motive to explain or rationalize past behavior, but because we use it to *predict*.

In our everyday dealings with other human beings we must be able to predict or anticipate what they will do next. Otherwise we could not associate with others. When we meet another person we must be able to say, "He is my friend. He will treat me well." or, "She has a wicked temper. Don't cross her." or, "He can't make up his mind." Trying to deal with others in total ignorance of what they might do next would be a paralyzing experience, so much so that we might all run from our communities and families to live, and very shortly die, in total isolation.

The problem with *motives* in real life is that they are not available for direct inspection. Whatever they are, they exist inside people; no one has ever seen love, revenge, hunger, or loneliness. How then do we know they are there? The answer is that we do not know; we make a series of more or less educated guesses based on what we can observe, and we act on these guesses. Sometimes we act cautiously: "He seems to be in a good mood. Maybe this is the time to ask him . . ." Sometimes we act rashly, as if we were absolutely sure: "She hates me. She won't be satisfied until . . ."

The cues on which we base these guesses are incredibly varied. They include physical characteristics: size, weight, hair color, and so on. They include characteristics modified by learning: a swaggering walk, a calm and resonant voice, an elegance of gesture. They include behavioral traits unconsciously displayed: posture, gesture, muscle tension. They include very evident mannerisms: what a person chooses to talk about, what words he or she uses, what dialect he or she speaks. Some of the sets of cues are culturally conditioned and must be understood in their appropriate contexts: an American engaging in conversation behaves very differently from a Japanese, or a Syrian.

The business of sorting out such cues and interpreting them as indicators of motive and subsequent behavior is obviously the key social technique of all human beings and always has been. As a result, the whole business of cue-selecting and cue-interpreting has been enriched—or confused, as you prefer—by centuries of accumulated wisdom, tradition, superstition, and knowledge.

There are many differences between drama and life, but the basic one is that drama is an art—it deals in things that are *made* by human beings. The version of human life which drama presents is necessarily artificial; may resemble life experiences, but it is never the same as "reality."

Characters in drama, like all artificial constructs, are much simpler than their models. In life, one may be motivated in thousands of ways, and the cross-relationships among motives may be uncountable. Real people offer myriad cues, gross and minute, to their motives. In drama, the playwright may choose to tell you that only one or two motives are important to a particular character in a particular situation. A character in a play may offer only very few motive cues: a harsh voice; abrupt, clumsy movements; a blunt, insensitive attack on all human problems he or she faces.

But writers must know much more about their characters, becoming biographers, whether writing fiction or fact. They need to develop a clear notion of the motives that are essential to a character, and to that end must know what has happened to the character in order to produce these motives. Finally they must know what the character is like externally—because, as we have said, the external facts about a person are all that we can truly experience. A writer, therefore, begins to write a character sketch, asking and answering questions like:

> Where was the person born? Where did the person grow up? What was the person's family like? Rich or poor, immigrant or native-born, country or city?
>
> How intelligent? Intelligent about what, in what ways? How educated? In schools and colleges? On the streets? Is my character self-taught?
>
> How tall is the person? What does my character weigh? What color eyes? What kind of hair? What other unique physical characteristics?
>
> What does the person like most? What other likes and dislikes? Is there anything that annoys him or her?
>
> How does this person allow him or herself leisure? Where does my character live? In what style? Is this person rich or poor, young or old?

The questions could be endless, but you must stop somewhere. Where? At the point where you begin to feel that you character is a living entity you know well but don't completely understand. The character must come alive, or you can't write him or her. If you understand him or her fully, there are no more surprises for you and the character is dramatically useless. You will learn from experience when you can stop; and when you must.

We suggest that you begin by creating your characters on paper—writing down the crucial facts as you come to understand them. Not all writers do the job in this way; some are able to make a character in the mind, with a minimal amount of writing. We feel that until you have mastered the process, at least, you had better write it down.

You have undoubtedly heard or read that sometimes characters "come to life" for an author and "run away with the story," dictating lines, reactions, episodes the writer had not previously thought of. To some extent characters must come to life; when you write, you must be able to see the scenes, the actions; you must hear the characters speak before you write down the dialogue lines. When you work on a script, you are not dealing in cold, lifeless materials. Aristotle said that drama is "an imitation of the actions of men," which is to say that it is as vital, as dynamic, as life itself.

WRITING THE CHARACTER SKETCH—FICTION

Character sketches are an essential part of the treatment, at least if a reader is to get the feel of your story. Writing character sketches is not a particularly complicated process. If you are writing for your own purposes, simply to bring a character to life, you can do the sketch in any way that pleases you, as long as you pay attention to (1) motive, (2) how the character got to be the way he/she is, and (3) external characteristics that indicate motives. When you go on to include all or parts of your sketches in a treatment, however, there are conventions to be observed. Most often, the sketch as included in a treatment will run no more than a page in length and often will be much shorter. When the character is introduced into the story, you first write a line or two to suggest the nature of his or her problem or primary motivation. Then you may include a few sentences—perhaps a paragraph or two—explaining who he/she is, appearance, and function in the story. A discussion of the character's background may or may not be inserted in the treatment; biographical exposition is something the writer needs to know, but possibly should not inflict on his audience.

The following pages taken from a TV movie of the week treatment should illustrate how important character sketches can be, and how they are to be incorporated in the body of the treatment.

WILLIAM LAWRENCE BOULANGER, late 40s, University of Chicago Law School, J.D., honors, U. of C. Law Review, heads the third largest law firm in the country. He's a tax expert who can smell a loophole when one doesn't exist on paper. He has been to the top of every mountain, experienced everything he wanted to experience—but the one thing above all that keeps him alive, that pumps adrenalin in his veins, is the prospect of making a deal. Putting people together, money together, jetting around the world to solve a problem. He loves nothing better than to sit in his penthouse Suite on the 17th floor of the Drake Towers overlooking the outer Drive, the shoreline and Lake Michigan, the yachts and sailboats which bob in a pool of sparkling water and plug into the rest of the globe with his phone. Presidents, Prime Ministers, Foreign Ministers, Ministers of Finance, William Lawrence Boulanger connects scheme with scheme, person with person, governments with governments because *money* ties them all together.

It's the feeling of the deal, the juggling, the closing, that counts for him— that's the heart of the matter. The emotion stops with the solution, and then he's onto something else.

He's not a good man, not a bad man. But he's remarkably successful because he gets things done—for a price. He has enough wealth, so he doesn't have to wear it. He lives in a baronial mansion in Lake Forest, but it's not ostentatious. He has the best of everything, but he doesn't enjoy it.

As soon as he hangs up the phone in his office, drives the hour to Lake

128

Forest, and faces his personal life, Boulanger the hard-nosed financial genius becomes Boulanger in turmoil. His personal life is in shambles. A wife is "resting" in a lovely peaceful "resort" staffed by psychiatrists and all the medical help and modern technology money can buy, with pills to run her moods up and pills to slide the moods down. She's committed because she's . . . crazy . . . no, that's a bad word, she's suffering from depression and anxiety. Nothing serious. Prognosis: probably it'll last a lifetime.

His son, in his 20s, a college dropout off somewhere in Europe. No calls. No postcards in months. His daughter is in the Sadler Wells Ballet School in London. She loves him for three days a week, and hates him for four. At least they speak to each other.

Boulanger is talking to a client who has a couple of million he wants to shelter when DANNY KRUG comes into his life. One of Boulanger's friends has set up the meeting. Krug, in his late 40s, is tall, with black wavy hair and deep-set, green eyes.

He classifies everything. He classifies Boulanger as a genius and himself as an almost. That's what life has been for him up to now. Almost a painter in Europe. Almost an actor in Italy. And now a charismatic dreamer who is almost a publisher in Los Angeles. He's created a too-obvious magazine steal from Playboy and Penthouse and Boulanger wants to know what he's offering that's new. More than the others do. More girls. More nudity. More style. Danny's gotten photographers to shoot on deferred fees, artists to produce layouts on deferred fees, a gifted Irish writer, his buddy, who doesn't believe in himself, to write the copy on a deferred fee, a printer to run off 300,000 issues on a deferred fee, and no one to distribute without money up front. He's nickled and dimed his way all the way up to the barricade. But now the union wants $100,000 up front before they load his magazines on the trucks and roll.

He's in debt, no credit, an almost.

What's his collateral? Hunger and drive—if that made a meal, Danny would be feasting.

William Lawrence Boulanger listens politely, with a fixed expression and tells Danny he'll get back to him in a few weeks.

Three weeks later. The money's there for Krug. But the money has to be a silent partner, for personal reasons. William holds two million dollars in a blind trust. Krug gets 45 percent of the voting stock, the silent partner has 45 percent, and Boulanger owns a 10 percent swing vote.

Danny balks at the mysterious partner, but he has no choice.

We find out where the money is coming from after Krug leaves.

The first paragraph gives us the character's name, age, educational background, professional background, and chief motivation in life. The second paragraph rounds out the character by giving us more information about his manner of living. The third paragraph sets up the beginning of a conflict by mentioning the strain his profession has put on his family life. Finally, the fourth paragraph merges the character sketch into the story line by introducing Boulanger to a new character with his own problem.

For another example of character sketches look at the television pilot script in appendix E. Since the script was for a television pilot rather than an ongoing series the writers had to prepare a set of brief character sketches for all of the major characters. Not all of these characters would appear in the pilot script itself, but each one would make recurrent appearances later in the series.

One producer of a television comedy pilot wrote twenty pages of character descriptions for each of the major characters in his series. The pilot was sold, but probably this sort of devotion to characters is not really necessary. Don't feel that you must write a full-length biography for every character you create. Do, however, spend a good deal of time and thought on your characters; do write sketches appropriate to the sort of script you are undertaking. Without interesting characters, no dramatic script means much.

CHARACTERIZATION IN NONFICTION SCRIPTS

What we have said so far about characterization in fiction scripts applies as well to the dramatizing of actual events—or to writing history or biography or presenting contemporary problems in dramatic form. It applies as well to documentaries and similar productions that use actuality materials rather than scripted ones. There is structure in *cinema verite* as much as there is structure in a film fully scripted before it is shot. The difference is that in a scripted film the structure is written into the script; in an *actuality* film it must be discovered and edited out of the footage.

Some of the structure of an actuality film will emerge in the preliminary research and can be built into the scenario that guides the director in his or her shooting. (There is usually a high ratio of footage shot to footage used in such films, but no one shoots completely at random and hopes for the best.) But for the most part, the structure of actuality is developed in the editing process. This means that the writer, with or without the director, sits down with the film editor and begins to construct sequences that have meaning and dramatic tension out of what has been recorded on film and sound. Thus, the film will have continuity and significance even if the subject matters deals with fragments of life distorted or perverted in the experiencing.

What you are doing in this case is conducting or arranging a film rather than writing it. Your situation is different from that of the musical conductor or arranger, however. In your case, it is as if a musician had composed a great quantity of music, rather loosely related, and turned it over to you. You must select the right segments of music, see that they fit each other, and arrange them in a meaningful and effective sequence. Any composer would be horrified to have this sort of thing happen to his or her compositions. No one is horrified when it happens in film because everyone recognizes that you, the writer, are actually the creator of the final work. A number of writers become directors simply because they want to compose films from the very beginning, and not just after the fact of shooting.

Robert Ford's film, *The Corner*, provides a good example of how the *actuality film* is made. This documentary produced in the 60s deals with the life of a Chicago street gang, the Conservative Vice Lords. Ford, realizing the need for careful research if the film were to be made at all, established friendly relationships with several members of the gang and began by recording some fifteen hours of conversation with them. He told the young men that he did not want to impose his own preconceptions on the film and invited them to suggest episodes for shooting. Taking his cues from the taped conversations and from the suggestions of the gang members, he then shot what he hoped would be sufficient footage to make the documentary.

At this point no theme or structure for the film had emerged. Ford remarked, with a touch of gallows humor, that he had never before worked on a film that seemed to consist entirely of outtakes. He had to rely on what was, after all, a fair probability that there was a pattern in his tape recordings and footage; the challenge was to find it. The film did indeed find its pattern and meaning in the daily round of life as it turned around "the Corner," the neighborhood geographical center of the lives of the Vice Lords. Even a verbalized statement of the theme of the film could be, and was, found in the tapes.

There are differences between showing real people performing real actions in an actuality production and dramatizing real people in real situations in a scripted production. The major difference is that in the dramatized production *you* are in complete control of the action, while in the actuality production you are not. In the latter, the action is ongoing; you are an observer and a recorder. You can say, "Stop the camera," *but the action continues in spite of you. In dramatizations the action continues because of you.*

There are many films, videotapes, and audiotapes that use a dramatized format to present facts. One type is the dramatized history or biography. Many of the major Bicentennial television programs were of this sort, as was *The Missiles of October*, presenting the Cuban Missile Crisis of some years ago in completely dramatic form.

A major work of this sort was an historical dramatization written and produced by Stephen and Eleanor Karpf on the building and use of the first atomic bomb. There had been several documentaries that dealt with aspects of this subject. There had also been at least one feature film that centered on this set of historic episodes. There had not, however, been any statement that tried to present, in full and accurate detail, the entire sequence of events the Karpfs covered in their script.

The terms *histo-drama* or *docu-drama* mean the dramatic reconstruction in full detail of an actual event. The *histo-drama* is not didactic. "We are not instructing the audience," the authors say. "We are following the tenets of good drama, using totally authentic detail and a real situation." Events and characters in such a drama are given qualities; drama emerges from the meticulous arrangement of fact and is not forced upon fact.

The research the Karpfs undertook for their script was awesome in its extent. They interviewed scientists who worked on the Manhattan Project, their families, politicians, and everyone available who had some experience to report. They consulted the huge archives of information on the series of events that led to Hiroshima and Nagasaki—from collections of papers in Washington to the Harry S. Truman Library.

The authors discovered that those connected with the Manhattan Project seemed to have been constantly aware that they were making history and consequently felt impelled to record very exactly day-to-day events. "The scientists," they remarked, "in the course of their work, would make notebooks of their experiments, recording what was happening and where they were at such-and-such a time. We were able to find out where Enrico Fermi was on every day from his arrival from Italy in early 1939."

This sort of documentation the Karpfs justly feel to be extraordinary. "For instance, we have the transcripts of the decision of where and when to drop the bomb on Japan. We know exactly where [the decision makers] were. We know they were at lunch. We haven't gone so far as to find out what their menus were but we do know exactly where the decision was made."

What distinguishes the *docu-drama* from earlier kinds of biographical and historical dramatizations is the necessity for this sort of meticulous, minutely detailed information. The point of the entire exercise is to reconstruct past events with characters not created but seemingly revived, moving on the screen as they once did in real life.

Elanor Karpf says,

> The most obvious kinds of information about historical characters are their public faces, and their pronouncements to the world, and their appearance in the great public moments. What we've done with such characters is not only to take these public moments in their lives which are well-documented in libraries, but to delve into them as people, to develop them as characters just as we would develop fictional characters.
>
> If we were going to write a story about a scientist, we would develop him as a character (by showing) his idiosyncrasies and his likes, dislikes, fears, ways of speaking, ways of dealing with people. We do the same thing for a real President or a real scientist.
>
> For the present script, we've done many in-depth interviews with friends and associates of our characters. We've talked at great length about how they dealt with people, how they talked informally, what they did in their daily lives. With this sort of information as a base, we can construct an image of a real person making real decisions.

In spite of this elaborate research into events and character, the Karpfs still insist that they are dramatists and that their principal skill in this respect consists in recognizing, drawing out, and stressing the essential dramatic elements in character and episode. They see little basic difference between their function as writers of histo-drama and their function as writers of fiction: "Our first obligation is to our audience, to give them an entertaining and an important piece of filmmaking."

WRITING THE NEWS: PRINT AND NONPRINT

You may be able, without much trouble, to see how history and biography turn to theater: melodrama, farce, and sometimes tragedy. But the news is different. News reporting is *reporting*: factual, objective, impartial. Or is it? We turn now to three newspaper stories published in a Chicago daily: the first a feature article, the second a piece of sports reporting, and the third a fairly straight news piece. Our point is that each of the three stories is built around a specific conflict, as is fiction; each involves dramatic characters, progresses through a dramatic episode, and foreshadows things to come. A news story seldom presents a complete dramatic action, as does a feature film or a three-act play; the drama of news is ongoing, rather like the drama of a television serial. Each story is an episode and not complete in itself, although it implies a beginning and foreshadows further development of the action.

In the first article, published originally in the Chicago *Sun Times* on June 13, 1975, the drama unfolds on a downtown Chicago street. The location is a singles bar which was, at the time of the occurrence, attempting to attract an ultra-prosperous clientele—the "beautiful people," as the phrase was then. A group of white-collar workers decided to stop in at the bar for a drink before going home. Four of the men were black. Out of the group, the four blacks were refused admittance—on the grounds that they were intoxicated. The blacks protested, with no effect. One of them happened to recognize a man who was passing the bar, Senator Charles Percy. Senator Percy was asked to arbitrate the dispute and the four men were admitted. The manager of the bar later told a reporter that at least two of the four men were drunk, and that he admitted them only because Senator Percy "started talking about my liquor license."

The story is one of conflict with a conventional dramatic structure—a beginning, a middle and an end. The four men are turned away. They protest, unsuccessfully. Percy intervenes, and the conflict is temporarily settled. The implication is that more such confrontations will take place in the future. This sequence could easily be filmed as part of a fictional feature film. It could also make up the entire action of an open-ended educational film for social studies.

The sports story develops as a sort of comic detective piece. It is an attempt to reconstruct an episode that took place during a game between the Los Angeles Angels and the Detroit Tigers. Members of the two teams seem to have engaged in a "twenty-minute bench-clearing brawl" provoked by a fast, inside brushaway pitch. A highlight of the squabble occurred when one of the Angels emerged from the dug-out carrying a baseball bat—which, however, he did not use on the Detroit players. The melee was evidently a confusing one. What really happened? Who was to blame? The comic incongruity lies in the contrast between the essentially trivial, juvenile nature of the episode and the fact that a great wire service should see fit to investigate and report on it. The comedy is developed in a sequence of charges and defensive statements made by the various persons involved. The drama of the farce is resolved by the revelation that there would be no consequences of the event: no suspensions, no fines, no action. The episode is indeed trivial and the treatment appropriately light, but the structure is basically the same as that of the feature story.

The third story, a UPI release, takes its lead from a government report: "Up to 30,000 Americans may be suffering skin cancer because of the erosion of the Earth's ozone layer caused by aerosol sprays and other sources." The story continued with a series of reactions from various persons and organizations, ranging from the DuPont Company to the Council on Environmental Quality. There was no agreement on the validity of the report's conclusions.

This account was not quite a hard news story. Indeed, it bordered on what the historian Daniel Boorstin has called a "pseudo event"—that is to say, the expression of a dire prophecy or controversial opinion of the sort always available to news reporters. Such reports always take the reporter, and the reader, into the realm of fantasy; like invented or traditional fantasies, they pose the question, "What will happen if . . . ?" In the case of the present story, and of most such news stories, the prophecy is scientifically based and the resultant drama becomes as much science fiction as *Buck Rogers* or *Star Trek*. Here we find everyone threatened with apocalyptic doom as aerosol sprays intended for insects or odors instead eat relentlessly away at the ozone layer protecting us all from ultraviolet radiation. Since it is difficult to project future events as literal fact the story cannot actually report about the end of life on earth. It can simply set up the situation familiar to students of science fiction: the imminent danger, the warnings, the easy disbelief. Any good fiction writer could proceed from this point to invent the rest of the story.

The tendency to merge fiction and nonfiction in media finds many forms. News stories and documentaries, as we have noted, are written as if by novelists and dramatists. Conversely, many of the dramatic programs on television—some of the police procedural series, the medical program *Lifeline*, many of the made-for-television movies—take on the appearance of documentaries. A number of feature-length films, such as Altman's *McCabe and Mrs. Miller* and *Nashville*, try for the look and feel of a *cinema verite* reality. This is less surprising when we look at the backgrounds of some of their directors, producers, and writers.

William Friedkin, who won an Oscar as director of *The French Connection*, started his career as a director of documentary films for WGN-TV, Chicago, and later for WBKB-TV (now WLS-TV, the ABC affiliate in Chicago). He also had some experience in directing live television. His experience in Chicago was entirely with documentary.

A case in point, which shows clearly how documentary techniques bridge over into fiction, was a film Friedkin directed that was so controversial it has not been aired to the present day. The subject was a man named Paul Krump, convicted of killing a police officer and sentenced to die in the electric chair. Instead of questioning the legality of a death sentence, Krump and his lawyer sought a commutation of the sentence to life imprisonment on the grounds that Krump had been rehabilitated. Eventually Otto Kerner, Governor of Illinois at that time, stayed the execution and Krump's sentence was reduced to life imprisonment.

Both the unaired Krump film and Friedkin's later *The French Connection* are brutal and savage in their thrust and remarkably similar in feeling. Friedkin directed Krump much the same way as he directed Gene Hackman and Roy Scheider in *The French Connection*. That film is fiction. Krump's documentary is nonfiction. *Both deal with reality*. That one is fact and the other fiction makes less difference than one might suppose.

Friedkin is not the only popular director who came from a documentary background. Robert Altman, whose work we have mentioned, learned his trade directing industrial films. Arthur Penn, who directed *Bonnie and Clyde,* has done documentaries. So has Steven Spielberg, who has a string of directing credits including *Jaws* and *Close Encounters of the Third Kind*. A sizeable number of directors, producers, and writers of the 1950s and 1960s had their early professional experience working on documentaries and propaganda films for the military during World War II. This tendency will probably continue for some time to come.

chapter 9

Writing Narration
for Fiction and
Nonfiction Scripts

THE MEDIA AND THE
SPOKEN WORD

We have already noted that media productions employ several very different languages in complex combinations. There are the visual images, in color and black and white, in film and video. There are natural sounds used in various acoustical settings. There is music. And finally, there is the spoken word.

Spoken lines are either part of dialogue or narration. Dialogue is action, though it may sometimes be used for exposition. Narration is talk about action and appearances and may also present commentary and analysis of action. Which type of speech is used in a script, and with what stress, depends upon the medium as well as the purpose of the production. For example, on the modern stage, story and character are exposed principally through dialogue supplemented by some nonverbal action. Narration is rarely used. On the Elizabethan stage, the forms were dialogue and monologue, but so written as to convey appearances and analysis of action as well as action itself. (Elizabethan plays are as visual as modern film scripts, but much of the visual element is conveyed through the rich poetic language they employed.)

Between sound, music, and speech, speech is most flexible. In any sort of a dramatized audio presentation, dialogue is the means of carrying the action forward, of indicating motives, even of suggesting the look and emotional feel of scenes. But some script formats rely primarily on narration and use dialogue as a means of supplementing the narrative line. In traditional radio formats the stress used depended to a great extent on whether the writer chose the conven-

136

tion of presenting an action dramatically (as on the stage with little or no narration), or of treating the script as a story. Both conventions survive in audio formats today. When materials are dramatized and produced in the studio either narration or dialogue may be stressed. In actuality broadcasts, recorded segments are carefully edited and connected with narration.

Let's say that you have been assigned to write a one-hour mystery for radio. The story is about a television news reporter and his field producer who plan and arrange the kidnapping of an attractive young heiress. Bob Walling and Mike Jackson, the television newsmen, having set up the kidnapping, are also assigned to report it. Eventually they offer themselves as intermediaries between the authorities and the kidnappers.

The script may begin in this way.

MUSIC	*MYSTERY THEATRE THEME UP FULL, THEN TO BACK . . .*
NARRATOR:	Kathy Farlin boarded the Number Three bus from campus on her way downtown to meet her father.
SOUND	*SNEAK IN SOUNDS, INTERIOR OF MOVING BUS.*
NARRATOR:	As usual, the bus was crowded and the passengers pushed all the way to the back.
VOICE:	(SOFTLY) Miss Farlin?
KATHY:	(STARTLED) Yes?
VOICE:	Do what I tell you and you'll be all right.
KATHY:	What?
VOICE:	Don't turn around. I have a gun. Now, we're coming to a stop. You get off here.
SOUND	*BUS COMES TO A STOP.*
VOICE:	Get off. Now!
MUSIC	*BRIDGE, THEN SEGUE TO . . .*
SOUND	*TV NEWSROOM: KEEP IN BACK.*
EDITOR:	Mike, come over here quick!
JACKSON:	Watcha got?
EDITOR:	Just off the City News wire.
JACKSON:	Let's see . . . Farlin's kid? Kidnapped?
EDITOR:	Yeah. In broad daylight. There's no ransom yet but Farlin's holding a press conference at three. His estate. I'll break you and Walling for that, and Smith's crew can cover the fire.

This is an example of conventional radio usage. Brief narration supported by sound and music introduces the story. Once the story is launched, dramatic dialogue makes the story move. The script would be divided into at least three major segments, each of which would be introduced by narration. The narrator might return at the very end of the script to round off the production.

Video productions are similar to audio, carried by words, but with a strong visual component. A live television play produced in a studio is rather like a stage play, relying on dialogue to make most of its points and create most of its effects. Visuals are always present, of course, but they are usually rather simple, consisting of close-ups and two-shots of people engaged in talk. The made-for-TV movie, since it can use actual locations in addition to studio sets, relies much more heavily on visual story-telling and often is not much different from a theater film. Sit-coms like M*A*S*H can be produced on a sound stage and with proper lighting made to appear as if the exterior scenes were really shot outside.

Television documentaries at one time relied heavily on filmed interviews, even though they were not of great visual interest. Today, with extremely mobile and portable cameras, there is no longer any reason for documentarians to be limited to the studio.

WRITING NARRATION AND DIALOGUE FOR NONFICTION AND FICTION SCRIPTS

First, some general rules: We suggest that you avoid two practices as much as you can: the use of literary narration in film documentaries, which tends to compete with the visual images; and an over-reliance on dialogue in dramatized factual or educational films.

A pretentious treatment of a documentary subject makes the use of overblown, rhetorical narration an irresistible temptation. We suggest that no matter how moving and impressive a documentary subject may be, always try to write your narrative lines in the plainest style possible.

If plainness does not seem to work, you can always revise your narration in the direction of the literary and the poetic. But the old advice to writers still holds: in revising, when you come to a phrase or a passage that seems to you especially elegant and well conceived, blue-pencil it. Your script will probably benefit from the surgery.

Narration: Some General Rules

The narration used in nonfiction and fiction scripts is generally rather simple, straightforward, utilitarian prose. Its principal function is to inform. This means it must be understandable without being obtrusive. Don't make the mistake of supposing that an overblown line creates a dramatic effect. It can become catastrophic when the narration is so bombastic it all but buries the dramatic dialogue.

In a film about the life of Pierre August Renoir, the French Impressionist painter, the writer had inserted one purple sentence into an otherwise effective narrative passage. In this part of the script, the narrative—read by the gifted actor, Vincent Price—describes Renoir riding a bicycle down a roadway. The path is still soaked and muddy from a downpour earlier in the day.

VIDEO	*AUDIO*
DISSOLVE TO:	VINCENT PRICE VO:
96. #3 LANDSCAPE	. . . The surface was still slippery from rain when Renoir began bicycling down the path. He skidded in a puddle of water and fell on a mound of sharp edged stones . . .
	Hot irons shot through his body and all he could hear was the tremor of his own breathing . . . Renoir managed to pick himself up—his right arm discolored because it was broken . . .

Price was uncomfortable with the "hot irons" line and so was the writer after he heard Price read the entire speech.

Here are some further suggestions:

Write short sentences instead of long ones, simple instead of compound-complex. Easy understanding is a function of sentence length.

The most natural and understandable sentence order is subject-verb-object, with appropriate adjectives and adverbs inserted. Sentences which invert this order always require a little extra effort to understand.

Use active verbs rather than passive ones. A style in which passive verbs are frequent is always confusing since it presents a reader with a series of actions no one seems to have performed. The statement "I struck him" is simple and direct. The passive form, "He was struck by me," stresses the action and the person acted upon, but almost omits the actor. Consistent use of passive verbs makes for an impersonal, dull, and confusing style.

Use the shorter, more familiar word in preference to longer and possibly more pretentious ones. Short words that turn up in almost everyone's vocabulary are immediately understood, while less familiar words must be guessed. Of course familiar words, because they are much used, tend to be ambiguous. A word like *run* has hundreds of possible meanings. So don't sacrifice precision for familiarity; use an uncommon word when it conveys a precise meaning or a shade of meaning that a shorter familiar word does not.

Use as many references to people as possible, personal pronouns and common nouns with strong human connotations (child, father, woman, etc.) as well as names of people. People understand statements about people more readily than statements about things. Even when you talk about things, talk about them in terms of their importance to people.

For example:

AUDIO
It cost John Levinson $50,000 to construct this building back in 1920. He and his brother laid

out the plans, excavated the dirt, even poured the concrete for the foundation. They hired four other men to lay the bricks, and when it was all over they had built a landmark. Today, the building that the Levinson brothers literally built by hand still stands on the same corner. A thousand people have signed leases for office space over the fifty-eight years it's been standing. On the corner over there used to be a soda shop. Then it was a grocery store, and then the son of the man who owned it took over the store next to it and turned the whole place into a discount store. The law offices of Miller and Miller are still there. Leo Miller retired twenty years ago. But people in the neighborhood still remember him. Anybody who'd walk in with a problem got help from "old man Miller." His son Donald admits things have changed and maybe he's a little more selective now but he still gets traffic off the street just as his father did in the 30s and 40s.

The Levinson Building. It has been repainted about ten times in the fifty years. Tuck pointed six times. Its roof tarred and asphalted three times. New windows put in ten years ago. Coal used to heat the place, natural gas now. But the brass elevators, two of them are still as they were when their metal doors first swung open.

A documentary about a building: we humanize the subject by making the bricks, mortar, steel, and glass as much a part of the building's character as the tenants.

Finally, we suggest that you buy, study, and use some basic reference books: as good a dictionary as you can afford, *Handbook in Writing* by Legett, Mead, and Chariat, *Modern American Usage* by Nicholson, *Modern English Usage* by Fowler, and *Roget's Thesaurus* for checking synonyms.

Use these works concientiously and regularly; possession of a high school or even a university diploma does not mean, these days, that you know how to write simple and correct English.

The primary function of narration is to describe an ongoing action, although a narrative passage may include statements about how things look, sound, feel, and so on, and may even comment on the value or meaning of the action. In writing narrative you may use four distinct kinds of writing: *scene* writing, which tells how things and people behave ("One man broke from the crowd and began to run down a side street"); *summary* writing, in which you tell briefly about an action that in fact covered a long period of time ("In spite of a short-age of workers, the foundations were laid within three weeks"); *descriptive* writing, which sets forth the appearance of people and things ("He wore a work shirt and jeans so covered with metal studs and sequins that he seemed to blaze in the sunlight"); and *comment,* in which you explain the significance of some-thing or express a feeling about an action, a scene, or a person.

A narrative style that runs largely to scene writing will be fast-moving, simple to understand, and probably engrossing. Most contemporary writers of books and magazine pieces have cultivated this style of writing; it works equally well with video or audio narrative.

A style that employs a great deal of summary is not usually effective. Summary writing moves too fast, and loses too much vivid detail. It is useful to bridge scenes—that is, to cover a series of actions not important enough to be reported in detail. If you can possibly avoid it, never use summary writing at the beginning or end of a script, or at the beginning or end of key sequences; these are positions of major stress that require scene writing.

Description is important in print narrative; without it a writer could not convey a visual image of people and places in a story. This holds true for audio narration. In video and film writing the pictures take over most of the functions of description. In any case use description with some caution, for it is essentially static; in order to describe what a person looks like, or the appear-ance of a particular house on a particular street, you must stop the movement of your story. Most present-day media writers do not write very long passages of description. They limit themselves to occasional descriptive sentences and phrases sprinkled into a narrative that most of the time is describing action of some sort.

In print narrative, comment was once a popular narrative tool. For example see almost any 18th or 19th century novel; the writer felt free to break into the story to make moral observations, explain actions, and moralize freely. Comment is rarely used today. Modern authors tend to keep themselves and their opinions out of the story; they seldom adopt the convention of directly conversing with the reader. Instead, reactions expressed in narrative are usually attributed to a character within the story.

Media narration is much more hospitable to comment, perhaps because radio and television have developed a tradition of editorializing to viewers as part of their reporting techniques. In general, if your script purports to tell a story as if it were fiction you will probably use little or no comment in the narrative portions. If your script is presented as explanation, reporting, or analysis, how-ever, you will probably use some comment, perhaps a great deal of it.

Here is an example of good narration that was written within stringent limita-tions, from the film *Point of Pride.* It was commissioned as a public relations and sales film by the G&W Energy Products Group, manufacturers of highly sophisti-cated machine parts, for clients and others in the industry. The subject matter is technical so the narration had to be precise, phrased in the language current to the industry at the time. Of course the film had to be made as understandable and interesting as possible.

Note how the writer, Greg Madsen, works out these problems in the following passage:

55. WORKMAN SETTING UP PLASMA TORCH

NARR:
In this business, what looks ordinary is sometimes quite exceptional. This man is preparing to cut a piece of stock that will be worth more in its raw state than the average American automobile. That's seamless copper-nickel piping, the starting stock we used to create components for the main seawater system in the Thresher and Trident nuclear submarines. The contract presented a high financial risk, but we handled it fairly well.

56. SUPER: SUBMARINE BLUEPRINT.

57. PLASMA CUT BEGINS. DISSOLVE TO ...

VOICE (OVER):
In creating the main seawater fitting for 12 of the first attack submarines, we had the unique experience in this industry of not scrapping a piece and not being obliged to submit a single piece on deviation. This was really an outstanding accomplishment.

58. JAY MACHINE IN OPERATION.

NARR:
The Navy specs were very clear—as always. Briefly, there wasn't an existing manufacturing technique or tool that could do the job. So our designers developed what we call "The Jay Machine"—a cold forming press with built-in rapid controls. The Navy gave us the job on the basis of the blueprints and on our proposed processes to meet specific properties. They felt our approach was a major revolution in manufacturing high-reliability components.

59. THRESHER ON SURFACE AND CRUISING.

VOICE (OVER):
Our philosophy in this particular instance has been to take precise dimension stock and then, under controlled conditions in the Jay Press as it was developed, forming the final part to the required dimension so that there is no machining required—other than maybe the end bevels and maybe a little slight conditioning if there is a scratch. Essentially, after it comes out of the

60. SUBMARINE TEE ON LAYOUT BENCH.

	Jay Machine, it is 95 percent ready to ship.
61. THRESHER UNDER WATER (STOCK)	SFX: SONAR PINGS.
	NARR:
	We understand the implications of failure. Lives depend on the integrity of our work, the quality of our products.

Point of Pride, if shown on prime time television, would never have damaged the rating of *Kojak* or *The Mary Tyler Moore Show. The Godfather* would undoubtedly be a greater attraction at your neighborhood movie theater. Nevertheless, with its necessary limitations, it is a highly successful film. Accuracy demanded that the writer employ an abstruse technical vocabulary, but did not prevent him from writing his narration in simple, direct, well-constructed sentences. Moreover, he was able to alternate his narrative passages with prerecorded voice-over segments done by employees of the company. Perhaps most important of all, the technical processes of manufacturing were cast in human terms; "this man is preparing," "we handled it," "our philosophy." Placing the story in a human perspective turns it into drama—a story of human ingenuity in solving difficult technical problems in order to save the lives of men who work under the sea.

Notice, too, that in *Point of Pride* the narrator deals in comment—"In this business, what looks ordinary is sometimes quite exceptional"—and in summary. The voice-over passages carry a good deal of the story line, aided by the visuals. Description through words is not too necessary in a film since the visuals themselves convey the appearance of things and actions. Taken alone, the narration in this script would not be well-balanced, but in context, with the voice-over sections and the visuals, it works admirably.

Here is a variation on this system of balancing taken from a script intended for audio production. The script deals with American life during the 1920s. Like other scripts in its series, the format is the dramatized essay. The narrator discusses features of life during the 1920s, referring to and quoting materials from a variety of books. Direct quotes from the books are read by actors, and music is used in a fairly traditional manner.

NARRATOR:	A casual leafing through Mark Sullivan's *The Twenties,* the sixth volume of his massive history called *Our Times,* provides a wealth of factual instances. For as everyone knows, the 1920s provided America with those remarkable social inventions, the marathon dance, the innocent bystander, and the great athletic hero.
MUSIC	*IN AND BEHIND . . .*
VOICE ONE:	A dingy hall littered with worn slippers, cigarette stubs, news-

papers and soup cans, reeking with mingled odors of stale coffee, tobacco smoke, cold broth, chewing gum, and smelling salts was the scene of one of the most drab and grueling endurance contests ever witnessed. There is nothing inspiring in seeing an extremely tired, pretty girl in a worn bathrobe, dingy white stockings in rolls above scuffling felt slippers, her eyes half shut, her arms hung over her partner's shoulders, drag aching feet that seemed glued to the floor in one short agonizing step after another. The sun sifted in. Reporters and substitute dancers washed up after a fashion. Outsiders stopped to glance inside. And still the phonograph continued grinding out its slow, level jazz until one wanted never to hear jazz again. Breakfast was served at 7:30. After that, the dancing was more like dancing.

MUSIC	*UP AND SEGUE TO A NEW THEME.*
VOICE TWO:	February 15, 1924. Senator Frank L. Greene of Vermont was accidentally shot and wounded as an innocent bystander during a pistol fight between prohibition agents and bootleggers on the streets of downtown Washington.
MUSIC	*UP AND SEGUE TO A NEW THEME FOR . . .*
VOICE THREE:	This is Graham McNamee speaking. Picture to yourself a cadaverous face deeply etched with the grooves that bespeak ascetic self-denial and years of rigorous training. A sad face, radiating grim determination, the corners of the mouth drawn down to heighten the forbidding aspect. Red Grange looks as though he means business. His bearing, his walk, his posture are impressively dramatic. He is the all-time, all-American halfback in flesh and blood.
MUSIC	*UP AND OUT.*
NARRATOR:	Well, Red Grange played football and he was a great idol in his day. And innocent bystanders were shot and killed in the streets of American cities. The trouble with the fable is that we talk as though these things happened to everybody, as though they were all that ever happened to anybody; and this, of course, is not true. There were in the twenties Chicagoans who never saw a gangster or a machine gun. There was plenty of nonflaming youth. There were probably one or two American citizens, though this may strike you as improbable, who never during the entire decade played Mah Jongg or bought a share of stock.

In any script there must be a story line dealing with human beings or with strong human connotations. In an audio script there must also be vivid visual elements. In addition, there may be elements of explanation, commentary and sometimes admonishment. Notice that in the above example the scene writing, the presentation of specific dramatic action and the visual elements are handled with quoted material. We see and feel the weariness of the marathon dancer, we watch as a senator is pistolled in the streets of Washington. This leaves the narrator free to summarize, interpret, and express his feelings. In this sort of script, if the books referred to were rather general and theoretical in their content then this pattern would have to be reversed; the narrator would have to carry the story line and provide the visual cues.

In terms of basic style, although this script on the 1920s is admittedly "literary," the writing is quite simple and direct: short, simple sentences, a basic vocabulary, and most important of all, constant insistence on a human perspective.

THE NARRATOR AS DRAMATIC CHARACTER

In any script for any medium, the narrator is always characterized to some degree; by the fact that narration is spoken by an individual human being if by nothing else. The problem for the writer is how much to stress the individuality of the narrator, and how much to make the narrator a functional part of the story.

In some films and filmstrips, especially those of a direct instructional nature, the narrator may be relatively impersonal. In others, the narrator may serve more as a dramatic character, as seen in Scott Craig's excellent documentary on the history of Chicago, *The Giants and the Common Men.*

EXTERIOR OF AN ELEVATED TRAIN. IT PASSES OUT OF SIGHT THROUGH THE TREES.	*NATURAL SOUND.*
CAMERA SLOWLY PULLS BACK FROM THE TRACKS TO REVEAL A CEMETERY IN THE HEART OF THE CITY.	THE MAN: (VOICE OVER) Graceland Cemetery. Chicago, Illinois. *MUSIC: SOFT, SIMPLE.*
SERIES OF SEVERAL WIDE SHOTS SHOWING THE UNUSUAL NATURE OF THE MONUMENTS OF GRACELAND. DISSOLVE SLOWLY FROM ONE TO ANOTHER. TILT UP FROM THE BACK OF A STONE TO FIND A MAN READING NAMES ON THE STONES.	

CU *THE MAN.*

THE MAN: (VOICE OVER)
Here, written in stone, are the names that made the city . . . and built the midwest. Now they are dust, yet alive in the minds of the living.

CUT TIGHT TO A SERIES OF NAMES ON THE STONES. DISSOLVE FROM SHOT TO SHOT.
- ALTGELD
- PINKERTON
- PALMER
- SULLIVAN
- SENN

John Peter Altgeld.

Allen Pinkerton.

Potter Palmer.

Louis Sullivan.

Nicholas Senn.

DISSOLVE TO *THE MAN;* HE IS WALKING SLOWLY THROUGH THE CEMETERY.

Here . . . in the midst of the city . . . they lie side by side.

SUBJECTIVE CAMERA SHOT FROM THE POINT OF VIEW OF *THE MAN.* CAMERA MOVES ON MANY OF THE STONES. WE CANNOT MAKE OUT THE NAMES.

Names that made history . . . Names that we have forgotten, or never knew . . . Stories enough to fill a thousand novels.

BEGIN TILT UP TO RYERSON TOMB.

THE MAN: (VOICE OVER)
These stones can speak clearly to us, if we will listen.

CUT TIGHT TO THE NAME *RYERSON.*

MUSIC: STRONG CHORD.

Here the narrator is a real person, with a real visual presence, who acts as surrogate, or stand-in for the viewer. Because he is a real person, and because he knows much more about Graceland—and the history of Chicago—than the viewer does, he is more than a simple viewpoint device; he is the connection between the viewer and history. He leads into the history, but remains detached from it. In this sort of script, the narrator has little to do with the dramatic action or with description; he or she summarizes, explains, comments.

A more complex use of narration occurs in a script called *One Palace F.O.B. Chicago.* Written for an NBC-Chicago production of a special program on the *Treasures of Versailles* exhibit then showing at the Chicago Art Institute, the script attempts to tell the story of the Palace at Versailles, using film footage, 35mm slides, and some shots of art objects included in the exhibit. Following preliminary historical research, the writer—before visuals were available to him—chose to tell the story of Versailles in terms of a series of linked narrations and conversations spoken off-screen by the major historical characters involved in the story. Although this tentative draft was rewritten and much modified to suit visual possibilities, a good deal of it remained in the final production. Thus, the script uses a narrator and, in addition, uses narrative monologues by such personages as King Louis XIV, Louise de LaValliere, and so on. Following is the section of the script which introduces the reign of Louis XIV.

SLIDE #21, LOUIS XIII MANOR HOUSE.

NARRATOR:

By the time of his death, in 1643, King Louis XIII had built a simple chateau which, though later embellished, has been preserved as the core of the huge palace.

DISSOLVE TO:

Battles, love and splendor interweave in the long reign of Louis XIV.

SLIDE #22: BATTLE OF ROCROI.

Battles? Five days after the death of his father, the battle of Rocroi is won.

SLIDE #23: LOUIS XIV AS A CHILD.

The new king is a child, but a magnificent child.

SLIDE #24: PALACE FROM ORANGERIE.

His first love, and perhaps his last, is Versailles, which he visits in 1651. But it is ten years before he can begin to create there the fantastic dream-palace which he must have envisioned long before. He finds three remarkable men: LeVau, the architect; LeBrun, the painter; LeNotre, the landscape gardener. With their help—and over the violent objections of his treasurer, Colbert—he begins to create Versailles.

SLIDE #25: WESTWARD VIEW OF THE PALACE.

SLIDE #26: WESTWARD VIEW, CLOSER SHOT.

SLIDE #27: LOUIS AND COURTIERS.

MUSIC: IN BG, A GENTLE, ORCHESTRAL THEME OF THE PERIOD.

NARRATOR:

In part, Versailles was intended as a setting for the young and charming Louise de la Valliere, a setting of which she became a happy ornament.

SLIDE #28: LA VALLIERE.

LA VALLIERE:

Not happy, monsieur. I was, in a way, the most reluctant of visitors to all that sad magnificence. It is true that I loved the King; it is true that I bore his children. But I never loved the crown or the court. The tournaments, the fetes, with which Louis honored me were nightmares of love and shames.

DISS. TO: BUST OF LOUIS.

LOUIS XIV:

IN THE FOLLOWING DIALOGUE BETWEEN LOUIS AND COLBERT, CUT FROM CU OF ONE BUST TO THE OTHER.

A King's loves, like other splendors, are not to be hidden. In 1662 I became the Sun King, *le Roi Soleil;* an antiquarian named Douvrier designed an emblem for me: a sun darting its rays upon a globe, with the motto "Nec pluribus impar." I was a young man and a young King then, but I knew that I was destined to a life of triumph and golden splendor, in which there could be no small loves or small secrecies. Versailles was my symbol.

COLBERT:
And a very expensive symbol it was, too.

LOUIS XIV:
Ah, Colbert! My treasurer! My old penny pincher!

Here the narrator remains the storyteller, although the characters in the story are aware of him. He shares the narrative function with them, so that the story of Versailles can be told from several points of view. This was made necessary by the fact that in the story of Versailles there was no single human protagonist; the story had to be told by a series of voices, tied together by—among other devices—the words of a narrator storyteller who stands somewhat outside the action.

The remaining possibility, of course, would be to make the narrator both a storyteller and an actor in the drama. This is sometimes done in biographical and historical scripts that deal with topics more unified in time than the story of Versailles.

Summary

It seems reasonable to say that the narrator in a script is never completely impersonal. He or she always speaks as an individual; the writer must decide how far the narrator is to be characterized. The reason is that facts must be seen in human perspective to be comprehensible at all. At a more complex level, as we have pointed out repeatedly, all nonfiction is dramatic; drama provides the framework within which we understand and react to information. Even the news is reported to us by "real" individuals with distinct personalities. Critics sometimes complain that television viewers and, at an earlier period, radio listeners have tended to choose their news sources on a basis of personality, public image, and so on, when clearly they should have considered other, more rational factors. We do not find this tendency of viewers surprising, or indeed a subject for criticism. Some of the most successful newspapers have been those that faithfully expressed the personalities of their often eccentric publishers. For better or worse, this appears to be the way in which we get our information.

chapter 10

Writing Dialogue for Fiction and Nonfiction Scripts

The study of dialogue is one of the most important and engrossing tasks a writer can undertake. Your raw material is humanity and your main way of representing human beings is through their speech. In the media, this is particularly true of the writer who attempts either an audio or television script. In motion pictures, dialogue is an important, but not always the only medium for telling a story. In television, with its small screen and low levels of visual information, talk is important, as it is on an audiotape. As the writer of nonfiction scripts you may invent dialogue, modify actual conversation for dramatic purposes, or edit real talk into meaningful sequences. In any case you need to know something of the mechanics of dialogue construction and the basic skills of dialogue writing.

THE BASICS OF WRITING DIALOGUE

Often in fiction, and sometimes in nonfiction, we write dialogue with an economy of movement never encountered in real life. What people actually say, as you can learn by listening to a recorded conversation, is often ungrammatical, verbose, and roundabout in phrasing. Words are often used because they sound right, not because they convey the correct dictionary meaning. To show you the difference, here is a dialogue sequence from a film on consumer education. The scene is an employees' lunchroom. Ms. Finchley, an elderly, alert woman, and Juanita, thirtyish, are just unpacking their lunches.

149

JUANITA:
You want some coffee?

MS. F:
Not that mud. I've got my own.

JUANITA:
Okay. (SHE RETURNS TO THE TABLE, OPENS UP HER LUNCH BAG.)

DURING THIS EXCHANGE HENRY AND ADELLA ENTER. HENRY IS A BLACK MAN IN HIS EARLY TWENTIES, ADELLA A GIRL OF ABOUT NINETEEN. THEY EXCHANGE GREETINGS WITH JUANITA AND MS. F.

MS. F:
How's the big world out there, Henry?

HENRY:
Cold. Rainy. Miserable. Everybody hates everybody. It's a jungle out there, Ms. F.

MS. F:
Nice of you to say so, Henry. Makes me feel all warm and cozy. You want a taste of my paté? It's homemade.

HENRY:
Thanks, Ms. F, but I got my peanut butter and jelly right here.

JUANITA:
Didn't you bring a lunch, Adella?

ADELLA:
Allen's getting me a sandwich. I need to gain weight.

AT THIS POINT ALLEN ENTERS WITH SANDWICH BAGS IN HIS HANDS.

ALLEN:
Here we are. (HE LAYS THINGS OUT.) One giant Mooseburger, with double chocolate malt. That's me. And for Adella, Polish sausage heavy on the mayo, one Boston cream pie, and a double strawberry malt.

MS. F:
(SIGHS.) I must have gone wrong somewhere.

Prior to this, the conflict has already been briefly established. The scene above is intended merely to establish the setting of the film and introduce the other characters.

A scene of this sort, though it does not advance the story, is important; for without it the characters, setting, and problem would be less than believable. At the same time, since the length of the complete film will not be over fifteen minutes, the scene must be handled with utmost economy. The dialogue, taken line by line, is very tight. There are few sentences that could be shortened or eliminated without making an actual cut in the content of the scene. There are, however, two such content cuts possible. One, which was made in the final draft of the script, begins with Ms. F's line, "You want a taste of my paté? It's home-made." and runs through Henry's following speech. Another possible cut would be Allen's speech beginning "Here we are" and running through Ms. F's succeeding line. Consider whether this second cut should have been made. The over-riding consideration in the end would be time; the speech does not advance action and would be one of the first to go on that account. On the other hand, it does help to characterize Allen and to create a believable setting for the conversation to follow. Decisions on tightening scenes and dialogue are usually based on considerations of this sort.

The tendency of writers of dramatizations is to produce a rather tightly written scene. It is sometimes desirable to retain a certain amount of dialogue "padding" in a shooting script, so that cuts may be used to adjust a scene to a desired length. But in the main the economically written scene is a proper goal to aim for. Such scenes are relatively easy to produce and play, and the technique of writing the dialogue is fairly simple to master. The keynote is economy of language, which may be achieved through use of a dialectical structure (see chapter seven). The skills you need are the ability to hear dialogue before you write it, a willingness to revise and edit, and a feeling for the dialectic of a scene.

Sometimes—perhaps more frequently in fiction than in nonfiction scripts—a writer will produce sequences of this sort stripped down to abstractions. For example, consider the following passage from an audio adaptation of Oscar Wilde's novel, *The Portrait of Dorian Gray:*

HENRY:	(ASTONISHED) In love? With whom are you in love?
DORIAN:	With an actress.
HENRY:	That is rather commonplace, don't you think?
DORIAN:	You would not say so if you saw her, Lord Henry.
HENRY:	Who is she?
DORIAN:	Her name is Sibyl Vane.
HENRY:	Never heard of her.
DORIAN:	No one has. People will someday, however. She is a genius.
HENRY:	My dear boy, no woman is a genius. Women are a decorative sex. They never have anything to say, but they say it charmingly.

Notice how the tight, rapid movement of the first seven lines, from thesis to antithesis and on, slackens on Dorian's two-line speech, which appears to transcend Lord Henry's objections but actually prepares the way for the true synthesis, Lord Henry's observation on women. This arrangement serves two purposes: the final, lengthy speech rounds out and concludes the short sequence, while the opening series of short, antithetical speeches builds up to and highlights the concluding epigram. This method was of special interest to Wilde and indeed is a very useful way of developing verbal comedy. In this story, as in his plays, the *bons mots* very often form the psychological center of sequences of dialogue, while the structure of an individual scene is a mosaic of such sequences.

Long, alternated speeches, in which characters talk at some length without interruption are less frequent in the media. In an audio production, a single voice talking on and on becomes boring; to sustain interest in such a speech, the lines must be heavily structured, almost like poetry; and even in that case, a heavy burden is placed on the performer. In film, with its primary stress on visuals, single voice speeches must be broken up to reinforce visual images.

Long, alternated speeches in any medium tend to demand a movement and pacing of their own which is relatively slow, and in comparison with more conventional scenes, quite complex. The soliloquies in Shakespearean drama, for instance, are usually staged as set pieces, carefully blocked to achieve movement and point, and they still require extraordinary skill of the actor. This sort of dialogue cannot be successfully paced; the actor and director must adapt themselves to the lines instead of adapting the lines to their preconceptions.

How this works may be seen in the following dialogue from an audio script on the atom bombing of Japan in 1945.

VOICE: But at least I saw Nagasaki from a distance that day—it was very nice.
                It's hilly country; the hills rise sharp from the water.
                They're green, outlined and shaded in brown, with a kind of faded blue tinge to the air.
                On a hazy day you could narrow your eyes and find yourself living in a Japanese print.

NARRATOR: You couldn't see the city from there?

VOICE: The city was behind the hills.
                You'd never have guessed that.
                But don't let me fool you; the Marines looked at the hill and thought, "What a tough place to land."
                It would have been, too;
                I thought about that myself.
                But I thought more about the city behind the hills, what it was like.

NARRATOR: You stayed outside all day.

VOICE: All day. It was growing dark when we went in.
                I was on the bridge at sunrise;
                We had worked all night at unloading.

The harbor and the shacks on the beach took on the outlines
of day.
About 7:15 a woman came out of one of the shacks and began
to hang up washing.
It was Monday morning.

Dialogue usually advances the story line; it is action, not description or comment. (As we have already noted, these latter functions may be left to the narrator.) Conventional dialogue is most often used and is important in helping to develop and identify characters. Such dialogue rarely displays an internal pattern of its own. *Alternate speech* dialogue, if it is properly written, does develop an individualized pattern. It has rhythm, it has repetition and parallelisms of structure, and it achieves design through the selection and distribution of figures of speech. If it does not achieve an internal design through the exploitation of some or all of these factors it is nothing but too many words. This sort of dialogue must be written as if it were poetry. As a scriptwriter you must choose the style of dialogue that best suits you and your subject. In general you will be safer if you follow the most conventional style.

Most good script dialogue is colloquial, not literary. Dialogue should *suggest* people talking; it is not a transcript, but an imitation of reality. The writer, more than anyone else, should realize the differences that exist between formal written English and the language we speak. In speech we may use many colloquialisms, slang expressions, and coined words that would be dubious or even incorrect in formal literature. In speech, we play havoc with the sentence (almost purely a convention of written English) and speak in grunts, single words, or elliptical phrases. Formal English is precise, carefully constructed, premeditated language, while spoken English is spontaneous and loosely constructed (but eloquent at its best).

Dialogue is an art that plays back and forth among the real, the realistic, and the artificial. As a scriptwriter you must be a master of the various languages and dialects of spoken English. You must be able to blend and combine them to suit your purpose.

First and foremost dramatic dialogue must be speakable. It has to be read aloud. A scriptwriter must cultivate a knack for hearing dialogue. So read it aloud as you write.

The cultivation of an ear and a voice for dialogue will soon teach you what to avoid. Alliteration is always risky. Any actor may flub lines of the "Peter-Piper-picked-a-peck" variety. Any sort of sound repetition, whether it is alliteration, rhyme, or assonance, should be employed with great caution. Combinations of sibilants are especially bad on the air because they cause the actor to hiss.

In an audio script, try to set up scenes for naturally contrasting voices. The voice *is* the character in a sound medium. As identical twins may cause confusion in the flesh, so similar voices may cause confusion on the air. Differentiate your characters by age, sex, speech style, and dialect as much as possible. Avoid introducing more characters into a scene than are absolutely necessary because problems of character identification multiply with increasing numbers of voices. Self-identifying voices are better than those who must be re-identified each time.

DIALOGUE AND CHARACTERIZATION

In addition to advancing the action of a script, dialogue contributes a great deal to the characterization. Remember our earlier comments on the creation of dramatic character—that your purpose is to reveal the inner motives of a character by showing outer, observable characteristics. The variety of individual peculiarities in speech being endless we cannot pretend even to hint at them all here. We can, however, point out certain types of speech characteristics and suggest their possible relation to motives.

Habitual choice of subject matter can reveal character. This notion is found in extreme form in Dickens's character Mr. Dick, whose conversation circled compulsively around the odd topic of King Charles's head. But even with less compulsive people, the idea remains valid. A person may be described in terms of speech, by the topic he or she discusses habitually, by choice of language, favorite expressions, and so forth. As an exercise, listen carefully to the talk of someone with whom you spend a good deal of time; jot down the topics he or she discusses, and returns to, note any repeated phrases or sentences, indeed all repetitions in his or her talk. Then imagine that you have only these notes to tell you about the character, that you must visualize him or her and understand motives from a study of these observations alone. What kind of character would you imagine? How close would your imagined character come to the real person?

Actually, of course, habitual choice of subject matter might almost be reduced to a consideration of vocabulary. Vocabulary is commonly taken to be an indicator of intelligence, education, background, associations, and so on. Certain general types of vocabularies may be distinguished. For example, John Steinbeck used rudimentary, inadequate vocabulary to create a character in *Of Mice and Men*. The simple, two-dimensional world of the weak-minded Lennie is mirrored in his choice of language. Indeed, Steinbeck uses almost no other device than word choice to suggest Lennie's character, except to convey an idea of Lennie's great strength through description and the reaction of other characters to him.

Tightly knit occupational groups are always likely to create special vocabularies. Railroad men, at least until recently, had a very colorful special language of their own. Army slang is a special professional language. Various criminal groups speak their own argot. Linguists and philologists, amateur and professional, have studied and reported on various kinds of argots, slang, and jargon. These reports, when they are well done, can be extremely helpful to the writer. They should, however, be reinforced by personal observation.

Character and character reaction may also be suggested through the manner of speech. The grammatical structure of dialogue may suggest basic character traits or, more frequently, temporary emotional states—whether, for instance, a character speaks in short, terse sentences or in rounded, orotund periods; whether he breaks off a sentence to fumble for words; whether his sentences are precise and to the point or loose and rambling. Observe the differences in character and mood in the following examples. First is a sequence from *One Palace F.O.B. Chicago* in which Marie Antoinette faces the mob at Versailles.

"The mobs surrounded us during the night. They were hungry, no doubt, but they were also full of hate.

"Early in the morning, some women tried to storm the Palace.

"The crowd came as far as the Marble Staircase. There were yells and pistol shots.

"I watched all this. The King was meeting with his ministers.

"I was standing by a window in the King's Chamber. Monsieur de la Fayette came and told me that the people had asked that I appear on the balcony. My God, I was frightened, but what could I do? I pushed my children aside. I remember that I said, 'Very well. Even if it means death, I will go!'

"I stepped out and faced the crowd. It was very strange, really. The shouting died down, the guns were lowered. Nothing happened at all."

Next, a segment from *Children of the Colonies*, an educational film showing details of the lives of early New England colonists. Brian who tells the story is a young boy living with his parents in New Hampton, east of Boston, in the late 1600s. The family is visited by Captain Jack Jensen, a sea captain who is Brian's uncle.

BRIAN

When my mother brought forth her standing salt of silver gilt which she had from *her* mother in Wessex, I knew that I would long remember this day. I had already smelled and partly seen what we were to eat—a fine dish of stewed eels, a spicy pompion pie, a haunch of venison and other good things.

AS HE SAYS THIS, THE MOTHER BRINGS OUT A LARGE AND ORNATE STAND-UP SALT CELLAR, AND PLACES IT IN THE MIDDLE OF THE TABLE. THEY BOTH PAUSE BRIEFLY TO ENJOY THE EFFECT.

BRIAN

At last my mother told me to bring wax candles—the sweet, green candles made of wax from bayberries which I had picked—and set them in our holders and light them.

AT A WORD FROM HIS MOTHER, BRIAN RUNS TO A CORNER CUP-BOARD AND BRINGS OUT THREE BAYBERRY CANDLES WHICH HE SETS INTO CANDLESTICKS AND CAREFULLY PLACES ON THE TABLE.

In William Goldman's *Butch Cassidy and the Sundance Kid*, Butch and the Kid are being chased by the "Superposse." We come in at a point nearly halfway into the script.[1]

CUT TO

A CAMERA SHOT FROM AN ENORMOUS HEIGHT. IT IS AS IF TWO GREAT BLACK CENTIPEDES WERE RACING. IN FRONT, THE HOLE-IN-THE-WALL GANG, MOVING LIKE CRAZY. BEHIND THEM, THE SUPER-POSSE, NOT LOSING GROUND. THE TERRAIN AHEAD OF THEM IS FLAT. ON THE OTHER SIDE LIE HILLS.

CUT TO

THE HOLE-IN-THE-WALL GANG, STILL SHOT FROM ABOVE. THE SOUND OF THE HORSES IS LOUD. THEN BUTCH'S VOICE IS HEARD.

BUTCH

(SHOUTING IT OUT) Scatter!

(AND LIKE A SUNBURST THE GANG FRAGMENTS, EVERY MAN TAKING A DIFFERENT DIRECTION, EXCEPT BUTCH AND SUNDANCE, WHO RIDE TOGETHER.)

CUT TO

BUTCH AND SUNDANCE REACHING THE CREST OF A HILL. SUNDANCE IS FIRST AND AS HE GETS TO THE TOP HE PAUSES JUST FOR A MO-MENT, GLANCING BACK. BUTCH IS JUST A STEP OR TWO BEHIND, ALMOST TO THE TOP HIMSELF.

BUTCH

How many of 'em are following us?

SUNDANCE

All of 'em.

BUTCH

(STUNNED) All of 'em?

HE IS BESIDE SUNDANCE NOW AT THE TOP OF THE HILL AND HE TOO PAUSES, LOOKING BACK.

CUT TO

THE SUPERPOSSE STILL BUNCHED, COMING AFTER THEM. IN THE DISTANCE AND SAFE, THE REST OF THE GANG RIDE AWAY.

CUT TO

BUTCH, FURIOUS, POINTING OUT THE REST OF HIS MEN.

BUTCH

(SHOUTING AT THE SUPERPOSSE, POINTING AT HIS MEN) What have you got against those guys?

[1] Reprinted by permission of International Creative Management. Copyright © 1969 by William Goldman.

CUT TO

SUNDANCE TAKING OFF, BUTCH A STEP BEHIND.

CUT TO

THE SUPERPOSSE. THEY JUST KEEP COMING.

CUT TO

BUTCH AND SUNDANCE RIDING AS FAST AS THEY CAN.

CUT TO

THE SUPERPOSSE. THEY ARE GOING AT EXACTLY THE SAME PACE AS BEFORE. THEY ARE ALL IN THE SAME POSITION IN THE PACK. NOTHING HAS CHANGED. THEY ARE LIKE A MACHINE.

CUT TO

BUTCH AND SUNDANCE, GOING, IF ANYTHING, FASTER THAN BEFORE. BUT THE STRAIN IS BEGINNING TO TELL. THE SUN WAS HIGH WHEN THIS BEGAN. NOW THERE ARE SHADOWS. AND ON THEIR FACES, STRAIN.

CUT TO

THE SUPERPOSSE COMING ON, MORE LIKE A MACHINE THAN EVER.

CUT TO

BUTCH AND SUNDANCE. THEY ARE APPROACHING A SPOT WHERE SEVERAL TRAILS ARE INDICATED. AT THE LAST MOMENT THEY VEER LEFT, FOLLOWING THE LEAST LIKELY PATH.

CUT TO

BUTCH AND SUNDANCE RIDING ON. THE SHADOWS ARE DEEPER NOW. SO IS THEIR STRAIN.

CUT TO

BUTCH AND SUNDANCE. ABRUPTLY THEY HALT.

BUTCH

I think we lost 'em. Do you think we lost 'em?

SUNDANCE

No

BUTCH

Neither do I. (AND THEY ARE OFF AGAIN, RIDING FLAT OUT.)

Let us look back at the first of these three examples. Notice that in the speech given to Marie Antoinette there are few if any eccentricities of style. The Queen speaks in a colloquial but rather elegant way. Her lines do not suggest a French dialect, but their rhythms permit an actress to read them in dialect. The story is told in a bare, stripped-down way to increase tension. Finally, the movement of the lines is light and flowing so that the actress reading them could create hesitations followed by little rushes of words, a rhythm indicating the Queen's terror.

Both the narrative and dialogue lines in the *Children of the Colonies* segment are relaxed and low-key to suggest the mood of pleasure and ease. Certain factual details—the bayberry candles, the pompion pie, and so on—help to create a sense of the period. Some of the vocabulary and occasional obsolete grammatical forms are used to the same end; the speech is not historically authentic in detail—if it were the viewer might have trouble understanding it—but it suggests the period.

In the Goldman script the dialogue is very sparse; the author wisely uses visual action to tell his story. Nevertheless, the placing of the dialogue is important. Notice how the terse spoken lines tend to cap and summarize an action sequence. Notice, too, how in the last fifteen words Goldman manages at once to advance the action of the scene and to add to the characterizations of Butch and Sundance:

> "I think we lost 'em. Do you think we lost 'em?"
> "No."
> "Neither do I."

The ability to say so much with so little dialogue is a mark of the skilled professional scriptwriter.

Little need be said about the matter of pronunciation as a factor in dialogue writing. Pronunciation can suggest locale, the education of a character, or his or her recent environment. The main problem for the writer is suggesting pronunciation in a script since English is not a phonetic language. (No matter what dialect of English you speak, you do not pronounce "though," "bough," and "cough" in the same way.) The words "I can't go to town today," read by a Southerner, a Kansan, and a Down-easter would produce three strikingly different sets of sounds. How does one convey this difference? Unfortunately, as Bernard Shaw remarked, playwrights cannot write their dialogue in phonetic symbols. Their next best expedient is using the standard alphabet to convey differences in pronunciation as accurately as possible. The difficulty with this, as may be seen in Shaw's *Captain Brassbound's Conversion,* is that dialogue almost needs an interlinear translation to be intelligible. Many writers do not attempt accuracy in recording pronunciations in their dialogue. They sometimes use a phonetic spelling to convey a characteristic variant in pronunciation, and rely on content, grammatical structure, and intonational pattern to convey the rest.

Good dialogue writing can be learned, with a lot of practice, by those who understand how important the ear is and use it as much as possible.

Let's say you have a scene in a high school where for a semester a teacher and student move closer to an eventual confrontation; the film you're writing is about this tension and conflict. You obviously can't write a semester's worth of antagonism in a half-hour script. But you can find the high point in the conflict which sums up those periods in the teacher/student relationship that can't be shown in their entirety in the film; and then start playing the scene from that point. For example:

STUDENT

Leave me alone.

TEACHER

Sorry, not this time.

STUDENT

You gonna tell me how great life is and all that crap.

TEACHER

No.

STUDENT

You're gonna try reverse psychology.

(beat)

You can stick that reverse psychology up your gazoo

TEACHER

Hey, Bernie, I'm not the enemy.

STUDENT

You're not nothing, man, to me, to my ol' lady, to this school.

(beat)

We're both two big fat zeerooes.

TEACHER

Okay, we're two big fat zeroes. What are we going to do about it?

STUDENT

Nah . .thinnggg.

TEACHER

We're going to cut this bullsh . . .

STUDENT

Hey . . . he can even swear, listen to him.

TEACHER

And start talking to each other. Real talk. No games anymore. So I can make sense and you can make sense.

STUDENT

(mocking)

Talk to me, teacher.

TEACHER

Or you'll walk out of this place and be dead.

(beat)

Because after me no one is going to even give you two seconds, Bernie. No one.

STUDENT

How do you know, Mr. Smarts?!

TEACHER

I don't have to know. You have to.

(beat)

See you tomorrow, Bernie.

STUDENT

What makes you think you will?

TEACHER

Tomorrow, Bernie. Bye.

TEACHER WALKS OFF LEAVING BERNIE ALONE IN THE ROOM.

Try writing a conflict exercise. Create a scene. Develop it on paper. Motivate your characters. Make them come to life. Think about experiences you've seen that may resemble what you're writing about. Draw on life. On your fantasies. On your own anger. Tell the story in narration or dialogue. Say it clearly. Simply.

Then write a scene using only visuals. Motivate it entirely from the camera's point of view.

Again we repeat: curiosity is the writer's essential virtue. Study is the writer's life. Listen to people, observe, record. Take notes of how they speak. Get or make tapes of different kinds of people in different kinds of situations. Analyze their vocabularies, their speech patterns. Read the works of writers who have learned how to write narrative and dialogue well. Experiment. Nothing can be more valuable to you than an understanding of the sound of a spoken word, and an ability to suggest it along with all its complex meanings on paper.

chapter 11
Writing
Television
News

Learning to write television news is an excellent preparation for learning to write longer and more complex kinds of scripts. The difference between writing an SOF (sound on film) news clip, which may run a page or two, and writing a short documentary, which may run ten pages or more, is not great. If you can think of a two-minute news clip as a mini-drama then the writing and editing of it isn't so difficult. You must ask yourself: "What is the conflict in this story? And how can it be said and shown in a matter of seconds or minutes as a complete dramatic package with a beginning, middle, and end?"

This approach to news isn't in the least novel; the most deliberate use of it was probably made by *Time Magazine*, beginning some thirty years ago. The editors of *Time* decided that although reporting the facts would give their readers a knowledge of events, an understanding of their meaning and how they worked could be communicated only if the facts were put in a dramatic framework. Today, a newsmagazine will start off the lead paragraph in a news story in less traditional manner:

He had tried every trick in the book—and a few new twists as well—to avoid his day in court. As President, Richard Nixon refused to appear before the Watergate grand jury and the Senate Watergate committee and shunned the House Judiciary panel that was steadily building the case for his impeachment. He put out sanitized White House transcripts and cloaked himself in questionable claims of national security, Executive privilege, and the constitutional separation of powers. Even after losing his Presidency and receiving a full pardon from his successor, Nixon held his tongue, protected now by a painful phlebitis condition that made any court appearance a threat to his life—or so his doctors said. But the long campaign of defiance and delay finally came to an end last week at Nixon's sunny San Clemente retreat. There, the former President formally took an oath and testified for eleven hours on the wide range of subjects still under investigation in the aftermath of Watergate.[1]

Newsweek, July 7, 1975

Conservatives in the news profession will certainly object to this sort of reporting; the hard news requires only thirty-two words out of approximately two hundred: the account makes no pretense of objectivity and indeed goes beyond slanting the story to actually fictionalizing it. But there can be no doubt that the story reported in this style does capture the reader's attention.

Television news reporting picks this dramatized style and reinforces it. Although obviously slanted stories on television are usually marked as editorial or commentary (newsmagazines and sometimes newspapers fail to make this distinction), the increasing use of film and videotape in television news programs through which the viewer is given a front-row seat in the news theater has made inevitable an increasingly dramatic TV style.

The older style of TV news shows can still be seen on some local shows with a low budget and minimal staff, and on the five-minute newscap most stations offer just before sign-off. In this style a newsman comes on the air for five minutes, or fifteen, or half an hour and simply reads news copy on camera or over mounted cards that display artwork, blown-up glossies, or photo newswire stills taken from the press services. Here is a sample of news handled in this style:

CARD PIC OF SHARIF SIRHAN

Another Sirhan brother is on trial—Sharif Sirhan, brother of Sirhan who is now on San Quentin's death row for the assassination murder of Robert Kennedy.

Sharif will stand trial on Monday for an alleged disturbance he provoked at a Pasadena hospital last March. A third brother, Saidallah, was taken there following a traffic accident on the same day . . .

LIVE ON CAMERA

Debate on a controversial ordinance that would control telephonic burglar and fire alarm devices was postponed in city council today and scheduled for next week.

Elsewhere in the news tonight . . . President Nixon again called on North Vietnam to start withdrawing its troops from South Vietnam . . .

In Saigon . . . the allied command says three Americans have been killed and thirteen others injured in sharp fighting around Tay Ninh (Tay Ning) City . . .

An Egyptian leader close to President Nasser says the Soviet Union soon will present a package of peace proposals for the Middle East . . .

The Irish Republic's Prime Minister, Jack Lynch, has won a slim but apparently decisive lead in legislative elections . . .

MAT CARD PIC OF CAIRO, ILLINOIS AFTER RIOTS

And finally, in Cairo (Kay Roh), Illinois . . . citizens acting as special deputies have been ordered off the streets of racially tense Cairo where an overnight curfew is still in effect.

The sports and the weather in a moment . . .

COMMERCIAL OR SUSTAINER
SLIDE: SPORTS

In sports . . . it has been a bad day for the California major league baseball teams.

The Giants lost to the Phillies 8 to 7, the Padres dropped their game to Houston 4 to 2 and the Angels were walloped by the Twins 8 to 1.

The Dodgers had a travel day and are scheduled to play Cincinnati tomorrow.

SLIDE: WEATHER

The veil of low morning clouds will blanket most of Los Angeles this morning but the clouds should break by mid-morning. The rest of today will remain bright and clear.

This evening's low reached 62 . . . the high expected for today . . . 75.

SLIDE: THE LATE REPORT

. . . And that's Eyewitness News at sign-off. This is _____, reminding you that on weekdays get the details from Bill Bonds at 4:30 in the afternoon and again at 11 p.m.

Although this particular newscap was given in 1969 the format has not changed to this date, and the sign-off recap mirrors the scripting of the earliest television newscasts back in the forties and fifties.

This style of writing employs the fact/conversational tone, especially useful when few or no graphics are used. Except in sports stories, few adjectives are used. Such news stories answer the conventional questions *who, what, when, where* and possibly *how*, much as a straight newspaper story would. The style is plain and direct. The drama of the story is not stressed by the newswriter; it is built into the story if it exists at all.

In fact, the writing style of most TV newscasts is relatively plain and straight-forward. Even if events justified it, you would probably never turn out copy like this (however radio news copy might incorporate some or all of these lines because the copy is quite visual):

> Chicago is quiet after a night of rioting which turned the city into a battlefield. Downtown Chicago resembled Dunkirk or Dresden after the fire bombings; over the Loop area hung dirtied clouds of gas, stained a ghastly orange in places by occasional fires. Every once in a while pockets of gunfire erupted almost like the score for a choreographed and orches-trated ballet—surreal, except that this *was* war. A war of poor and middle class citizens stricken by the ravages of a ten-year-old recession and infla-tion which finally sent its victims into the streets in uncontrolled terror.

These events seem most improbable; but if they did take place, and if tele-vision stations were still functioning, newswriters would still not turn out this sort of purple copy (unless it was for radio). No doubt mini-cam footage or videotape would show the devastation of the city and snatches of the continuing action, but the spoken copy would still be relatively unadorned.

Simplicity is the great virtue of a solid newswriting style. This is the idea of headline writing. Headlines, however terse, can still tell a complete story:

LIBRARY TO SLASH HOURS, FIRE 400
CARDINAL CODY REBUKES SCHOOL-CLOSING CRITICS
REASSERTS HIS AUTHORITY
SENATE TO PROBE HOUSING SCANDAL

To convert headline writing to newswriting for television, you simply take the headline, loosen it up a little, then tell the store in a more conversational way.

For example:

LIBRARY TO SLASH HOURS, FIRE 400

BAKER ON CAMERA

BAKER:
This afternoon the Chicago Public Library announced that it would cut library hours and fire four hundred of its employees as part of an economy move to make up for a $1.5 million budget deficit.

The job cuts will affect four hundred part-time employees, according to Louis Lerner, who is vice president of the Public Library board.

Lerner also told reporters that beginning July 1st, all branch libraries will be closed either Wednesday or Thursday.

Never try to overpower a news film story in the writing of it. If your story is that "fifty people were attacked by a school of killer sharks off the coast of Florida yesterday," say it that way. You don't have to say "mauled by a school of killer sharks" or "mauled by a school of killer sharks on the rampage." The line is not necessary if the footage the camera crew has shot tells the drama on film. All you need is ten seconds of copy to get into the film sequence.

Why? The television news director needs ten seconds of live copy to get into a film clip; it takes ten seconds from when the director calls for a *ready film* to *take film. Ready film* is the cue given to the operator in *telecine*, the room where still slide chains (slide projectors) and 16mm and 35mm projectors are located. The film editor usually puts on at least ten seconds of black leader before the first frame of film appears. A television news director needs these seconds to make sure that the right clip is up, or a blank does not occur on the screen instead of a picture. Think about seven television monitors plus the on-air monitor that a news director has to watch, all at the same time. There's a monitor for all the slide chains (projectors), a monitor for all the 16mm and 35mm projection chains used, and monitor(s) for the videotape machines in use. There is also a monitor for television commercials and public service inserts for the show. That's why ten seconds to get into film clips, videotapes, commercials, slides, and so on, are absolutely essential.

There are two ways of getting into *sound on film* (SOF) news clip. First there is the standard opening, where the anchorperson reads the opening copy live, followed by the SOF clip. The second way is where a live on-camera opening may be shorter than ten seconds, followed by five to ten seconds of silent footage and then the sound-on portion. This arrangement doesn't break the ten-second rule because ten seconds are required to get into a sound clip, since the sound portion of a film runs ahead of the picture. For the first five seconds the camera is on the anchorperson, then the next ten seconds he or she is talking over silent footage. The last lines of the anchorperson should fall just short of the pick-up point of the sound on film piece, so that the last word said on the studio copy should be followed by a beat, then the first word of the SOF.

There is absolutely no way a director can go through a newscast without proper cues to tell him or her when one film clip or videotape story or live copy will end. These *end cues,* also called *outcues,* include both video and audio cues wirtten into the news script. As an example, here is the script for a news special *Organized Youth Football: Are Parents Dangerous?*

```
PART #5                              TAPE:
SPORTS DOCUMENTARY                   AIR DATE:
SIL/SOF
COLOR
TOTAL TIME: 2:56
```

NOTE: A AND B ROLL IN SYNCH
KEEP POT OPEN ON *B* ROLL FOR STU UNDER

STU LIVE

Today is our fifth and final report looking into the game of organized youth football. It's a rough and competitive game where the youngsters are pushed to their limits.

:10 V.O. S/U FILM
Establishing shot

It's not unusual to find the nine, ten, and eleven year old kids playing just as hard as the pros do. But what about injuries and immediate medical attention? Is the medical attention

MORE . . . . . MORE . . . . . MORE

adequate in these games?? One father felt it was.

1:13 SOF

SOF

at apx 1:23

(OUTCUE . . . "I like football.")

CUE STU FOR V.O. S/U :25
                    S/U
:25 V.O. SIL FILM
MONTAGE ACTION SHOTS OF
ORGANIZED YOUTH FOOTBALL.

Maybe he's right, but there still is another part of our story which we haven't shown you yet.

We said organized youth football is rough and it can and does cause injuries. The youngsters play hard and their parents cheer them on for more action. But yelling in the grandstands is safe for the parents; after all, they're not on the field where the action is. That's where their children are. Only when a boy gets hurt does the yelling stop. We were there when the yelling stopped and saw what a boy goes through when he has suffered an injury.

:03 SIL FILM
:42 SOF
TO CONCLUSION

HERE THE AUDIO POT CAN BE HIGH—
WANT TO EMPHASIZE THE BOY'S PAIN—
HIS CRIES!

SPORTS DOCUMENTARY #5
VTR
PLUS LIVE IN STUDIO TAG
2:40 SOT
DUMP OUT ON CLOSEUP OF BOY'S
FACE AT 2:40
LIVE TAG

Maybe that young boy shouldn't have cried out . . . because if his coaches expect him to play like a pro . . . he should behave like a pro.

Perhaps there should be bonuses for these 9 and 10 year olds . . . a winning season to mean an

increase in his allowances . . . and what about
pensions? Maybe there should be a fund started
for those boys who are injured and forced to
retire at the age of 12. Or better yet . . . maybe
we should take a little bit of the organizing out
of kids playing football and put in a little more
enjoyment . . . after all . . . isn't that what
growing up is all about?

Since this was a five-part series the script is simply marked Part #5. Next the
kind of documentary is identified: SPORTS DOCUMENTARY. The film footage
includes both silent and sound sequences. This fact, and the order of sequences
is shown: SIL/SOF. The film is a COLOR presentation. And the TOTAL TIME
for that particular show is 2:56. Near the top center of the page appears the
directions:

NOTE: A AND B ROLL IN SYNCH
KEEP POT OPEN ON *B* ROLL FOR STU UNDER

An *A and B roll in synch* means that there are two synchronized rolls of film
running through two separate projection systems at the same time. News film is
shot and processed on the same day within a matter of hours, and most is shot
on single system with both the sound and visual tracks on one piece of film.
The only way dissolves can be made, or bad cuts covered on the air is to have
two sequences of film *A and B rolls* running in synch. For example, the mayor
of a city is answering a question. The writer doesn't have time for the whole
answer, which may run five minutes. His producer only wants a minute and
thirty seconds for the total clip. So the writer, with the editor, figures out a bite
of sound on film that makes sense. But to edit this bite and put it in a new
sequence may mean that the mayor is looking up at one instant and has his
head down and eyes shut at the next. This is a comical effect. To prevent it,
sound can be used from the *A* roll, and the *B* roll can cover with another
picture, either directly part of the scene or relating to what is being said. In the
case of a mayor's press conference the *B* roll might be of news reporters and
camerapersons who are set up in the room, or a shot of the mayor talking from
behind the podium. Or if the mayor is talking about a particular section of the
city, the *B* roll could be footage of a building, or a series of buildings in the
neighborhood referred to by the mayor. But the *B* roll isn't always shot as
silent footage; it is often sound footage. The *B* roll can act as an additional
sound track.

The second part of the director's instructions, *KEEP THE POT OPEN ON B
ROLL FOR STU UNDER,* means that the *B* roll in this documentary *does* have
sound, and that sound is to be left on, but kept under voice of the sports anchorperson for this particular documentary. What the producer or writer wanted was

sound throughout except for part five's introduction, so that S/U on the script means sound-under—in this case, under the narration of the sports anchorperson.

The opening of the last part of the series on *Organized Youth Football* is live—STU LIVE. There are approximately ten seconds of live copy and then the sound-under portion begins for ten seconds —*:10 V.O. S/U*

Establishing shot

For ten seconds the sportscaster's voice is over sound on film footage.

The director marks the script about five lines above the point where the SOF begins. Five lines marked for cue above the SOF gives the director enough time to call for the SOF roll. This SOF runs 1:13, which is marked on the left-hand side of the page. A newswriter must have *all* times down on the script, although there are occasions when the script goes down to the studio ahead of the film and the editor hasn't been able to give the writer exact times yet. If this is the case, when the times are available they are called into the control booth for the director, assistant or associate director, the technical director, and anyone else, including the sound person, who must have this information.

Since the first ten seconds of the film were used for a S/U (sound-under) sequence, this time is added to the full SOF of 1:13 to give a total of 1:23. At approximately 1:23 that portion of the SOF ends. The director needs an OUT-CUE to know when he should cue the sportscaster for more live copy—in this case the live copy is VOICE OVER. Such cues are written in this manner:

at apx 1:23   (OUTCUE. . "I like football.")
CUE STU FOR V.O. S/U :25

Which means at apx 1:23 (into the SOF portion) where the clip ends with someone saying, "I like football," cue the sportscaster for twenty-five seconds of voice-over narration on a sound-under film track.

The next sequence calls for :25 V.O. S/U FILM, MONTAGE ACTION SHOTS OF ORGANIZED YOUTH FOOTBALL. This means that for the next twenty-five seconds the writer has called for a montage of action shots showing youngsters competing with each other in rough contact, coaching, scrimmage, actual game. This sequence is to be in sound, but the sound is to be reduced so that it is under the voice-over copy, which sets up a scene in which a youngster gets hurt.

The last sequence on the film is a :42 SOF that runs to the conclusion of the documentary. In this sequence we see and hear what it's like for a youngster to sustain a painful injury. This statement is better expressed as SOF, sound on film, rather than through narration. The audience actually sees how a nine-year-old player lies motionless on a football field, how he struggles to breathe, how the pain stays with him as he's carried off the field. But the fact that he's breathing is enough for the referee to blow the whistle, wave his arms, and start the action on the field again.

Of course the writer/director was looking for drama in filming this documentary. His assignment was to look for danger, and if he found it, to film it. The film prompted a flood of telephone calls, both approving and indignant, to the station over which the documentary was broadcast. The film made its point. Why? Because it made effective use of the techniques of television news reporting, and because it was correctly structured. News *is* drama; and this brief documentary parallels in its methods the work of good playwrights, screenwriters, and novelists.

chapter 12
Writing
Advertising
Copy

The first commercial on American radio was broadcast over Station WEAF, New York, on August 28, 1922, almost two years after radio first became a part of our national life. The commercial was sponsored by a real estate developer and offered cooperative apartments for sale in a new building, the Hawthorne Apartments. The commercial was a sales pitch, read by an announcer, that lasted between ten and fifteen minutes. It began not too subtly as a tribute to the genius of American writers, notably Nathaniel Hawthorne, and eventually suggested that residents in the Hawthorne building might conceivably come, by osmosis, to share in the author's talent and distinction. The original commercial cost the sponsor one hundred dollars and is supposed to have produced some sales.

Oddly enough, most radio broadcasters did not immediately turn to the sale of commercial air time as a means of financing their operations. In the early days radio stations were subsidized—by manufacturers, newspapers, religious groups, and so on—and were not really supposed to show a profit. In addition, there was a common feeling that radio should not be used as a vehicle for advertising; Herbert Hoover, then Secretary of Commerce, expressed this attitude vigorously. However, as the years went by radio became more popular and more expensive. With the appearance of the networks—the NBC Red and Blue Networks began operations in 1926 and 1927—radio became too popular and too expensive to operate as anything but a commercial venture.

Since then, American radio and television have broadcast millions of commercials and will no doubt continue to do so as long as they function. Commercial copy has to be written and produced and this chapter discusses some of the procedures involved.

BROADCAST COMMERCIALS: SOME BASIC FACTS

Broadcast commercials—especially those done for television—are more expensive and involve more skilled human effort than any other item of programming. Some sixty-second television commercials can and have cost as much as a one-hour dramatic production. It follows that an assignment to write a script for such a commercial is not one casually handed out to a free-lance writer. Commercials are developed, written, and produced in advertising agencies and production compaines by large and complex organizations.

As a viewer or listener, you may regard commercials as a nuisance, trivial and sometimes rather silly, but in the world of broadcasting they are taken with total seriousness. They are thought to be crucial in the sale of billions of dollars worth of consumer goods every year, and the business of producing and airing them is in itself, in terms of annual budgets, a major industry.

Commercials are of course intended to be persuasive. They are supposed to persuade viewers and listeners to use one brand of detergent rather than another, or to drive one make of automobile rather than another. When advertising goes into politics, commercials try to sell candidates in much the same way that they sell packaged foods. Oddly enough, it it usually difficult and sometimes nearly impossible to tell just how successful these efforts at persuasion are. Advertisers know how well their products have sold, and politicians can certainly tell, after the fact, whether they have been elected or not, but it is hard to measure how much of their success has been due to a television or radio campaign. Too many other factors enter into the consumer's or the voter's choice. Nevertheless, in a competitive world, advertisers and political parties continue to spend money on broadcast commercials because no one really knows what would happen if they did not.

Although commercials are persuasive in intent, they are almost always dramatic in concept and usually in form. A commercial, whether it is ten seconds or sixty in length, presents a problem and a solutuion, shows character growth, has conflict, and possesses a beginning, middle, and end. The world these miniature dramas depict is not really the world in which the viewer lives, but an idealized version of it or at least of a world to which the viewer can aspire.

Commercials tend to be, either by implication or direct statement, highly critical of their audiences. Their teeth are dirty, they are smelly, they lack the respect of their neighbors, and so on endlessly. Fortunately the solutions they offer are simple ones; a particular brand of toothpaste makes the user sexually irresistible, one make of car results in higher social status. Commercials are, in their way, a public conscience—forever whispering of our failures and deficiencies, which could so easily be remedied.

HOW COMMERCIALS ARE DEVELOPED

To begin with, somebody, usually in an advertising agency, gets an idea that may be developed into a strategy acceptable to a client. The idea may come from a copy writer, an art director, a creative director or a vice president, an account executive, or the head of the agency. It may be an original notion or an attempt to top a campaign for a competitor's product. What matters is that the idea is seen as having possibilities by someone in a position to make decisions. Ideas sometimes come from clients, who take them to the agencies handling their accounts.

If the idea has possibilities it is passed along to the "creative department." In large advertising agencies there are often a hundred employees working in a "creative department." Usually they are divided into groups numbering anywhere from four to ten, with each group supervised by a creative director. Under the creative director may be an associate creative director, a copy supervisor, and copy writers; in the same group will also be art directors or art supervisors. Each group works, as a team, on as many as five projects at a time. Often one group will compete with another on the same campaign, so that a single client may have as many as twenty persons working on advertising. On occasion, if in fear of losing a client's business, an agency may put most of its creative personnel to work on a single campaign. This may be done for several reasons. One may be the fear that unless the agency succeeds in reversing a downward trend in sales the client will take his business elsewhere. The client may also be impressed by seeing a great number of people working on a new approach to his problems; it shows the client how hard the ad agency is driving its staff to come up with product approach positions and solutions.

The development of an advertising campaign begins with a meeting called by the creative director. The problems of the project and any ideas are laid out for the group. Then the group separates into pairs, usually one copy writer working with an art director, and the work begins. Rough ideas are developed in written copy and storyboard visuals. During the first stages the copy is sketchy, consisting of a rough statement of a theme for the advertising. The art director then begins to produce sketches that point up the visual aspects of the theme.

Most competing products basically do the same things in about the same way. For example, automobiles that sell for about the same base sticker price and offer the same wheelbase, width, height, and gas mileage are difficult to distinguish except in terms of styling and accessories. American cars costing seven or eight thousand dollars are likely to be similar in most fundamental respects, so that engineering or styling differences may be the only satisfactory basis for a marketing approach.

One group, in developing an automobile commercial, may decide to concentrate on engineering. The writer comes up with the idea of showing styling engineers at work, with one of them speaking voice-over to explain why he thinks the car he has designed is good. Another group may hit on the notion of stripping down the car, frame by frame, until all that is shown is the chassis. Then, through special effects, the doors, hood, back, front, top reappear, with an offscreen speaker talking about such selling features as doorbraces, unibody welding, and so on. Another group might decide that the history and tradition of the car is a selling feature and begin to shape up a commercial that shows the development from classic models of years gone by to the present one.

It is worth noticing that, at this stage, copy writers do not really write very much copy. Their real value is as an idea person, a conceiver or perceiver.

Ideas at this early point in the development of a campaign are remarkably similar to those developed by a playwright or novelist starting work. The commercial turns around a dramatically stated problem, just as a novel does. It involves characters, actions, and conflict. In commercial advertising, as we have said, the resolution is always a quick and happy one offered by the product being sold. Public affairs advertisements, such as those sponsored by the American Heart Association or the American Cancer Society, are strikingly different because their problems are usually presented without being resolved, always with the overhanding threat of a tragic ending. If you do not have the yearly check up . . . if you do not stop smoking . . . if you continue to eat cholesterol-laden foods, you may decidedly not live happily ever after. If we go by commercials alone, we must conclude that industries are always extremely optimistic concerning human life and happiness, while organizations devoted to the public welfare are never so.

Throughout this process the writer's ideas are constantly scrutinized and tested by the creative group. After a dozen or more different campaigns have been developed in rough form, perhaps eight or ten are chosen to represent the group's various approaches to the merchandising problem. These are eventually brought before a creative review committee in which the members of a number of groups take part.

Let us assume that you are a copy writer who has been going through this procedure. By this time, if your concept for a commercial is considered good enough to be submitted to a creative review committee, a number of things have happened.

1. You and your art director have produced a version of the commercial in storyboard form. At this point the commercial looks somewhat like a series of rough sketches for a comic strip. Visually, it has been broken down into a sequence of panels sketched out in pencil. Beneath each panel the copy is written out, so that each panel has a visual and perhaps

a narrative line or two that advances the story. Once this simple story-board has been accepted by your creative director, you move into the stage of finished art work. This means that the storyboards are redone in color on large cardboards. The copy is typed on adhesive tabs which are stuck beneath each visual panel. Possibly the typed copy is also pre-pared separately and blown up by the graphics department to four or five times the size of a typed page. This is mounted on a separate board.

2. You have gone over your campaign with your creative director several times before entering the conference room, and either your creative director or you and your art director will make the presentation. At this point the creative review committee is still an internal affair; the client thus far has no part in it.

3. The creative review committee may work for an entire day, or even for several days. Usually agency administrators, from vice-presidents to the owner or president of the agency will be present.

4. Some of the campaigns have advanced, not only to the stage of finished art work, but to the next step beyond. This step entails a sort of preliminary production of the commercial. Studio time is booked to record *scratch tracks,* which may include an announcer to read the copy and musicians and singers to perform music and lyrics. Scratch tracks are usually approved by a creative director when he or she feels strongly enough about the value of the campaign or its chance of being chosen to see it developed as far as possible.

5. You and your art director may be called on to act out your commer-cial before the committee, and to explain the reasons for doing it in the way you have.

6. Usually the copy writer goes over each label on the storyboard. The effectiveness of such performances is important; at this point you, the copy writer, have changed hats again and become an actor. If the campaign is more visual than verbal the art director will make the presentation. Again, depending on the nature of the commercial, you and the art direc-tor may make the presentation in tandem.

7. After the presentation, the creative review committee may elect to go over the material, criticize it, play the role of devil's advocate, and offer initial feedback. At the end of a creative review committee session, deci-sions are made on all the campaigns submitted: to drop some of them, to advance others to the next stage, sometimes to move a campaign to client-ready status.

Obviously these review committee sessions are nerve-wracking and difficult and demand much more of a writer than the simple ability to write good copy. The pressure develops from the fact that decisions made here presumably influence sales of the client's product, perhaps to the tune of millions of dollars, and certainly determine whether the agency will prosper or go bankrupt.

At this point we can fill in more specifically what the writer does in develop-ing a commercial. To begin with, the format for writing copy is the same as documentary—the divided page with video instructions on the left side and audio on the right. All camera terminology and scene blocking is written in simple headline style and typed in caps. The dialogue is typed in lower case and double-spaced.

Suppose that your group in an agency is told to produce some campaigns for "Happy Sandwich Bags." You probably will spend a day or so working up rough ideas, although it's not unusual for a copy writer to think he or she could sit down and write the whole campaign in an hour.

You have been given some guidelines for the project in the form of material prepared by your marketing and research department, and possibly a memorandum of the client's feelings and suggestions. With this material you start to rough out some possibilities for a commercial. It is wise to produce several such possibilities, and to submit the best of them last. The first idea you submit will probably not be acceptable, and you will need better ones to follow up. This situation may seem illogical, and perhaps it is. However, you must realize that developing an advertising campaign is a process of exchange, dialogue, and manipulation—between creative teams and directors, between the agency and the client. Advertising people and their clients are used to having projects grow rather than having them come into existence full-blown.

The material that you have before you tells you that most sandwich bags have similar features and perform the same function—preserving foods for later use. You know that Brands X, Y, and Z are fairly popular and have divided the market rather equally among them, except for the share your client's product gets. Your problem is to shift this balance, to capture a bigger share of the sales.

You know that there is really nothing about the product itself that makes it superior to any of the others. The possibility that remains, then, lies in the nature of the miniature drama you are about to create. If you can invent a character who will capture the public imagination and become a trademark for the product, your problem may be solved. You begin to think about characters. Cartoon characters have been over-used. So have harassed housewives whose happiness seems to depend on some minor issue of housekeeping. Harassed fathers seem a little remote from the problem of keeping sandwiches fresh. You finally remember your grandmother, who used to make sandwiches for every kid on the block. Cooking, to her, was as important as breathing. Eventually you create "Grandma Happy".

Grandma Happy, however, is not the conventional, Norman Rockwell type of grandmother. Indeed, she is so contemporary that she's comical—she jogs and exercises, wears a state university sweatshirt, and rides a sandwich cycle, a three-wheeler restaurant on wheels. Naturally, she keeps her sandwiches well-preserved, as she herself is, with Happy Sandwich bags.

Your first draft might look something like this:

HAPPY SANDWICH BAGS
"GRANDMA HAPPY"
:30

Date

EST. GRANDMA HAPPY DOING
EXERCISES
CUT TO:
GRANDMA HAPPY

CUT TO:
TIGHT ON GRANDMA
CUT TO:
DISPLAY: GRANDMA HOLDING HAPPY
BAGS UP TO CAMERA.
CUT TO:
CU ON HAPPY BAG BOX

CUT TO:
DISPLAY

CUT TO:
GRANDMA PEDDLING HER SANDWICH
CYCLE UP TO A CONSTRUCTION SITE
FULL OF HARD HATS.
CUT TO:
A WORKER WALKING TOWARD HER,
WHILE THE OTHERS BUY SANDWICHES.
CUT TO:
GRANDMA AND NORMAN

CUT TO:
GRANDMA HOLDING UP HAPPY BAG
AND CONFIDING TO VIEWER.

CUT TO:
GRANDMA PEDDLING AWAY

GRANDMA:
You think I'm well preserved.

GRANDMA:
You ought to see how I make my sandwiches.
GRANDMA:
I use Happy Bags.

GRANDMA:
With the fold lock top.

GRANDMA:
This flap in—this flap over.

GRANDMA:
Roast beef on lettuce today, boys.

GRANDMA:
Hi, Norman.

GRANDMA:
Here's your carrot.

GRANDMA:
Norman's into natural things like carrots—so I
wrap *them* in handy bags, too!

GRANDMA:
Keeps it fresh like it was just pulled out of the
ground. Happy Sandwich Bags. Keeps things
well preserved. I ought to know!

As a dramatic character Grandma Happy will never compare with any great
heroines, but she might enjoy a life in television like that of Mr. Whipple, the
mild-mannered grocer whose chief motivation in life was protecting Charmin
bathroom tissue from the bruising touch of maddened housewives. For better or

worse Mr. Whipple had a long and more successful career on the screen than nine-tenths of the television and film performers now living.

THE POLITICAL COMMERCIAL

Political commercials are seasonal; they flower during major political campaigns where large campaign funds are available. Production costs and broadcast air charges are extremely high, and the result is that a candidate for major public office must be wealthy, have good credit, or have access to very large funds contributed by supporters. In a presidential race, considerable use will be made of radio and television throughout the campaign period; in a congressional election, funds available for this sort of persuasion may be reserved for a last-minute, pre-election push.

Political commercials, in theory, deal with the issues before the voters: taxes, inflation, energy, foreign policy. In practice, since they are dramatic statements, they tend to concentrate on the character of candidates—what Aristotle called their *ethos*. A commercial is a little play designed to present Candidate X as a person of intelligence, character, and good will toward prospective constituents. If the opponent, Candidate Y, is referred to either directly or by implication, he or she usually is shown to be lacking in one or all of these excellent qualities. Issues are discussed with reference to the candidates: X has a long record of preaching low taxes and economy in government, whereas Y has consistently favored heavy government spending.

Whether a campaign is seen as "clean" or "dirty" depends largely on whether candidates talk mainly about themselves or their opponents. If Candidate X's commercials show X to be an admirable person superbly qualified for the office being sought, there will be no criticism, even if the claims are in fact somewhat exaggerated. If, however, the commercial portrays his or her opponent as dishonest or dangerously incompetent, a reply in kind from Candidate Y is invited, and the campaign is likely to become "dirty". Obviously, charges against an opponent can raise serious legal problems, and radio and television stations normally refuse to air commercials containing them, unless they can be substantiated.

Political commercials are, or should be, even more carefully considered and researched than commercials for consumer goods. They should focus on one issue at a time, presented in a context of human motives and actions. The copy should be lean and crisp, without much adornment. For example:

ANNOUNCER: Representative. Doe votes his conscience, not his pocketbook. That's why you put him in office, and that's why you ought to keep him there. He's a voice that no one owns.

His opponent is spending three quarters of a million dollars of other people's money so he can get elected. Do you want

someone who can buy his way into government? I don't. I
don't think you do, either.

Keep Representative Doe in Washington. He hasn't got a lot
of rich friends who want to get richer. He relies on you. Vote
for him next Tuesday.

In summary. Whatever their specific purpose, commercials are among the
smallest of broadcast forms and are intended to do one of the largest and most
difficult jobs possible in the media—change and shape behavior. In that combination of smallness and potential power lies their fascination and challenge for the
media writer.

chapter 13

Where
the Writer
Stops

Where does the writer's job end? It would seem logical that when you've finished the final draft of a script your responsibilities are over. Unfortunately, logic and filmmaking sometimes have an adversary relationship. Unless your contract says specifically that your job as a writer ends with completion of the final script, you may very well find yourself on location making script changes as the filming goes on.

WRITING DURING PRODUCTION

In some documentary specials the narrator may be a celebrity of national prominence who has always had a hand in making script changes. (This is especially so in California.) This habit doesn't change when the star leaves Los Angeles and does a film in Chicago, New York, or someplace else. Usually these specials are well budgeted, so extra money is built into the budget for writing to be done on location. Always ask whether your services will be needed on set or location, and if the answer is yes, build an additional amount into your fee to cover the extra assignment. The best way to reach a figure is to come up with a per diem expense rate for on-location writing (an additional $150 per day was the going rate in 1979, although some writers ask, and get, more).

Changes on the set are usually minimal and the narrator usually wants these changes primarily because he or she feels more comfortable using one word or phrase rather than another. Every well known actor or actress has, or thinks he has, a public image, a special unique identity. This image must be established early in the script, and the lines spoken by the star must always be character

179

lines. Just as Archie Bunker and Lieutenant Kojak are different dramatic characters, who sound differently, so are Burt Reynolds and Vincent Price.

In shooting a television commercial, the head writer and either the associate
creative director or the creative director are always on the set to handle script
changes asked for by the client. The same situation may prevail in shooting a
documentary. The producer may want the writer on all the locations making any
editorial changes the camera narrator may request, especially if the narrator is a
television news anchorperson. Again, most of the changes are in style rather than
content. By the time you're reached the shooting stage, the content should be
approved and locked in. When the cameras are rolling, it's too late for research.

The usual reason for script changes during production is to eliminate any
discrepancies between script and visuals that could not have been anticipated before filming. For example, the script may call for the narrator to talk while
walking, but when the movement is blocked out in rehearsal it appears that the
narration takes longer than the movement. To make the move effective, the
narration has to be cut down.

Some producers, directors, and actors kid about how they improvised a lot of
the dialogue while shooting a particular feature film. They seem to take great
pains in telling anyone interested in hearing, especially newspaper writers, how
the script had to be torn apart and literally reconstructed on the set. Needless to
say, this kind of talk makes for poor relations between the screenwriter and his
or her critic(s).

The problem of changing a script in production is a lot more common than
one may think. Perhaps the biggest perpetrators of "change on the spot" are the
hyphenates—the writer-producer, the writer-director, the actor-writer-director,
whose hands are in the pie even before the dough is mixed. Because they wear
so many hats it's difficult for one part of them to tell the other part to stop.
There *is* such a thing as overkill.

But often script changes during production have less to do with ego or other
kinds of "in-fighting" and much more to do with seeing something happening
that no one could predict in scripting. An actor or actress builds on a mood or
motive far beyond what even the writer(s) had in mind, and to allow the actor or
actress the freedom to explore means making certain allowances in the script.
Depending on the contract either the writer makes the changes or the director,
actor, or producer may initiate the revision. And it may not always be line
changes. The writer calls for a certain scene, the director sees it in another way,
his or her way happens to be better, and the producer acquiesces in favor of the
director's choice. Or it may be the producer who sees something else, or the
director of photography. There has to be this kind of give-and-take. Who can
argue with this if the end result turns out better thanks to the "extra" effort.

In short, all the research and pre-production location scouting you have done
may not solve all the problems of the production. Only when you are actually
on the set, rehearsing the scene, do some problems emerge. When you are on the
set and changes are called for, the best way to respond to these requests is *calm-
ly*. When someone calls for a change that must be made quickly, allow yourself

a moment to collect your thoughts, and another moment to see the whole scene in context. Always have the script in front of you, and learn how to talk out your ideas rather than depending on a pencil, pad of paper, or typewriter. The key to quick script changes really is a knack for extemporizing dialogue or narration. Verbalizing dialogue or narration is an absolutely essential technique. Some writers speak their lines to anyone who will listen. Others "hear" the characters or narrator in their minds. However the hearing is done, good dialogue and narration *must* be "heard" or they will never be speakable. Print is just a handy way of "fixing" dialogue; its real existence is in speech.

Sometimes the writer is not specifically requested to be on the set. However, this need not prevent him or her from watching the production, always with the producer's approval. Watching as your script is produced is a highly educational, if sometimes painful, experience. Especially if the experience is painful, be quiet and observe. What you have to say is in the script, and at this point no comments, complaints, or suggestions that you can make will help. In your script you've spoken to the producer, the director, the actors, the narrator, and the technicians. How do they interpret through their respective skills what you have written? Have they understood what you meant to say? Do they find more in the script than you had expected? Which of your ideas seem to work? Which do not? Visiting the set or studio while your script is being produced is especially recommended for beginning writers. You will learn a great deal, appreciate the services performed by other members of the production staff, and find excitement in seeing your script transformed into the completed production.

HOW MANY REVISIONS?

The nature of your writing services will depend on the needs of the producer. If you are not asked to be on the set during the film, your services will end on completion of the final draft. Normally there are three drafts; first, revised, and final. It is wise to have these obligations also spelled out in your agreement with the production company and/or producer, especially if you are not represented by an agent or protected by a guild.

If you are writing nonfiction and your contract calls for three drafts, the first one normally should be completed from two to three weeks after approval of the final treatment. It will probably run longer than the final draft, need polishing, changes in scene, possibly changes in point of view, and generally will serve to show the weaknesses, if any, in the concept.

The first draft is really a blueprint. You've laid out the scenes in rough dialogue or narration or both, tried to write the necessary transitions, developed structure to a point where there is a flow of action and the story, presumably, moves forward. You may experiment with a few ideas—your own or those given you by the producer or client. If these ideas do not work they can be cut; if they do, they will be approved and incorporated in the second draft.

Once the first draft is approved, usually within a week of its presentation, the second draft is begun. Generally, it should be finished within a week. If you've followed instructions in revising the first draft, this should be no problem. The problems of the second draft arise when you think you have understood all the changes asked for on the first draft, and write the second, only to discover that you misunderstood what the producer wanted. It is absolutely necessary to make sure you understand every change called for before you begin writing the second draft.

Second draft approval should mean only minor revisions on the third and final draft. In the final draft you polish the writing, tie together any abrupt transitions, lock in on all the scenes, indicate final camera movement and angles when necessary, enter important stage directions, and indicate the kinds of mood if music is used, or specific musical selections or original music if that has been contracted. The time given to write a final draft, after approval of the second draft, is anywhere from a few days to a week, depending on the total time allotted for the production. Obviously, if you have six months from concept to final script, you'll have more than enough time to complete all the drafts, and more than a few days to complete drafts after approval on the preceding draft is given.

Occasionally, a final draft involves more than minor changes. In that case, the deadline given to make the changes may (1) be commensurate with the number of changes to be made or (2) still be requested within a few days.

The fiction scriptwriter takes basically the same steps to completing a property, with some differences. Usually a screenwriter's or television writer's services are contracted in steps: story outline, treatment, first draft screenplay or teleplay, second draft, and final draft. However, the writer and producer may agree on additional revisions, as many as it takes to make it right.

The first draft script is rough at best and shows weaknesses that need to be strengthened. The writer has anywhere from one month to six to complete this draft. Then the studio, network, producer(s) may hold the property for a few weeks or a few months before giving it back to the writer to rewrite based on their suggested changes and the ones the writer has also come up with during the intervening period.

The producers may want the second draft within weeks or months. A studio may write a contract in such a way as to tie up a property for over a year (just in the writing), because this way they can keep a tighter control on development monies, hold back final payment much longer, and spread out initial payments over a greater period of time. As you can see, there's an awful lot of cost efficiency in filmmaking.

Normally you're nearing the 6-month mark by the time you've started writing the third revision. You may have weeks, months, or longer to finish. Your services may be no longer required once the third or final draft is completed. (Indeed, it's possible that any draft could be your last if your option is not picked up.) But that doesn't mean the writing is over.

The writing stops when it is absolutely impossible to make any further script changes. And that may take place even after a preview print is released to a select audience for review. Changes can occur even then, providing there's money in the budget and no conflict in talent availability.

WRITING AFTER SHOOTING

The procedure we have outlined above assumes that production does not begin until a complete script is available. This assumption holds for dramatic productions of all kinds and for most educational and instructional films, video and audio tapes. It is not usually true of documentaries, television news programs, or indeed any kind of production that deals in *actuality* (unstaged) materials. In such productions the shooting or recording comes first, and the full script later. The reason for this practice is that a full script for a documentary consists of narration that explains, comments on, and connects the actuality materials.

For the sake of simplicity, let us suppose that you have contracted to write a documentary film. The first script you prepare will simply lay out the shots needed and perhaps the order in which they will appear in the film. The film is shot, edited, and arranged in sequence. At this point you write the narration, most or all of which will be voice-over dubbed into the sound track.

Why this seemingly backward procedure? Essentially, there are two reasons. One is that some films are not complete in content until the editing is finished: you don't know all the scenes available until after you've shot them; you aren't sure whether some of the scenes called for in the script will fit; if the story is timely it may be subject to sudden change in dramatic content, requiring new visuals or information. For example, the NBC documentary *RTA: Yes/No* on a referendum for setting up a new transportation activity was aired before the referendum took place. There was no way of pre-scripting everything because the issue itself was changing daily. People changed their minds, new people expressed views. There was simply no way to provide, beforehand, unity to the script; no way to write a lead-in and lead-out until after the sequence was filmed and edited. The second reason for the procedure is time. Time also tells you what can be written. If you're shooting random shots (in the sense that you have little prior control over their content), not until these shots are filmed and cut will you know what the final sequence looks like, and the time of each segment in it. The combination of SOF and silent footage, properly edited, will determine how much time you have left for your narrative track. Some of the narrative and voice-over may have already been shot on location and is included in the SOF time, so now all you are left with is some narration, primarily lead-in, lead-out, and transitions to be written.

Nearly all television news copy is written *after* the film is screened for the writer and editor. Some television news documentaries, especially the mini-documentaries (so-called because they are usually five-minute segments presented during news shows) are fully scripted after they are shot. Sometimes these mini-documentaries are re-edited into a half-hour special later on in the year. If that happens, a revised script is usually written to fit the re-cut version and to include any new information not available during the first series.

Whether the film is to be fully written before or after principal photography is determined by the executive producer or the producer. In general, as we have said, the practice of writing the narration after the film is shot is followed where actuality materials are involved. Industrial and educational films are almost always fully scripted before production. What this means is that educational and industrial productions are shaped to fit the pre-conceptions and requirements of their producers and sponsors. Documentary and news productions are much more likely to be shaped by the nature of the events with which they deal.

WHERE DOES THE WRITER STOP?

Where does the writer stop? Sometimes not until the film is a few hours away from airing. Sometimes after the final draft. Sometimes on location while the film is being shot. Sometimes after the first draft because the production has been cancelled or re-scheduled for a later time. Sometimes when the writer's contract calls for a *step deal*. (In this arrangement, each stage of the scripting must be approved before you go on to the next. No approval, at any stage, means that you stop there.)

In general. When and where you finish a script depends entirely on your arrangement with the producer. Be sure that your agreement is both specific and clear. Misunderstanding on this point can turn an interesting and satisfying assignment into confusion, frustration, and anger.

chapter 14

The Writer

and

Technology

Basically, a writer for the media needs to have some technical knowledge, but not a great deal. You do not need to know how to run a camera or edit, but you must know what a skilled cameraperson or editor can do. You need not be able to run a control board or pick sound or music cues, but you must know the possibilities of sound. Of course, here as elsewhere, the more a writer knows about the media, the better off he or she is. What we'll do in this chapter is review the major equipment most often used for film and tape and then try to define some of the technical language used most frequently in media scripts.

THE EQUIPMENT

Probably the very first documentary that received national attention was the film *Nanook of the North,* shot by Robert Flaherty in 1920. His film, made in the Hudson Bay territory of Canada, is credited with the world coming to recognize the documentary. *Nanook of the North* has been played more times than *Gone with the Wind.* There is *no* documentary filmmaker to this day who has had such a remarkable distribution record as his. Flaherty shot on location, processed his film on location, and in effect was his own writer, producer, director, cinematographer, and editor. Flaherty's equipment was comparatively light and withstood the rigors of sub-zero air.

More than a half century later we're back to fairly light equipment. Modern cameras are more advanced than the one Flaherty used, but the documentary method of using them, from *Nanook* to *Woodstock, American Revolution Two,*

185

or *The Salesman,* is essentially the same; documentarians use the camera as a non-interfering device recording people as they do what they normally do.

In the fifties and early sixties with the advent of more modern equipment, particularly hand-held cameras, we saw the emergence of *cinema verite*—going out and filming reality as it was going on. *Cinema verite* filmmakers happily discovered that given the right set of circumstances people would do on film what they would ordinarily do with the absence of a camera and sound equipment—if the filmmaker and the people he or she were recording struck a relationship of mutual trust. Sometimes mutual distrust and antagonism was the arrangement. Antagonists may enjoy the company of other antagonists and feed on this mutual abrasiveness. Either way, actuality was being recorded on film.

Another dimension was also added: the relationship between the filmmaker and the subject, and the camera itself and the subject. Occasionally, the people being recorded did special things for the camera, not in the sense of "hamming it up" but in the sense that the filmmaker and camera generated a whole new relationship with the subject(s). Don Pennybaker discovered that when he made *Don't Look Back Now,* a film about folk singer and folk hero Bob Dylan, that the film was as much about Dylan's relationship to Pennybaker and the camera as it was about who Bob Dylan really was. The same was true with *An American Family,* the story of the Laud family, which Craig Gilbert spent two years shooting and editing. Rightfully or wrongfully, the Lauds became American folk heroes, possibly the first "documentary" media family. The Lauds separated on film and subsequently filed for divorce, another television first. But after all, television was the medium which gave us *Bride and Groom,* where couples were married on the air. The televised breakup of a marriage seemed only a logical extension.

A number of portable cameras came on the market, most notably the Eclair which was much used by documentary filmmakers. The Eclair makes little noise; it weighs roughly twenty-five pounds and has a quick-change magazine which permits almost continuous filming (five seconds lost for every eleven minutes of film), whereas normal studio cameras take seven to ten minutes to rethread the camera once it runs out of film. Cameras today weigh as little as eight pounds. They can be reloaded almost instantaneously. The instruments for recording *actuality* grow constantly more efficient.

FILM VS. VIDEOTAPE

For a long time videotape was considered a studio system. Portable cameras and recorders took tape out of the studio and into the world, giving rise to predictions that tape would soon replace film. Videotape does offer possibilities that film cannot, the most important of which is instant printing, eliminating the steps necessary in processing film. In a sense, tape develops as you record on it so there's no delay in having to process videotape in a lab. The lab is the videotape recorder itself. The consequences of this fact were extensive: on-location use; the development of instant replay and stop-action (thanks to professional sports); animation; three-dimensional images popping out in darkened rooms (much the same principle used in Walt Disney's haunted house at Disneyland); the small porta-pack videotape systems with camera and backpack recorders, which help foster the underground television movement; and later, the mini-cam used by television news departments. All of these developments came within a relatively short period of time.

Most television directors, especially those directing news, agree that the mini-cams are a fact of life now, highly portable and mobile, but still not offering the kind of color quality that 16mm cameras can offer. In cases where a breaking story is close to the television station or a mini-cam location, the mini-cam can be rushed to the scene and have live transmission within minutes. However, the mini-cam is expensive to use, and the quality of transmissions is not always satisfactory.

It may be that 16mm is still the best system available for reportorial work, certainly for documentary work. Forty years of service all over the world, in combat, following naturalists in deep-sea research, covering a rock group in concert, showing the birth of a child, it's the best we've got going for us and probably will be for some time to come.

TECHNICAL TERMS A WRITER SHOULD KNOW

Writers should understand at least the most common technical jargon used in scripts, what these terms mean, and how to call for their use. We can break these terms down even further into camera angles, camera movement, sound and music effects, and narrative or dialogue effects.

Basically, narration is either *straight on-camera* or *voice-over*. The abbreviated symbol for voice-over is *VO*. When the narrator is straight on, his or her name is all that is necessary to type in caps.

Sometimes dialogue is spoken *offstage*, the character heard but not seen. In that case you type the character's name:

PAUL MARTIN

and then the abbreviation for offstage, (O.S.)

PAUL MARTIN (O.S.)

That's easy enough. But camera terms and other technical effects are more involved. The more common terms used and the reasons for their use are given below. The glossary provides you with a comprehensive list of terms and definitions, but let's concentrate now on the ones you'll most likely use over and over again.

Fade In	Think of a FADE IN as opening a window shade letting in the outside light and introducing you to a new day. The FADE IN begins the picture or a new scene, or shows a wide span of time difference between scenes.
	You can also FADE SOUND as you would a picture. In this case, one sound ends, and a new sound begins.
Fade Out	Just the opposite of FADE IN. Think of closing or lowering the window shade until the room goes dark. FADE OUT is used at the end of a scene or the end of a picture. If it's used at the end of a scene, we know that the scene to follow (on which you will FADE IN) represents a different time period. The end of the day. A week later. A month later. A year or years later. A FADE OUT goes to black on the screen.
Cut To	The next shot following the one before. An instant change of an angle or a scene. For example, you can CUT TO a CLOSE-UP from a LONG SHOT. Or CUT TO a building from a shot of a street corner. Normally CUTS do not mean a long change in time. But sometimes you can call for a QUICK CUT or a SHOCK CUT from an action taking place on one day to an action taking place the next day. Or from one scene to another. CUTS such as these have the effect of abruptness or shock value. CUTS from one scene to another or from one day to another surprise the audience, since the visual transition happens immediately.
	CUTS also provide perspective and show relationships. A CUT from a LONG SHOT of a beach to a CLOSE-UP of a girl crying. Or a CUT from a table with a bunch of papers on it to a CLOSE-UP of a letter that ends in the middle of a sentence. CUTS can mean *expectancy, anticipation, reaction.* CUTS can also convey *mood* and *action.*
Dissolve To	A DISSOLVE occurs when one image or scene and another image or scene begin to blend together, the first image losing definition while the new image takes predominance. Finally the DISSOLVE is complete, the old image is lost, and the new one takes its place. The speed of a DISSOLVE varies depending on the amount of frames an editor marks for the DISSOLVE to take place. The DISSOLVE is processed in the lab.
	DISSOLVES usually indicate lapses of time and often bring the story forward. Whereas a CUT is used often to startle the audience, the DISSOLVE is a soft movement. It can be poetic. It can show the strain of a mood, or heighten and sustain emotion. DISSOLVES can bridge scenes, act as transitions, and take the place of narration or dialogue in motivating a character in a moment of new growth or tension; we see this change taking place in a series of DISSOLVES, visually, rather than in words. The film *Love Story* used this technique throughout the movie.
	There are also MATCH DISSOLVES, which take a person in a scene and place that character in the exact same position in another scene.

DISSOLVES motivate more subtle feelings than CUTS—their use is, as we've said, to sustain a feeling or attitude.

Flashback

A term that means to dissolve or cut back in the past. For example, someone remembers an episode from childhood, and we FLASHBACK to that person years younger.

Flashforward

Dissolving or cutting to a time in the future A couple talks about spending two weeks in Europe and suddenly we have cut or dissolved to Europe and they're on the beach.

Or a man talks about wanting to win a sports car race. He continues telling someone how important that race is—we now FLASHFORWARD through a dissolve or cut to an instant of a sports car suddenly swerving to avoid hitting another car just out of a tight turn—then we CUT BACK to the man saying how he will retire after this race, he really means it, and now we FLASHFORWARD again as the same car skids and spins even further down the track crashing into the side rails, then we CUT BACK TO the same man saying that he will spend a lot of time on his farm with his wife and children and then we FLASHFOR-WARD to an ambulance stopping in front of an emergency hospital entrance and the man being wheeled into the open doors, then we CUT BACK to the same man saying that twenty years of driving is long enough, and then we FLASHFORWARD to a woman crying hysterically as a doctor says, "I'm sorry, we tried. There was nothing more we could do."

FLASHBACKS and FLASHFORWARDS are used for motivating both character and conflict, in a number of ways, including developing mood and attitudes, or suggesting impending disaster that we, the audience, know will happen before it happens to the character.

Natural Sound

Sound that is normally taking place in the scene you're shooting. If the scene is, for example, a crowded restaurant, the NATURAL SOUND is all the noise, people talking, waiters or waitresses putting glasses on the table, and so on. Whatever sound is a part of the action is considered natural sound.

Wild Track Sound

Sound that is either added to the scene after it is shot or sound having no rela-tion to the immediate scene at all. For example, someone is sleeping; the room is silent, but we hear the sound of a car door opening and slamming shut.

WILD TRACK SOUND is used like music, to orchestrate and heighten the intensity of a scene, to make the scene sometimes a little larger than life. We hear a clock ticking much more loudly than it normally would but we don't see it in a scene. This is WILD TRACK SOUND. Ingmar Bergman, the Swedish film-maker, uses WILD TRACK SOUND often in his movies, especially his earlier ones.

So far we've talked about effects done in a laboratory or in editing. There are some cameras which have devices built into them to make a dissolve happen while the camera, loaded with film, is being used to shoot the action (for example the 16mm Bolex). These instances are rare though; most of the cuts and dissolves are made at the editing bench on a work print which is to be conformed with the original print and then taken to the lab for answer prints and final prints.

Besides such effects you need to understand camera angles and positions, which constitute a special visual language. The conventions of this language must be observed. Do not arbitrarily write in a CLOSE-UP or a LONG SHOT unless you have reasons to use them. The most common camera angles used are: CLOSE-UP, LONG SHOT, and MEDIUM SHOT. Then there are modifications of these: TIGHT CLOSE-UP, MEDIUM CLOSE-UP, and WIDE ANGLE SHOT. Added to these are OVERVIEW or AERIAL SHOTS, PANNING and TRUCK-ING, ZOOM-IN and ZOOM-OUT, and DOLLY-IN and DOLLY-OUT. It is not enough simply to know these names; you must also know how and why they are used.

Close-Up (CU)

A shot of a subject, usually from the shoulders up. CLOSE-UPS often motivate and show certain dramatic emotions, reveal intensity, show strain, pain, thought. They can often have a harsh effect, and used with SLOW PAN, where the camera *turns* either left or right, or by a TRUCK where the camera *moves* either left or right, the feeling can be uncomplimentary, adversary in nature.

A TIGHT CLOSE-UP (TCU) could mean the difference in perspective from someone's face to someone's eye.

Medium Shot (MS)

This occurs when the subject is about three-quarter full-frame or less. A shot from the waist up would be a MEDIUM SHOT. Often used as MEDIUM 2 SHOT (M2S), which means two people in the frame. A MEDIUM SHOT does not give the impression of isolation as does the LONG SHOT. It is also a less dramatic shot in terms of visual motivation. If you show someone walking down a deserted street on a LONG SHOT, you create a visual impression of loneliness or isolation, desperation, or possibly impending danger. If you have a CLOSE-UP of someone shuddering with fear, the effect is strongly dramatic. The MEDIUM SHOT, however, neither isolates the character nor stresses emotional response. It is primarily a transition shot of less emotional force than a CLOSE-UP or LONG SHOT.

Long Shot (LS)

The LONG SHOT shows the subject and other things in full frame. For instance, a LONG SHOT can show a desolate beach at dusk, the waves lapping up on the shoreline and someone suddenly moving into frame. Except for that person the rest of the beach is empty. We have created a mood of anticipation without ever introducing a word of dialogue or narration. Who is the person? Why is the beach so empty? Is it safe? Does that person have suicide in mind? Or is the person there to meet someone else? LONG SHOTS can create these moods and prompt these kinds of questions. They can also establish a scene, like the opening statements in the first paragraph of a book's chapter.

A LONG SHOT can show a PANORAMA VIEW (another camera term) and create the same impression of a horizon that a painter may wish to convey in a work of art. Think of a sunset in northern New Mexico, the blue sky darkening, the mountains casting colored shadows in the background, an adobe shack with a little garden patch, a swatch of crusty mud caked with dry cactus stretches from the roadside to the mountains, almost endlessly. This lonely land seems somehow crowded with the ghosts of generations—Indians, conquistadores, mountain men, even telephone linemen. This sort of scene, and its feeling, can be conveyed in a LONG SHOT.

Wide Angle Shot (WS)

The WS is used when distortion is called for in a script. Perhaps a character is under such pressure that reality, for him, is stretched out of shape—a football player is out on a field and suddenly he realizes that fifty thousand people are looking down on him. He feels as if the whole stadium has turned on him. With the WIDE ANGLE SHOT, the image is stretched on each side of the frame and the effect is much the same as that of a carnival amusement mirror that stretches your image.

Zoom-In, Zoom-Out

A telescopic way of filming gives the impression of either spying on someone or something, or picking a subject out for greater scrutiny. This camera movement should be used sparingly since it is distracting and can be jarring to the viewer.

Dolly

A shot done with a camera mounted on a dolly truck, which can be moved by hand or motorized; you've seen scenes where the camera is moving down a hall as the subject moves through the same space. The DOLLY allows you to get inside or into the action more than a static shot will. And if you want your audience to feel as if they are "touching" the action, then a DOLLY shot may be called for.

Aerial and Overview Shots

Both really the same thing, these shots convey an omniscient or panoramic view. They are seldom used because they call for both time and extra equipment.

Superimposition

Purposely blending together two or more images to show a double or triple exposure. This is done to show dream sequences or character essays, or cover a lot of time in one scene. Often the SUPERIMPOSITION conveys a poetic feeling, especially when done in a soft focus. People's names or titles can also be SUPERIMPOSED over a picture of either that person or what he or she is talking about. Television news film clips use the SUPER often. Other graphics can be supered over pictures as well, including maps, facts taken from materials such as legislation, or quoted remarks.

For a listing of other technical terms, refer to the glossary at the end of the book. The ones presented here are those you'll use most often and should understand completely. If you think of them as a kind of film grammar, this will aid you in choosing which ones will provide the most meaningful effect possible.

An example of why a writer chose to use a specific camera angle when he prepared a shot sheet for a film crew sent up to cover the tragic aftermath of a flash flood in Southern California should illustrate the importance of camera angles, and how they select from a dramatic event the most powerful elements. This is the way he told the story:

> A TIGHT CLOSE-UP is always used to emphasize drama in a documentary. In a documentary on the Los Angeles floods, one of the scenes was shot at an evacuation area set up by the Coast Guard. There was a man waiting near the heliport, which was close to a river already spilling over with water. The man was waiting for his son. He had been told the boy was being flown in. What he wasn't told was that his son was dead. When the helicopter landed, the stretcher taken off, and the boy's head covered with a blanket, the reaction on the man's face, and then his eyes told part of the story. We intercut from his eyes to the raging river to the men carrying the stretcher, back to the father's eyes again.
>
> Narration wasn't necessary. Just the NATURAL SOUND, the sound present at the base camp, and the man's face torn with grief was all needed to tell the scene.

To make the marriage of the visual and the word complete you need to know what the camera can do for you, what sound can do for you, what an editor can do for you, without necessarily having to go out and shoot, record, and then edit the whole thing yourself.

In summary. Camera angles are used to show relationships, and not always in a physical or spatial sense. A LONG SHOT of a young woman walking down an isolated beach tells us more than the fact that she prefers the beach to a sidewalk. The scene conveys isolation, loneliness, or maybe tranquility; the point is that the LONG SHOT in a script can be used for more than just satisfying a spatial requirement. Camera angles are also used for *moods*. How do you know which moods mean which angles or distances? Emphasis is one of the keys. What do you want to emphasize? What is it that your script is saying? What is the best visual way to convey your ideas? These are some of the questions you should be asking yourself in determining the kinds of camera shots to call for.

A film is structured like a piece of music. You have a theme and then a variation of that theme. You have soft moments. Moments that are hard, ironic, tragic. Moments that are funny, thoughtful, restful. Camera angles and positions are an essential part of that structure and movement.

chapter 15

The Mistakes
You Can Make:
A Summing Up

Writing is a craft, though not like carpentry or bricklaying. A carpenter making a table and a bricklayer making a wall begin with plans and specifications to which the finished product conforms. A writer deals with a living process, and life is always somewhat unpredictable. In this book we have tried to discuss certain special kinds of writing for special media as a craft whose product grows and changes in the process of coming into being. We hope that as a professional writer for the media you will begin with our suggestions and then modify them as your temperament and your experience dictate.

So in summary we choose to talk about the various mistakes that writers can make and that most writers have made. We include many "don'ts" along the way. The reason is not that we are pessimistic about your abilities or negative about the business of writing for the media. The reason is that mistakes are specific and can be economically described. Describing the right way to solve a problem is much more complex, and in any case the "right way" to do one script may not be nearly so right in the next one.

Chronologically, the first cluster of mistakes you can make in scriptwriting occurs when you are reaching an agreement with a producer, and then meeting experts, consultants, and possibly clients' representatives for the first time. This whole early period in the history of any assignment, which is in the past by the time you write your first line, is a mine field.

In dealing with your producer, be sure that any agreements you make are clear, specific, and detailed. Get the agreement in writing. An oral arrangement may be satisfactory if you and the producer know each other and have worked together in the past; otherwise, it is not. Be sure that your responsibilities are clearly stated: how many drafts of treatment, how many drafts of script? And

193

where does your responsibility as a writer end: when you have done the last script revision, or when the production is in the can? What are the deadlines? Be sure that the agreement states the producer's responsibilities as well: how long will he or she take in reading your copy? How much will the producer pay, and in what specific stages? Never accept an agreement in which the producer promises to pay you "on acceptance" of your work. These two words could entitle him or her to refuse payment to you indefinitely. If what you write has any more than an immediate value, what will be your rights in the written script in the future? Could you, at some future date, use the material in the script on another project, or are you selling the work to the producer complete and forever?

These are only the business and legal aspects of your arrangement with the producer. There are other sides to your relationship, professional and personal. Clarify this relationship as thoroughly as possible, as early as possible. Otherwise, you may be preparing the way for an unhappy and frustrating assignment.

Sometimes a writer is forced to deal with failures and errors that are really the producer's fault. Situations of this sort may arise when a producer has not discussed a project adequately with a client's representatives, and simply leaves the writer to take over. We recall one of several such situations in our own experience. A writer had agreed to write a series of scripts for audio production dealing with great medical discoveries and modern subspecialties (paramedics, X-ray technicians, and so on) in contemporary medicine. The client was a large corporation that sold medical supplies of various kinds. The basic idea of the series was to dramatize some of the great medical discoveries of the past, and to give some information on present-day career opportunities in medicine. The client would be identified as the sponsor of the series, but would offer it as a public service in the field of job-counseling and education.

The producer of the series and the public relations director for the client had talked, but had apparently done little except express a mutual enthusiasm for the series. The writer consequently found himself dealing not only with experts in medical history, which he had expected, but with fifteen or twenty medical and paramedical societies through the public relations director, who was constantly fearful lest his company offend even one official of a single such organization. Caught between production deadlines, the historians, and the omnipresent possibility of enraging some medical group whose favor was important to the client, the producer, the public relations director, and of course the writer ended the series in a state near collapse.

In this particular case, expert consultants were helpful rather than troublesome; sometimes the reverse is true. Very often, problems with consultants—like problems with clients and their representatives—can be forestalled by a good producer. When they are not, they tend to fall on the writer. One memorable production in our experience was to be a TV special for an art museum dealing with an exhibit of paintings, sculptures, tapestries, and so on from the Palace at Versailles. The exhibit, sponsored by the French government, was fascinating and of great historical interest. The museum wished to publicize the showing, the television station agreed, the producer checked briefly with the art museum experts, a writer was engaged.

The writer felt that the most effective way to tell the story was to recount the history of Versailles, from its beginnings as a hunting lodge in the days of Louis XIII, to its historical climax as Louis XVI and Marie Antoinette fled the Palace in the days of Terror. The thesis was that here was an authentic and vivid bit of French history, lent by France to America. Everyone agreed. The treatment called for some film to be shot outside the museum, after which the cameras would move inside and tell the story as the works of art were examined. At the end, the viewer would emerge into the city streets of modern America as if he or she had just stepped out of a time capsule. All of this seemed excellent.

At this point, the experts of the art museum intervened. They explained carefully that, although the works of art had historical value, aesthetically they were something less than desirable. The museum did not really wish to be identified with such stuff on television. Telling the story of Versailles was a good idea from their point of view, but no filming of the works in the actual exhibit would be allowed.

For some days the writer and director pondered this problem. They could film outside the museum and even in the entrance-way to the exhibit, which might give them three minutes of visuals for an opening and a close. But what of the rest? For a while they considered going to a test pattern or a shot of the French tricolor while a voice said, "If you could see this painting of the young Napoleon crossing the Alps . . . as you would understand if you looked at the Houdon bust of Lafayette . . . by all means when you go to the exhibit look for the interesting painting of the surrender at Yorktown . . . ."

The art experts stood their ground. No filming in the exhibit. The TV station managers said they were committed to doing the show, and the writer and director would of course find a way to do it. Eventually the director was flown to Paris for a weekend. He shot a fair amount of footage at Versailles, but his triumph was in finding and leasing a collection of some 600 35mm slides of Versailles, the result of the lifetime hobby of a Parisian gentleman. So by editing film footage and laboriously selecting dozens of slides, then adapting the writer's research materials to the visuals, the director and writer succeeded in producing a TV special on an art exhibit without actually showing the exhibit itself. The program eventually won an Ohio State award for excellence.

In saying these things, we do not mean to ridicule experts as a class, or as individuals, or to make them seem anything other than what they are: a *potential* resource of great value. Note that we emphasize the word *potential*. Consultants to a film, television program, or slide film are subject-matter experts. They are not supposed to know anything about the media. Unfortunately, they often have the notion, shared with most people living in the United States, that they know everything about the media. This attitude makes for problems that must be resolved tactfully.

On the other side of the ledger, it is important to understand that you, as a writer, and the other members of the production team have at best a super-ficial knowledge of art, or French history, or urban sociology, or whatever the film is supposed to be about. If a consultant is willing to give you time, early in the production schedule, to learn more about his or her specialty, accept it. Learn. Even an hour or so spent learning during the research and early treatment stage of a writing assignment can save you days of revision later on.

Suggestion. In the early stages of working out an assignment, spend as much time as you can talking and listening. Don't avoid discussing the details of your assignment with the producer. Get them in writing if you can. Don't avoid seeing the consultants on a project, on the assumption that they will be a nuisance rather than a help. Learn from them. Learn everything you can. Find out espe-cially what your script should not say—the cliches, the popular inaccuracies, the obsolete notions on the subject. This talking-learning procedure will not be as time-consuming as you might fear. You can save time by doing homework, by preparing for these sessions. Besides, producers and experts alike are busy people, and talking to you may not seem very important to them. Nevertheless, this is the stage at which you must find out the difficulties of your assignment, antici-pate mistakes, and save invaluable writing time. Use your opportunities for all they are worth.

So you begin to write your treatment. We have said nothing in this book about *style* in writing. We've talked about structure, about conflict, about visual and dialogue pacing, about orchestration, but not about style, and for good reasons. In the long tradition of writing for print, style has been a serious consideration. Style is supposed to be the unique, individual way in which a particular author expresses himself or herself; "style is the man," says one of the standard definitions of the term. In this sense, style is everything a writer does that makes his or her work distinctive, distinguishable from the work of any other author. Style is something you acquire over a period of years.

There are supposed to be great styles and great stylists in print literature. Robert Louis Stevenson tells how he "played the sedulous ape" as a young writer, copying out long passages from the writers he admired, hoping that some of their elegance might rub off on him.

This view of style is not very much to our purpose as writers for the media. Kenneth Burke comes closer to our mark in commenting that style is "ingratia-tion," the whole complex of ways in which a work is presented to readers, viewers, listeners, so as to engage their attention, identify with their interests, and so on. If we are to use the term *style* in this sense, it must be applied to a finished production, not to the script alone. Here, style is the product of col-laboration, in which the writer has a major share.

So there is not very much temptation for a media writer to become over-concerned about style and, frankly, we feel that this is fortunate. Even for print writers, *a style is slowly developed, cannot be forced, cannot be acquired by imitation, and is best left to develop as it will*. For media writers, we suggest: forget about style. Write everything as well as you can, as accurately as you can, and as simply as you can.

When you write the *first draft* of a treatment, don't try to be too rigorous or self-critical. *Say what you mean, or think you mean, as well as you can—at that moment.* Don't edit too much in doing a first draft. The first draft is a place to put ideas in, not take them out. You can edit later. At this point, you want to encourage the concept of the script to grow.

But the first draft is not totally without controls. It is possible, if you write totally without inhibitions, to produce a great flood of words, free-associating, Klang-associating, letting your fingers do the talking. As a result, whatever pertinent ideas you may have had for the script may be drowned in bubble.

How you achieve a balance between no-control and total-control in writing a first draft is something only experience can teach you. You will make many mistakes by going too far in either direction, but they are inevitable, and you will learn from them.

There are occasions when all of this advice is not to the point. If a producer tells you, "I need this treatment by tomorrow and it has to be *good*," you are faced with the task of producing the equivalent of a second or third draft without having written the first one. In short, you are probably in for a long, hard night.

First draft treatments are almost always revised. The common mistake new writers make is spending too much time on them. If you are too slow and painstaking, you may dwell too long on one section of the treatment and have to race through the rest. An amateur's treatment can be easily recognized; the first few sequences will be carefully worked out, often too elaborately, and the closing ones will be barely sketched in.

When you start a first draft, write it straight through as quickly as you can. Then, if you have time to spare, go back and rework the sections that need it most. If you haven't time to rework them, make note of the necessary revisions and any further ideas you have for the treatment. These notes may be made on a separate piece of paper, or in the margins of the draft itself. Then, when you have the story conference with your producer, you can say, "This scene needs more research. What I did was to lay it out generally as you see it. When I revise, I'll try to rework it along these lines."

Almost all good writing is not written; it is rewritten. Young writers never believe this, for two reasons. First, they are hypnotized by the marvelous fact that they can get a piece of writing done at all. Second, they don't know how to rewrite. We can do little or nothing to break the hypnotic spell, but we can give some practical suggestions about the process of rewriting.

As you write your first draft, you will notice that from time to time you feel uncomfortable with what you have written. Initially, all that you may know about an early draft of a manuscript is that it doesn't "read right." This is a vague feeling, but important. The intuitive sense of hearing what is right, seeing what is right, feeling what is right, may be your only guide in revising.

Don't stop to repair a first draft whenever you feel uncomfortable. Complete the draft, and then go back. At this point you must read and reread your manuscript very closely, syllable by syllable, phrase by phrase, in an effort to sort out the good from the bad. Remember that the first draft of a treatment is not a completed work. It is simply the first stage in a long process, the end of which is a production script.

Another frequent error you can make in writing a first draft is not saying what you mean, or even not knowing what you mean to say. A good deal of revising may consist of asking yourself the questions, "What do I mean? What am I trying to say?" and not stopping until you are clear both in your own mind and on paper.

First drafts are usually verbose. Cutting the unnecessary is another, and essential, way of polishing a manuscript. You will find that very often you have taken hundreds of words to repeat what you have already said, or to explore tangents to your idea that never came out anywhere. Repetition is not always bad; for good communication, a certain amount of redundance has to be built into what you write. But repetition without purpose has to go. As for the tangents, if they yielded anything pertinent to your script, salvage them. Otherwise remove them, however fascinating they may be.

There is another question you should ask yourself constantly as you revise. It was a cliche of old-time melodrama, occurring in a scene in which one character was trying to describe some past event to another. He would talk and talk; his story would get longer and more complicated and seem less and less likely ever to reach its point. Suddenly the character would pause portentously and then say, "But why am I telling you all this?" It's a good question. It forces you to remember that you are not just spinning language, but talking to people out there who must listen and understand and be interested. Whenever you come to a part of your manuscript that seems to have strayed a little from the point, ask, "But why am I telling you all this?" If you can't find a good answer, then cut. There is a writer's axiom that has been kicking around for some time: "When in doubt, cut out."

Pay particular attention to the opening pages of anything you may write. Beginnings are difficult. Usually a writer will devise what seems, as he or she begins the draft, an interesting way of getting into the story—witty, dramatic, well-stated, and so on. On rereading your first draft, you must always consider whether you couldn't do without the wit and the drama, in the interests of getting into your subject. All too often, the answer is "yes." The opening paragraphs, or even pages, of a first draft represent a sort of warming-up period, after which the writer begins to write. The warm-up is important for the writer, but can certainly be spared for readers, viewers, listeners.

In general: cut everything that isn't necessary. Look with suspicion on anything that seems to you "beautifully written." Eliminate all private jokes, or references that can be understood only by you or your friends. Clarify the ideas of the script in your own mind and know the structure you are trying to create. Finally, always be aware of the audience for your writing—first, your producer and the production team, then possibly a client and his or her representatives, and eventually the great mob of people who may listen to your tape, see your film, watch your TV program, be forced to learn from your slide film. Why *are* you telling them all this?

Most important of all the aspects of developing, writing, and revising your treatments and scripts is the business of getting and testing ideas. The world is full of ideas for films, videotapes, and the like, but the good ones are still hard to come by. Ideas for scripts, or for scenes and sequences, come often enough from a glimpse, a snatch of reality, a series of impressions that flash across your mind. Ideas are developed from incidents that have happened to you, to someone you know, to someone you have read about. Ideas also come from the things that worry people, sometimes from issues that affect communities, nations, the world at large, sometimes from the persistent annoyances and threats of every-day life. Ideas come from park-bench arguments or fragments of restaurant conversations overheard, from the debates of community groups concerned about their neighborhoods, from casual social conversation.

But not all ideas are appropriate for a film, or a videotape, or a radio program. In some ways, the media writer is more circumscribed in his or her choice of ideas than the print writer is. The length of films, news shows, mini-documentaries for TV or radio is always a factor—more so, perhaps, than would be true for the writer of magazine articles. Also, the costs of production, at least for film and video, are very high, so that considerations of budget eliminate a good many ideas.

For these practical reasons, many ideas are called, but few are chosen. A hundred ideas may produce a dozen treatments, which result in two or three finished scripts, one or two of which may actually be produced.

With this sort of idea mortality rate, you will understand that a writer—among other people in production—has to be extremely fertile in producing ideas and very hard-headed in testing their merits. Aside from the practical considerations we have referred to, you must keep in mind other and more technical standards against which to test writing projects.

Always remember that your ideas must be translated into a specific medium, with a special language of its own. Some ideas work very naturally with radio, for instance, but can be expressed in film only with great difficulty. The point is not to discard notions that are less than ideal for a particular medium, but to understand that they must be stated within the confines of a particular medium. Never permit yourself to think that an idea is generally great, without reference to medium. Always think in terms of specific media languages.

A crucial test of an idea is whether you can state a theme for it in one simple sentence. There are many subjects that have a self-evident importance: inflation, crimes against the person, the role of religion in present-day life, women's liberation, and so on and on. But unless you have something to say about one of these subjects—until you can say what makes it important for you—you might as well forget about the project. The test question is: "What about it?" Someone says, "I want to make a great film about the problems of old people." The first question you should ask is, "Well, what *about* the problems of old people?"

What do you have to say that is new, wise, useful? If you don't know, file the idea until you do.

If an idea ever gets to the treatment, scriptwriting, and production stages, it must have a dramatic structure; there must be a story line, characters, a developing conflict. Conflict is essential to nonfiction writing, as it is to fiction. If an idea cannot be cast into dramatic form—or, more probable, if you can't see it in dramatic terms—discard it.

An extension of this observation is the Aristotelian cliche that a story must have a beginning, a middle, and an end. A nonfiction film or tape follows this prescription in one way or another. Whether your script deals with on-the-job safety, following the Rolling Stones on a series of one-nighters, or the proper methods of serving guests in a resort hotel, it must have an internal structure similar to that of a short story, a novel, or a play. In the case of the script on safety, you may begin with a body of research findings, suggestions, and legal information, and construct a fictitious play that conveys the essential parts of this information. If the Rolling Stones are your subject, your problem is to select out of twenty hours of filmed materials the two hours that will tell the story most dramatically.

Selecting, editing, and shaping actuality materials is a technique that is rarely taught in schools, but which has become of increasing importance to writers in recent years. Much contemporary writing since the advent of the audio recorder and the portable videotape recorder is really editing. The process works something like this: you tape an interview of someone, have the interview transcribed, edit the transcription, and finally retype the edited material into a coherent story. This seems simple enough; the difficulty comes in the process of editing.

Your first task is to find the story line, the dramatic line, in your material. Having done so, you eliminate everything that does not advance this line. Next, you edit for tension and climaxes. A good interview, like a good story or play, consists of a series of small segments, in each of which tension builds to a minor climax, is paid off, relaxes, and again begins to build. Tension that is constant becomes distracting, eventually unbearable. The pattern must be: build, climax, letdown, build, climax, letdown—with each new build starting at a slightly higher point of interest.

All "real" events involving people—a religious ritual, a football game, a courtroom trial—when they are controllable at all, exhibit much the same pattern. If you go to a courtroom and watch a trial in progress, especially one that is receiving press coverage, you will see the pattern clearly. Any trial lawyer knows the values of tension and relaxation; after a startling revelation or an exciting exchange between lawyers, there is always a period in which the trial returns to routine and everyone relaxes.

A filmmaker, whether he or she is shooting from a script or dealing with actuality materials, follows much the same procedure. In a dramatized production, a high climax will be followed by a switch in tone or mood. Extremely serious footage may be relieved by a comic touch. This means that sometimes you have to take a scene, look for the level where the tension is the highest, then break the tension at that point in order to build for an even higher level later on.

We mentioned earlier the necessity for writing economically. One way to achieve economy of words is to understand the many languages that are available to you in the media. For example, we communicate not only with words but with silences, not only with moving visual images but with the composition of individual frames, not only with "representational" sound but with the emotional overtones of sound. We know a good deal about such exotic subjects as "body language," or kinesics—enough to know that a human being maintains a constant dialogue between him or herself and the world through posture, gesture, facial expression. We know that the "natural" composition of a group of people—the spaces that separate them, the clusters they make, the touching and not-touching—says more about their interrelationships than fifty pages of type possibly could. All of these languages are available to you as a writer.

To look closely at only one example of the many media languages, notice the spectrum of meanings we can work with when dealing with *natural presence* sound.

1. A maternity ward, and the sound of newborn children. The brisk voices of the nurses. The intimate soft conversations coming from the colorfully-decorated rooms where mothers and fathers visit. The rather hard echo of hospital corridors.
2. A football stadium, and the yelling crowds. The cold November wind that blows across the field. The bands blaring away at halftime. The "outdoors" context, very different from the outdoors of a field in spring, or an empty box-canyon in the mountains. The vendors waving their banners and calling out to the spectators.
3. Water lapping on a vacant beach. The seagulls swooping overhead. The splash of a big fish, far offshore.
4. A singles bar with the customers stuffed inside like sardines, everyone talking at once, the jukebox blaring through half a dozen speakers. Although it's packed, the place sounds like a cavern, its walls vibrating with jabber, wails, and the clump of rock rhythm.
5. An empty deep old church painted in shadows, collecting soft memories of sound like a seashell, and someone barely visible kneeling near the first row of pews. Here the natural silence conveys a mood, a feeling.

These scenes are over-written intentionally to stress the factor of natural presence sound. Put them in a script, and the over-writing would convey to the director the sort of sound presence you wanted.

The point of all this is that, if you work with the several languages of the media fully, you can afford to be economical with words. The principle to follow in deciding how best to convey the story line of your script is to understand that (a) the various media languages are used together, never in isolation, and (b) the languages used in a given sequence should supplement each other, and never compete.

We have said that a film is sometimes built in the editing room. Such films have usually been shot from a brief outline or from nothing at all. Thus, the script is created as the film is edited. Either the narrative passages are written at the editing bench, or notes are taken there for later expansion. Usually these notes describe the action preceding and following the point at which the narration is to be used, plus the amount of time to be used for narration. Narration in this sort of film is generally used to bridge scenes, so the time allotted for it will usually be short. Here, for example, is an excerpt from a film in which narration reinforces the visual transition from one scene to the next:

We follow Maxwell, hand-held camera, as he walks into a small room, the size of a closet, to pour himself a cup of coffee. He's tired, and he has only a few seconds before he has to get up and start all over again.

SLOW DISSOLVE TO:

MATERNITY, and Dr. Maxwell is starting his rounds all over again.

SOF MATERNITY WARD

By Monday Dr. Maxwell had completed his first week as an intern. So far he had performed an emergency appendectomy, sent a little boy home with a swallowed coin left in him for nature to take out, and brought to life a young girl who had o.d.'d. This week Dr. Maxwell was on the maternity ward service.

SOF SEQUENCE.

Notice that this narration is quiet and understated, so that it will not overpower or contrast with the visuals too much. The weariness and determination of Maxwell, which we should get visually, are reinforced by the plain statement of what his responsibilities are, and what he has accomplished. The quietness and strength of the sequence should force a viewer to realize the awesome responsibility of the young doctor.

How you develop a sense for knowing when to allow the picture to move the action rather than opting for dialogue or narration to tell the story is based probably as much on instinct as it is on any hard and fast rule. This is why filmmaking doesn't have a specific style, why filmmakers have unique identities, and why the more successful ones can be spotted even before their credits appear on the screen.

How do you know when to cut from a rock concert onstage to backstage as the groupies, agents, and others pace up and back, or sit sullenly on an old sofa in one of the dressing rooms in sharp contrast to the frenzy taking place on the stage? If the film is about a "behind the scenes look" at what goes on at a rock concert you pretty much know that juxtaposing stage shots with backstage shots is necessary. But if the film is about the group performing, what tells you when to leave the group and develop a substory about the action taking place in the back rooms? Instinct may tell you. Your own fantasies and imagination may tell you. The point is, if you care enough about wondering just what *does* go on backstage, you'll translate this curiosity into visual images.

Somewhere along the line you must assume the role of audience. What are your interests? Are yours compatible with the intended audience for the film you're creating? Maybe they give you a clue that will help you decide how to interpret events and people. Never be afraid to commit your own curiosity to a project.

You must recognize that any given movement in a film grows out of the movement that has gone before, and implies the movement that is next to come. If you're on a close-up of someone who is looking off to his left, the next shot obviously will follow his glance. If a sequence is building toward an outburst of extreme anger or violence, a two-shot of the embroiled characters may be followed by an extreme close-up of the hand of one of them as it clenches and unclenches, or by a tight facial shot in which we see the jaw muscles bulging in the cheek.

Remember that every visual suggests a future action, which may follow immediately or may not come up for quite some time. But when you think of a total film as a mosaic, you realize just how each visual fits with the next. Every part in a mosaic that makes itself known advances a visual expression until the last piece completes the whole. *Just as true, each piece of film advances a point of view, until the total pieces complete a story.*

The above are all topics we have discussed, sometimes in different perspectives, earlier in this book. We repeat our observations both as reminders and as a way of showing the endless facets of media writing techniques. This chapter could readily be expanded into a new book, different from the one we have written but supplementary to it.

Instead of writing that book, we offer at this point a little catalogue of *don'ts*. They deal, as don'ts usually do, with severely practical matters rather than theoretical issues, but they may be all the more valuable to you for that.

Don'ts

Don't ever take anything about a writing assignment for granted. Find out.

Don't accept a writing assignment without having it spelled out in a contract, unless you are absolutely sure that a verbal agreement will be honored.

Don't count on promises, especially when they seem to be an expression of good will. Promises have a high mortality rate.

Don't believe that any first draft you ever write is really satisfactory.

Don't assume that you know what anybody else thinks or wants. This applies with special force to producers. Ask.

Don't think you'll look like a fool if you ask questions. It is always better to know than not to know.

Don't ever believe the old admonition to "look in your heart and write." Your heart is a splendid organ, and probably full of great things, but you need research—in libraries, through interviews and location scouting—as well.

Don't set aside certain hours of the day as the best hours to write. If you miss those hours, you then have an excuse to write nothing that day. If you must, you can write twenty-four hours of the day.

Don't be satisfied, when you're working on an assignment, until you have put in at least an eight-hour day.

Don't treat smaller and less complex assignments as if they were beneath your talents. Treat the most mechanical, cut-and-dried assignment as if it were the most challenging of your career. There is no point in being bored if you can help it.

Don't ignore your ears or your eyes as research tools. They are functioning throughout every waking hour of your day, but you must learn to pay attention to what they tell you. As Sherlock Holmes once said to Dr. Watson, "You *saw*, but you did not *observe*." There is a difference.

Don't be afraid to learn your trade from anyone who has anything to teach. Listen to producers, directors, technicians of all sorts. Ask production companies for sample scripts of past productions, and study them. Never ignore any chance to satisfy your own curiosity.

Don't be so hypnotized by your own words that you can't change them, or consider reasonable criticism.

We are convinced that all creative writing, whether it's writing television news copy, film dramatization, or writing the novel, is dramatic writing; that all creative writing must have conflict, character growth, rising tension; that there is a dialectic principle at work in a good script that builds through the conflict of thesis and antithesis to a resolution. A script is never static; it is a dynamic system. It has a living feel you will learn to recognize. A good script does not simply exist. It works.

appendix A
The
Writer's
Qualifications

There are probably several thousand practicing writers in the United States today. There are also tens of thousands of people who would like to "be writers," which usually means that they are attracted by the mystique of writing but have never managed to endure the pains and the discipline necessary to practice the skill. Still further, there is an uncounted number of people who do practical, bread-and-butter writing from time to time, not because they have any special interest in writing, but because the job needs to be done and there's no one else around.

The motive behind most professional writing is simple necessity. Most professional writing is done because most professional writers need the money. Samuel Johnson, a thoroughly professional writer, once said that anyone who writes for any reason other than money is a fool. The statement is extreme; there is also in the process of writing great excitement and genuine pleasure when the words flow well. But at bottom, Johnson, as usual, was quite right. The prototype for the media writer is not the young poet with flaming vision; it is rather a teacher in a junior college who needs some extra income and has found out that there is money to be made by writing educational films. Or it is a college graduate with a major in radio, television, film, journalism, or English who wants to make a living writing scripts. Other media writers may receive their training in the natural or social sciences. What is important is they all desire to write and are determined enough to learn. We are concerned with people who wish to write professionally—to make all or part of their living by writing—and are willing to bring to this task all the creativity, enthusiasm, imagination, and skill they command.

205

THE WRITER'S HABITS
AND PRACTICES: ACQUIRING
KNOWLEDGE

A Roman playwright once set down a line that applies to all writers: "I am a human being," he said. "I believe that nothing human is alien to me." In a period in which the workings of nonhuman worlds have come to seem more and more important, we may add, "Nothing animal, nothing of organic life, nothing of the inert universe, nothing of the possible worlds of the spirit is alien to me, or outside my interests."

Perhaps the words of a young writer who was asked to deliver a speech at a small college not too long ago can best sum up this idea. In part he said,

> "I'm only a writer . . . I deal in the politics of words . . . of human experiences . . . of dreams . . . of sadness. When I am at my best my pages laugh and sing and they also cry. When I'm at my worst my pages wait impatiently for me to make them come alive . . . to add layers of texture and shading until my pages become dimensional . . . I'm a painter. I'm a composer. I'm a rabble rouser . . . a provocateur. I'm a patriot. I'm the enemy. I wave the flag. And sometimes I hide from it. I'm a tender lover . . . I'm a hard bargainer. I'm sweet and innocent. I'm hardened and brutal.
>
> "I'm a writer.
>
> "This is my world. Welcome to it.
>
> "It's a world filled with the unpredictable . . . with blind spots and dead ends . . . with straight lines which out of nowhere, it seems, suddenly change direction. It's a world of ethics and erotica . . . pathos, and pleasure . . . and the writer sits in the middle of all this confusion like a sponge being soaked and squeezed . . . and if you really want to write you face a constant dilemma of values . . . yours and everyone else's.
>
> "This is a writer's world . . . this is our world."

It matters less who this person is than what he was saying. What we have tried to set in motion in our book, among other things, is the idea that writing begs its creators never to stop seeing or listening or feeling or questioning and this requires a discipline to lifelong learning, whether you wind up winning an Academy Award for writing a feature film or set your sights on writing nonfiction scripts. The steps to get there are really the same: an insatiable hunger for knowledge and an unshakable confidence in knowing that you can tell it in a special way so that other people can share in this discovery as well.

Recent slide films of which we know have dealt with the process of producing table salt, the workings of simple machines, and the activities of paramedical units. One of the authors co-produced, wrote, and directed a film dealing with a great hospital maintained by a university medical school. The other wrote a script dramatizing the psychological barriers to good safety practices in industry.

206

It would be a most unusual writer who could muster enough information to produce statements on all these matters out of his or her own training and background. Most media writing projects require a good deal of preliminary research; a radio series written ten years ago on medical discoveries required the writer to use the research facilities of an encyclopedia publisher, read twenty-odd books, and scan perhaps fifty more. The point is that the media writer must have the habit of study and the expert knowledge required to do simple research economically. The writer's education can provide a basis of information for much research. The hospital film, mentioned above, was certainly easier to make for a person with some knowledge of medicine and medical practice than it would have been for a total innocent. But of course prospective writers can't anticipate, when getting their education, the range of topics with which they may have to deal.

What sort of education, then, is best? We offer three bits of advice. First, study subjects that fascinate you. Never mind if you can see no immediate use for them. Most high school and college programs will force a certain unity on your studies; you will be obliged to worry about majors, and requirements, and so on. But when the opportunity presents itself, select courses in areas you simply want to know about, or courses taught by teachers with whom you want to work. Risk, even, the possibility of getting a mediocre grade in some course where you have more interest than ability to contribute. Study the early military uses of balloons, or Anglo-Saxon poetry, or the mathematics of probability, or Blackstone's commentaries on the English law. You will certainly get more pleasure and satisfaction from your education if you do this. We confidently predict that, if you make a career of writing, sooner or later you will find that what you have learned is eminently useful to you.

Second, think of formal education as an ongoing process. People who believe that they "are" educated when they have received a high school diploma, a bachelor's degree, or for that matter a Ph.D., have wasted their time in school. Education should be a continuing, lifelong process. People who try to cut it off at any given point in life are simply preparing themselves intellectually for the physical decline and dissolution they will shortly begin to experience.

Actually, continuing education for most of us is as near as the television set; some of the best documentaries and feature films produced are shown on public broadcasting stations and commercial television stations. In addition, the chances are very good that you live within range of a high school, a college, a good library, or some other educational and cultural center where you can study anything from organic chemistry to yoga and the Great Books of the Western World. We note again, the principle to follow in carrying on your education is to study what fascinates you. And if that happens to be a topic that seems wildly unlike anything you have every studied before, so much the better. One of the happier aspects of writers' lives is that they have a built-in, institutionalized explanation for being intellectually free. Nothing is inappropriate or alien to them, because it is all part of their profession.

Third, cultivate the habit of reading. We are all aware that the world of knowledge has changed radically in recent years: that information is to be found not in printed books alone, but in films, tapes (both video and audio), and the mechanized gadgetry of teaching machines. This is all true, and no writer should fail to make use of the products of the new media. But it is also, and still, true that the great storehouse of human knowledge is print, and that anyone who would enter it must have the skills and the habit of reading.

LEARNING THE CRAFT

For a long time, the usefulness of courses in writing and of "writers' groups" has been debated. Can writing be taught? Our position is that the skills of writing can be deliberately learned, and to some extent they can be taught.

Much of the information that can be garnered in writing courses is very basic, even mechanical. But it is necessary information for anyone who wants to write, particularly for the media we are concerned with, since they impose a great many technical requirements on the author's work. But the course in writing, or the regular meetings of the "writers' groups," has more to offer than this.

The classroom does bring together people whose interests in writing, life experiences, and styles vary greatly. This variety can be most stimulating, if the class members are reasonably tolerant of differences and anxious to be mutually helpful. The class can supply something the solitary writer needs and lacks: a sense of the human environment, of people around you responding to you and your work.

The classroom setting can and should promote a useful exchange of ideas. Some neophytes in the trade are almost neurotically afraid to discuss their ideas for fear of theft. Actually, ideas are not all that uncommon or valuable. An idea is anyone's property, at least up to the point where it is expressed in some tangible form. It is the actual work—the words in their sequence, the film, the sounds on the tape—that is valuable property and can be protected under law. There are few experiences more rewarding than being part of a group examining a writer's problem and, after a time, gradually discovering the sense and the texture in an idea which had somehow eluded its creator. The experience is exhilarating, and certainly one you should not deny yourself.

CURIOSITY AND THE SENSE OF WONDER

Since the beginnings of Western science and philosophy in ancient Greece some five centuries before the Christian era, our knowledge and understanding of the nature of the world and man has grown out of a persistent itch of curiosity. What is the world like? Where does it all come from? What strange creatures and re-

markable tribes live just over the horizon? How does it work? These and a
hundred other questions provoked men and women into observations and
searches that produced the novels of Tolstoy, the astronomy of Copernicus and
Galileo, the physics of Einstein, the lyrics of Sappho, the wonderful histories of
Herodotus, the epic tales of Roland and Odysseus.

Writers of any kind need to maintain this sort of fresh and innocent
curiosity—about people, their life styles, their eccentricities, their even more
surprising "normalities." If you don't like the word *curiosity,* perhaps you will
accept the statement that a writer must have a constant awareness of, and
interest in, the human environment. Whether people are ordinary or extraordinary, dull or fascinating, depends more on the observer than the observed.
A college student in a writing class, on hearing how Thomas Wolfe had presented
members of his family in his novels, protested that Wolfe must have grown up
in a really far-out family. He himself, said the student, wasn't so lucky; his own
family was pretty dull. Replying to this protest posed a somewhat delicate problem for the instructor; it seemed altogether likely that, whatever his family
might be like, the student himself was a pretty dull fellow. Humanity is always
out there, for you and everyone else, giggling and groaning, winning triumphs
and suffering defeats, getting through the day and devising the most ingenious
stratagems for making life bearable. If you are aware of people, and involved in
their lives, they become the most fascinating spectacle that can be imagined,
and if you can write even moderately well, you can convey a sense of that
fascination.

Since we are partly concerned with nonfiction (which has become more and
more popular in late years), you must also be curious about, and aware of, the
other, nonhuman environments that also surround you. "Ecology" has become a
fad word in recent years, but it is still perfectly correct to say that any good
writer is an ecologist, at least in the sense of understanding "the web of life,"
the intricate, living system of which we are all part, that which makes survival
possible. You must have a feeling for trees and water, sun and shade, vegetation
and animal life, the patterns of weather and climate. You may very well have to
write about any of these topics, and whether you do or not, they play a part in
whatever you do write about. People make no sense until you understand the
skies under which they live, the food that nourishes them, the air that they
breathe.

There are other environments as well: Marshall McLuhan and many others
have pointed out that our lives are shaped to a great extent by the universe of
science, invention, and technology to which we must accommodate ourselves;
there is also a social environment of folkways, customs, common beliefs; there is
even, if we are to believe the philosopher Teilhard de Chardin, an environment
of human thought that envelops our world very much as the atmosphere
envelops it.

In short, the world is a complex and wonderful place, and one of the great
rewards of the writer's profession is that you must be aware of the wonder. If

you are not, you cannot write. Writing always grows out of the sum total of the writer's personal experience, knowledge, and study, and if that is true, then a capable writer takes a daily inventory of life and keeps a mental diary as well as a written or spoken one.

One additional word on the subject of curiosity and awareness: if you are not interested in almost everything and everyone that comes to your attention, you shouldn't try to write. Above all, you should not become a professional free-lance writer, for this particular profession feeds and sharpens the appetite of those who are curious and frustrates and annoys those who are not. A free-lancer, especially in the nonfiction field, can find him or herself confronted with topics as widely varied as these: what it is like to be a policeman in Pasadena, California; how people contribute to their own accidental injuries and deaths; what a nonagenarian confidence man likes to remember of his criminal career; how you construct a television fairy tale for children that must point a religious moral; how midgets and dwarfs survive in a society of giants; what it is really like to be old in a society that believes in youth. For the aware person this is a rich feast, but the insensitive should not try to cope with it.

KEEPING TRACK AND PLAYING WITH IDEAS

Writers must collect materials regularly and keep them in some usable form. There are as many ways to achieve these ends as there are writers and the most common methods probably are quite familiar to you. Nevertheless, we think it worthwhile to present our own impressions of this important subject. The tools that are available to you are the notebook (which will involve the use of scissors and paste as well as the pen or typewriter), the tape recorder, the sketchbook, and the camera.

Since writers are, after all, writers, the notebook is probably the most familiar tool. Writers tend to make notes in the most unlikely situations, on anything that comes to hand and will take an impression: inside matchbook covers, on paper napkins, old envelopes, even parking tickets. Such odds and ends are all very well if they are regularly collected, amplified and translated a little, and kept together. Normally, this means keeping daily logs, diaries, notebooks for observations and ideas, piles of legal pads. It is best to date the beginning of each notebook, date each idea, if you can, and then date the end of the notebook once used. We have also found that clipping articles and items from newspapers and magazines, and even photocopying occasional pages of books, is a useful practice. These items may be kept in a separate file, but they are probably best included in your notes, along with any comments that occur to you. Some writers find it useful to catalogue and index their notebooks. We do not urge this because indexing this sort of miscellany can be most complicated, and we try to avoid activities that are substitutes for writing. However, once you have filed a notebook, you may wish to add a summary sheet to it showing the general content of the book for quick reference.

If you are not so used to the written word that other means of composing are uncomfortable to you, we strongly recommend the use of the pocket-sized tape recorder. Very good recorders with built-in and extension microphones, along with other useful gadgets, can be bought for around $100 and there are many models that sell for less. Generally speaking, the bulkier models are less expensive, but not necessarily less reliable. Since they operate on batteries and are fairly unobtrusive, these tape recorders can go anywhere. You can record your own ideas and impressions on cassette tapes, and of course they are invaluable for getting down conversations, sounds, and so on in precise detail. Very few writers who do nonfiction would use any other method for recording interviews. Writers of fiction find this procedure worthwhile, too.

The small tape recorder is also extremely useful for doing first drafts of any sort of material—at least, it is if you are accustomed to "talking your story," or can learn to do so. With the recorder, it is quite possible to talk through a rough draft of an hour script in a day, or to "write" a fifty thousand word manuscript in a week.

In writing scripts for film, slide film, or video tape, you must of course accustom yourself to thinking in visual images, telling your story visually as well as verbally. This is particularly true of motion picture film; film is *primarily* visual, and the best way to approach a film assignment is to consider whether you can tell the entire story in pictures, without using any words at all. This means, of course, that a writer's records will not be complete unless they contain many visual notes. The easiest way to get these notes is, of course, with a camera—again, a very small camera, preferably with a flash attachment, which can be carried without inconvenience, and costs as little as possible to use. If you happen to be a photographer of some skill, you may wish to use rather sophisticated equipment, but it isn't really necessary. A small snapshot camera, or a Polaroid, will work quite well.

There are evidently more amateur photographers at large than amateur graphic artists. Still, a modest knack for sketching can be invaluable to a writer. You need not really be any sort of artist, in the sense that your sketches are not to be shown to anyone else; you must simply be good enough to get down visual effects so that they mean something to you when you refer to them. If you can do a rough of a place so that the sketch preserves the physical facts of the scene, along with some sense of feeling and movement—if you can do a thirty-second impression of a person that conveys the lines of the figure, the flow of movement, the impression of a personality, that is more than enough.

Our point is that you, as a writer, should learn to use tools other than the pen and typewriter in building a stock of impressions, ideas, and facts for use in your writings. Experiment with these tools; play with them; use them not only to record and preserve material, but to discover and develop ideas for your writing.

STORYTELLING AND ACTING AS
WRITERS' EQUIPMENT

We devote special attention to storytelling and acting as qualifications for writers, especially media writers, because they are ancient arts that once were allied with writing and were even precedent to it. In this age of specialization, the alliance is not so evident.

Storytelling is one of the oldest forms of literature, perhaps the oldest. Storytellers have always done one of two things: either retold a traditional and familiar tale, making it fresh and new with their own inventions and variations, or taken a recent event and turned it, through art, into drama. Storytellers have always been regarded as liars of a sort; puritans beginning with Plato have charged them with this, and they themselves have usually admitted their guilt quite cheerfully, and even claimed it as a virtue. Of course, as Picasso once pointed out, all art is a lie; in the storytellers' case, their basic technique is to exaggerate, ornament, and vary for effect. The story they have inherited *is* art, but they hope to make it better. The raw events they pick up and tell about are nothing until they have interpreted them, re-ordered them, improved on them to make a great story.

Writers who understand how a storyteller functions are lucky; they have one of the essential qualifications for their work, because whatever they write—whether it is intended to educate, inform, move, or please—is basically a dramatic tale, and must be so understood. An account of how drug manufacturers use quality control in their work, or of the geography of Afghanistan, must be developed as a story, with consequences for living human beings, if it is to be understood. Writers should be good storytellers; if you are not, you need to listen to and study those who are.

Experience in the theater, and especially acting experience, is likewise invaluable experience for a writer. There are two reasons for this. There is no other place where the nature and structure of drama, and the reactions of audiences, can be learned so well—perhaps no other place where they can really be learned at all. An actor or actress who has faced an audience, has struggled to create a character, has felt the response of playgoers to his or her performance, thereafter has a special, even unique, knowledge. Besides, media writers deal in scenes, in visual effects, in spoken lines. You must be able to conceive your work in a dramatic form, so that it will convey its meaning through visual effects and through the sounds of the human voice. To restrict our comment to one aspect of this matter: very few writers can write good dialogue or narration who have not had to speak it to an audience. You need not have been a good actor or actress; probably you will be a better writer if you have been fairly bad as a performer, for in that case you know how passionately a weak actor will hope for support from the writer's script.

A SENSE OF LANGUAGE

There is a common and most unfortunate notion that written language has somehow become obsolete. Marshall McLuhan cannot be entirely blamed for this idea, although a haphazard reading of his works might well contribute to it. People who work in the media—especially in radio, television, and film—have realized for a long time that they deal in many symbolic languages other than words. They know, for example, that a film script is nothing in itself; it is not intended to be read by a general audience; it has no special significance until it has been translated into a sequence of visual images and sounds. They know that a script for audio production is simply a convenience that permits a group of skilled people to create and arrange meaningful sounds in a sequence. This sort of understanding is foreign to traditionally educated people, who tend to think of the written or printed word as a natural phenomenon ordained by heaven. To them, "writing" with sounds, photographs, animations, and so on, seems unnatural and possibly a little impious. One of those educators so often quoted by news feature writers recently proclaimed that American young people are semiliterate because "they would rather make films" than subject themselves to the hard, relentless demands of the speller and the grammar book.

On the other hand, one of the authors recently conferred with a college student who had given small evidence of literacy. The author pointed out to the student that his paper work, if done by a fifth-grader, might receive a mediocre but passing grade. But the student had a reply, couched in the best recent jargon. "I can't help it," he said. "Culturally, I'm really an oral type."

Our position on this issue may be stated in three propositions. First, there is no question that the new media deal in languages of colors, sound, and forms, and not in written words. The media writer must learn to think and create in these largely nonverbal languages. Second, the first proposition does not mean that written language is obsolete. These new media make necessary a precise, accurate use of language just as the sciences and technology do. A script, to be useful, must convey to director, producers, performers, technicians a series of facts, a sequence of feelings, a number of technical suggestions, in such a way that the writer's intent cannot be misunderstood. Third, the media do deal in spoken language, much of which must have the quality, the movement, the feeling and color of poetry. Such language cannot be improvised or roughed-out; it must be written. Moreover, all of us when we come to the visual and aural media bring with us our experience of written and spoken language. What we have learned from the language of speech and the language of print we gradually translate into pictures and non-verbal sounds.

It is quite possible to make a film, a videotape, or even and audiotape that conveys precise meanings and yet involves no script at all—or at least, no script in the conventional sense. But no one should doubt for a moment that good writing is a key skill in the production of works for the media.

213

A KNOWLEDGE OF THE MEDIA

Anyone who proposes to write for print need have little technical knowledge of the ways in which magazines, newspapers, and books are produced. The basics of print production are fairly simple, and after more than five centuries of printed books they are certainly familiar. The newer media are different. In some ways, they are technically more complex than print; being newer and perhaps more liable to change, the production techniques associated with them are less well known.

How much does a writer have to know about the process of producing a film, a film strip, a video or audio tape? Certainly enough to write a script intelligible to media technicians, and producible. But this is not a complete answer because, as we shall see, many writers for the newer media, in order to exercise control over the end product, themselves become producers.

The answer to our question, then, is this: a writer for the media must know at least enough to be able to speak and write the technical languages of production, in order to communicate with the specialists who will make the script into a finished product. Writers, at this stage, need not know how to use a camera, a tape recorder, or a movieola; need not be able to direct, edit, mix sound, or perform any of the other special tasks involved in production. Ultimately, if the writer continues to make a career in the media, he or she probably will need to learn some or all of these skills.

One of the principal functions of this book is to provide you, a writer, with basic knowledge about production as well as about writing techniques. These are some of the things you need to know:

1. *How a script for a particular kind of production should look, and what the technical jargon used in the script means.* A script for an audio production is not the same as a script for film production is not the same as a slide film script is certainly not the same as a play or short story manuscript.

2. *In general, what happens in the course of a production.* Producing a film does not involve the same routines as producing a videotape. A television production that employs the miniaturized television cameras does not work in the same way as a production using the big studio cameras. At very least, a writer should be able to sit in on any sort of production and understand, in general, what is going on, and why.

3. *The process of editing.* At one time, all radio productions were done live in a studio; all early television was produced in the same way. A script had to play from beginning to end without confusion or error, because there was no way of wiping out mistakes. Since the appearance of audiotape in the late 1940s and the increasing use of film and videotape a few years later, more recent productions have been almost all recorded and then edited into finished form. It is often said that editing is the key technique in filmmaking, and certainly in all of the media it is very impor-

tant. A writer needs to know how the editing process works, and what can be expected of it.

4. *Other specialties.* It is probably not essential for a writer to know much about highly specialized production procedures, such as the mixing of sound, the dubbing of a soundtrack on film, or the process of editing videotape as opposed to editing film. Nevertheless, it is certainly true that you cannot know too much about the media for which you write.

5. *What the media are like.* Many years ago, Marshall McLuhan and Edmund Carpenter wrote an essay called "The New Languages," in which they argued that each new medium of communication *is* a "new language," in the same sense that Mandarin Chinese or English are languages. If this true, they said, then film, for example, has its own vocabulary, its own grammatical structures, its own way of handling information, and the way of film is not at all the way of audiotape. Linguists agree that communicators can say anything that they wish in any language they can master, if they are patient and ingenious enough. It is theoretically possible to discuss astrophysics in the language of the Australian Bushmen, although it probably wouldn't be worth the trouble. Some subjects are undeniably easier to handle in one language than in another. So perhaps the same thing is true of the media. Some subjects can be presented rather easily and effectively in a slide film, but handled only with unnecessary trouble and expense on a videotape.

It follows that an understanding of the various media, their characteristics and uses, is a basic qualification of the media writer. How can you learn about production technique? You can find books in any library that will help you: books on film and television production, books on technical aspects of photography and sound recording, collections of scripts. Then there are schools: many colleges and universities today offer first-rate courses in writing, directing, producing, and performing for the media. Some high schools offer similar studies. "Continuing education" programs for adults occasionally do the same sort of thing.

There is, of course, no substitute for experience. If you can find opportunities to watch productions, and to listen to professionals in the field talk about their work, by all means take them. Such experiences are invaluable to a writer. The real school of experience, however, is the often painful one of watching a script of your own being produced. If you have any pride of authorship at all, it will almost inevitably be outraged in the normal course of a production. The reason is not that producers are stupid, or that performers are incapable of performing, but rather that your concern with the script is not quite the same as theirs; their experience and professional skills may be considerably greater than yours. We advise you, at least until you have built up some experience and skills of your own, to watch, listen, and open your mouth only to ask questions.

THE DISCIPLINE OF WRITING

In a small way, the discipline of writing is a perennial topic of discussion among people who are interested in the craft. We offer some generalizations, with the customary warning that they should be believed in moderation. They are these. People who "want to be writers" usually wait until they "have time." Amateurs wait for some great idea to strike them. Professionals, and people who wish to be professionals, write regularly, maintaining a suitable schedule; but their specific schedules and methods vary with the individual.

There are people who write best at three in the morning, and others who can barely function until ten in the morning. There are people who can work at writing for ten or twelve hours a day, and others for whom three or four hours is the limit. Some writers regularly turn out five thousand or more words a day, and others never get to the thousand word mark. Many writers can produce good first-draft copy on a typewriter; others are better off with a pencil and a stack of copy paper.

How many hours a day you write, or how much copy you need to produce, depends more on the kind of writing you do than any other factor. Thirty and more years ago, the pulp magazines offered an active market to writers. They used an enormous amount of fiction, and some nonfiction, and they were prepared to buy this material from anyone who could supply it; whether the writer was young or old, man or woman, established or new, didn't much matter. Probably the average price paid by the pulps was one cent a word; many magazines paid less, a few paid more, but in the main, a 5,000-word short story brought in $50.00. Even in those days that wasn't much, and the really successful pulp writers turned out a million words a year or more. That meant nearly 3,000 words a day, week in and week out. It also meant long working hours for the writer.

On the other hand, many extremely successful writers, from Hemingway to Kurt Vonnegut, have regarded a day that saw the production of five or six hundred new words as a very satisfactory one.

It seems appropriate, toward the end of this discussion on the writer's qualifications, to repeat an anecdote once told about Sinclair Lewis. Lewis, then at the height of his fame as a novelist, accepted an invitation to lecture on a university campus. He drew a large crowd of eager young people, most of them with the ambition to write. Lewis looked them over carefully. "Before I begin my lecture," he said, "I want to ask you one question. How many of you here want to be writers?"

Two or three hundred hands went up.

"Then," said Lewis, "what are you doing here? Why don't you go home and write?"

appendix B
Glossary of Terms
a Writer Should
Understand

ANSWER PRINT: The first print combining all the elements—visual track, sound track, music track, effects track—into one print for review by the producer for his or her approval or disapproval based on color and sound quality. If this print is acceptable the final prints are made.

BACKGROUND MUSIC OR SOUND: Music or sound subdued for background presence over the picture. Abbreviation for this is MUSIC IN B.G. (B.G. means background.)

BEAT: A pause between lines of dialogue to help heighten a new thought or feeling.

BLIMP: Soundproof cover in which the camera is enclosed to prevent the noise of its mechanism from being picked up by the recording microphone during shooting.

BLOOP: A popping or other nuisance sound over an edit splice in the film. A small opaque patch placed over the splice in the sound track smothers this noise.

BOOM: Crane-like device for suspending the recording microphone in mid-air and moving it from one position to another during shooting.

BRIDGING SHOT: Shot to bridge a jump in time or any other break in continuity.

CEL[L]: A rectangular piece of transparent celluloid holding one section of a drawing required in the making of an animated cartoon. Several cells are needed to complete the drawing, then these cells are placed one on top of the other.

CELLULOSE ACETATE: The flexible transparent plastic used since 1950 in the making of cinematograph film.

CELLULOSE NITRATE: Flexible transparent plastic, known also as celluloid, used before 1951 for the manufacture of standard cinematograph film, despite its high inflammability, because of its resistance to wear and tear.

CHANNEL: A recording and reproducing system used both as an input and output of electronic transmissions.

CLAPPER: Pair of boards hinged at one end

that are banged together in view of the camera at the beginning of a take to enable the sound-cutting print and the picture-cutting print to be synchronized on editing. The "clapper sound" appears as a pronounced fluctuation on the sound track, and then is related to the first frame in the picture showing the boards in contact. The name of the production, director, camera person, client, and writer are also chalked in on the clapper board, which has spaces for each, along with the "take number," the date of day's shooting, a playback date if the production is on videotape, and the production number.

CLOSED CIRCUIT: A television system whose signal is not broadcast but fed to the receiver by a cable, for a limited audience, usually within the same complex or building from which the signal is being sent. Also sent from owned and operated commercial stations so that affiliated stations can use network pieces supplied to them through a closed-circuit network feed, on local news shows.

CONFORMING: Matching and editing the master color negative with the edited black and white workprint to produce a conformed master negative. This process includes matching all elements, sound and music tracks, as well.

CONTACT PRINT: A print made from a master film (usually, of course, a negative) by the process of running the two lengths of film in contact with each other through the printer.

CONTRAST: From darkest to lightest part of an image.

CRANE SHOT: Moving shot taken by the camera on a specially constructed crane.

CREEPING TITLE: Title that moves slowly upward on the screen as it is being read.

DEPTH OF FOCUS: The range to which a lens will clearly focus near and distant objects at the same time.

DOUBLE SYSTEM: Separate tracks for visual and sound.

EFFECTS TRACK: Sound track of sound effects besides speech, music, and narration or dialogue.

EMULSION: Gelatin, containing silver bromide or silver chloride in suspension, with which film is coated in order to make it sensitive to the action of light.

ESTABLISHING SHOT: A long shot that introduces a scene.

EXCITER LAMP: Lamp in sound-head of projector that shines through the sound track onto the photo-electric cell.

EXPOSURE: Length of time a single frame of film in the camera is exposed to the action of light in shooting.

EXTERIOR: Term that means a scene taking place outdoors. Abbreviation is EXT.

FRAME: One of a series of single transparent photographs on a length of film.

INTERIOR: Term which means a scene that takes place inside. Abbreviation is INT.

LIBRARY SHOT: A stock shot, purchased or saved, that has been used on other films but is suitable to current production. War pictures used stock shots often.

MAGAZINE: Box or container in cinematograph camera or projector for holding the roll or spool of film.

MAGNETIC TAPE: A plastic tape coated with ferric oxide powder which, on being run through a variable magnetic field, can be made to register in a permanent form the impulses necessary for the reproduction of electronically produced sounds and pictures.

MAGNETIC TRACK: The sound track of a film recorded on magnetic tape, either separate from the picture film, or (in the case of striped film) on the picture film itself. (See *Optical Track, Striped Film.*)

MIX: 1 (Optical). Gradual merging of the end of one shot into the beginning of the next, produced by the superimposition of a fade-out onto a fade-in of equal length. 2 (Sound). Combining the sounds of several sound tracks for the purpose of re-recording them onto a new track.

MONTAGE: A creative juxtaposing of shots which indicates a succession of time and story in a very short period of time, usually running less than a minute in length.

MOVIEOLA: An editing device that projects film and reproduces sound on a small viewer; cuts can be made and the film re-wound to pass through the viewer again to see and hear how the edit works.

OPTICAL: Any device carried out by the optical department of a laboratory, requiring the use of the optical printer, such as a fade, dissolve, wipe, or other special effect.

OPTICAL TRACK: A sound track produced by the action of a variable light source on a light-sensitive photographic emulsion. (See *Magnetic Track.*)

PANCHROMATIC FILM: Photographic film sensitive to all colors.

PLAYBACK: Playing back a sound track during recording or shooting.

POSITIVE: Film in which the tone values of the picture correspond to those of the actual scene it represents, the dark parts of the scene appearing dark in the picture, and the light parts appearing light.

RAW STOCK: Sensitized film that has not been exposed or processed.

REACTION SHOT: A shot showing the reaction of a character in a film to something said or done in the immediately preceding shot.

REDUCTION PRINT: A print of smaller gauge than the master print from which it is made (for example, a 16mm print made from a 35mm negative). The size of the image is reduced optically to the size of the frame on the smaller gauge.

REVERSAL FILM: Film made for use in cameras which, when processed, becomes a positive print ready for projection.

ROUGH CUT: The first edited cut of assembled footage. A number of cuts may follow until the final cut is approved.

RUSHES: Prints of takes made immediately after a day's shooting so that they can be viewed by the director and other members of the crew either the day of shooting or the day after.

SHOOTING SCHEDULE: Film script in which the shots are arranged, not in the order in which they will finally appear, but in the most convenient order for shooting.

SINGLE SYSTEM: The combining of visual and sound on one film track.

SOUND TRACK: The strip running along one side of the film in which sound is recorded either magnetically or optically by a light source.

SPECIAL EFFECT: Any effect introduced into a film after shooting and during laboratory processing, e.g. mix, wipe, etc.

STOP-ACTION CAMERA: Camera that can expose single frames of film in successive order. Used in time-lapse sequences.

STRIPED FILM: Raw film stock that has magnetic striping down one side to record sound. Also called single system film.

SYNCHRONIZE: Sound track and visual roll moving at the same time so that both sound and visual appear natural.

TAKE: Single recording of a shot made during production. (Usually several takes of a shot are made, the best one being selected for inclusion in the completed film.)

TECHNICOLOR: A color process, involving the production in a special camera of three separate negatives during shooting, registering the blue, green, and red elements of the scene respectively, and the making of color prints by means of matrices made (through intermediary separation positives) from these negatives.

TIME-LAPSE CINEMATOGRAPHY: Very accelerated motion picture photography to show slow process, such as the growth of a plant or a complete sunrise to sunset sequence.

TRAILER: Very short film of two or three minutes' duration shown for publicity purposes or previewing a soon to be shown or released motion picture, documentary, or television show; especially, such a film composed of extracts from a longer film, and shown beforehand to advertise it.

WILD TRACK: Sound track recorded independently of any picture with which it may subsequently be combined.

WIPE: Technical effect "wiping" away one shot to reveal another.

appendix C
A Selling Proposal

It's common for a film production company to spend a few dollars for a writer to develop what is called a selling proposal. The company writes it off as necessary speculation to generate new business and, if a client buys the concept, the writer stands to make more money as the person who will write the treatment and script. The following is an example of such a proposal. It was written for a Chicago-based industrial and educational film company, *Phase 5 Productions*.

Package Description for
INTREPID BIRDMAN
Series of six films on
PROMOTING GENERAL AVIATION SAFETY

For openers 97 percent of the accidents involving private planes shouldn't happen. The problem is there are Sunday drivers on the streets and Sunday drivers in the skies. It's the ones in the skies who blemish the record of good pilots and plane manufacturers. This is what I suggest:

A character, a Walter Mitty type possibly played by William Windom who imagines himself in all sorts of adventurous situations—and an animated character who sits anywhere—on the wing tips, on top of the cowling, the tail, on Mitty's shoulders, an alter ego, a subconscience who can stop action, turn things around, right wrongs, etc.

The Mitty character in flying jacket, white scarf dashing around his neck, goggles, sees himself starring in Casablanca on a desolate runway with the fog

221

hanging over the air, and the mysterious young woman in red floating out of his arms. Our Mitty climbs aboard his plane and takes off in a peasoup where no mortal ever flies or tries.

Just as he's about to take off, our animated character calls for the camera to pan over to him, and before our Mitty can crack himself up, the plane goes back down. Mitty finds himself outside again in the arms of his lover and we see a sign which says *Grounded for the Night*.

Then just as we move out, and see Mitty and girl in silhouette, our animated character—INTREPID BIRDMAN—comes on screen and the instructional points of the story's beginning, middle, and end continue to be made. Maybe this film deals with instrumentation and navigation or PLANE COMMON SENSE.

Another film deals with take offs and landings. This time Mitty thinks of himself as a Cary Grant character in North by Northwest. All the Hitchcockian terror abounds. The chase is on and poor Mitty is tormented by a plane which takes off and lands perilously close to him, and all the wrong way.

Intrepid Birdman tries grabbing Mitty away from the prop wash. Just in time. Next our super hero grabs the plane. It stops. And in a few sequences Mitty has captured the pilot, handed him over to the authorities and then triumphantly turns around from the cockpit and says, "This my friend is how you take-off." The instructional points of the story continue being developed.

(The Mitty character can be named anything—the idea is that he is a dreamer, an adventurer but needs Intrepid Birdman to bring him back to reality.)

The animated character can be a logo for the plane manufacturer and the collateral benefits—print ads, trademark, etc., are infinitesimal.

This gives us a chance to do some super stuff with serious overtones always present. But instead of hitting people over the head with statistics and other garbage let's give them a "mini-movie" with a continuing character who is the dreamer, the adventurer, the leader, really all the ingredients that we ascribe to people who fly.

appendix D
A Treatment
for a
Television Special

Every year between Thanksgiving and the middle of December the television networks run "Christmas Specials." So do major department stores, but the merchandise is a little different. The ones the networks wrap come in all types, from journeys back into Christmas history, to variety specials, to dramas. Some are scary, some are coated with suspense (excluding monsters and other things that go bump in the night); others laced with humanism, morality, sadness, or humor are dramas that end happily. The following treatment for a Christmas television special falls into the last category and has a bit of an O'Henry twist to it.

THE NIGHT SANTA CLAUS
HELD UP CHRISTMAS
Story for a TV Special

You probably have never heard of Christmas City, Iowa. Very few people have. It's about 100 miles south of Des Moines, and, if you're travelling on the two lane highway leading to Christmas City at night, you'll pass it up without even knowing you've gone through. The only time Christmas City has its street lights on after dark is on Christmas Eve. Then all the houses in town, ten of them, plus all the stores, that means DALPETER'S BANK, MCCITRICH'S DRUGSTORE, STONEHABER'S GAS STATION, CULDANK'S BARBERSHOP and STEIN'S DEPARTMENT STORE, keep their lights on so that SANTA CLAUS, EVERETTE NORSON in real life, can see where he's going. Everett has a problem with night vision. It's hard for him to see in the dark.

As I said, Christmas City is one of those small unincorporated towns you drive through on the way to somewhere else . . .

The Story . . .

On this particular Christmas Eve, EVERETTE NORSON is in nearby Farmington Hospital nursing a bad case of rheumatism. Now, he's given his word he'll be bringing his sleigh through Christmas City that evening, but if all the others could see him writhing in pain the way nurse HOPKINS is watching, they'd all agree the town has a better chance meeting a Martian than hearing ole Everette as Santa Claus, "ho-ho-ho-ing" against the moonlight.

Walter Dalpeter, the banker, is already on his fourth beer as is Harry Culdank, the barber, Leo Stein, the department store owner, Calvin McCitrich, the town druggist, and Carl Stonehaber, who owns the PHILLIPS 66 Service Station. For the last 20 years all these men, the pillars of the community, have started off Christmas Eve the same way, a little smashed.

Culdank, who is pretty good at the piano, at least with his right hand, and Stonehaber not so bad as a tenor, pull out the old music sheets from inside the piano bench at DUKASIS' BAR TAVERN, and start leading the rest in song.

A train stops once a week unloading fertilizer. It happens that on Christmas Eve, an unscheduled box of fertilizer falls out of an open freight car, passing slowly through town, and a few moments later, a white scraggly bearded rosy cheeked, puffy bellied old man lifts himself out of the box marked in bold letters: KARNITZ FERTILIZER, brushes himself off clean, and looks around.

ARTHUR "WHIFFY" RAFFERTY, wearing a bright red ski jacket he found rummaging through garbage a few years ago during a train strike in Indiana, and a red stocking cap pulled over his head and ears, wipes drowsiness off his face, picks up his knapsack, swings it over his shoulders, and soon disappears in the darkness, heading toward those town lights he sees.

The first building he passes is a COUNTY ORPHANAGE which currently houses 15 youngsters from nearby towns.

One of them is a sparkling little 10 year old imp with a mop of strawberry blond hair that falls down her face and over her eyes. Her name is Kimberly, they think. Doesn't have a last name. And nearly everyone calls her POOLY, because the way her hair falls over her eyes, she looks like a pooly dog.

Pooly is on the second floor peering out of a window telling her friend, next to her, who thinks Santa Claus is for babies, that she knows Santa is going to show up.

But her friend teases her and leaves Pooly alone at the window.

Pretty soon she sees someone walking up toward the side of the Orphanage. And, as soon as the figure is touched by the moonlight, Pooly's eyes pop. Santa Claus!

And when she runs to the opposite side of the second floor and peeks out a side window, the next thing she sees is Santa Claus rummaging through the garbage, picking out a half eaten banana, and chomping into it with absolute abandonment.

Pooly is mystified by the sight of Santa, and just as bewildered by Santa's peculiar eating habits. In her excitement she accidently leans too far and bumps her head on the windowsill, which jolts Whiffy, who lifts his head up, squints, and then scurries off into the night again.

Pooly grabs her leggin's, coat, scarf, cap, and boots, sneaks out of the orphanage and within minutes is scampering after this strange Santa who feeds on bananas.

Meantime ole' Whiffy slips into town unnoticed and stops in front of the bank with a huge picture of the man who owns it stuck publicly enough on the front window. Whiffy studies the face and the words above and below it:

DALPETER FOR MAYOR

It's a cold night, and Whiffy's beating his chest to keep warm. The light coming from the tavern offers some escape, no matter how temporary. Not too many people take too kindly to hoboes who are looking for free handouts, even during the Christmas Holidays, but he tightens the collar of his bright red ski jacket, and holds it steady as he walks toward the place.

Inside Dalpeter and the others are sloshing down a few more beers and making the floor a mess with peanut shells.

Dalpeter's the first to see the figure leaning in the doorway.

"Hal-lay-lu-jah: What did I tell you boys. Ole Norson wouldn't let the kids down!"

What he sees through his fuzzy vision is Santa, which of course is Norson in his costume, which of course isn't Norson, but a bewildered, and then bemused Whiffy Rafferty.

"Have a beer ole' buddy before you get your reindeer out."

A mug slides across the counter.

Then a few seconds later, the keys to the bank!

"Toys are in the same place as last year," Dalpeter tells him. "Ho-ho-ho," Dalpeter bellows.

"Ho-ho-ho," Whiffy snorts in his beer, then grabs the keys, bows politely, and races to a gold mine, talking to himself all the way over.

"Whiffy, you got yourself the keys to Fort Knox!"

First he walks around, surreptitiously to the back of the bank until it dawns on him that whoever Norson is has always used the front, so why shouldn't he.

His hands and fingers are trembling. "Now get a hold of yourself, Whiffy. These good people are giving you a gift of their bank, least you c'n do is open up the darn door."

When he walks in his eyes pan the emptiness, and then lock in at the vault. "Man says the same place as last year. Must be the vault."

Sure enough it is. The bag of toys are there, and so are stacks of bills. Ones, fives, tens, twenties, fifties, and hundreds.

"M e r r i i i e e e e e e Christmas!"

After he stuffs as much money as he can into the sack full of toys, he stuffs his own sack in, closes the vault. Pets a cat that scares the heck out of him first when he rubs by his legs, and then walks out, locking the door, and leaving town.

Followed by another pair of eyes, Pooly's, who has watched it all through a side window.

Pooly knows every short cut in town and arrives at a cross road just as Whiffy trundles up.

"Hi Santa!"

Whiffy freezes in his tracks.

"I knew you were coming. The other kids were lying when they said you wouldn't be."

"Well, now, you can just run home and tell your mama and your papa and your brothers and yours sisters that you saw Ole Santa."

"I don't have a mama and a papa. I live in that orphanage, the one you took a banana out of the garbage can from. That one."

"Great," Whiffy mutters.

"How come you going this way? This isn't the right way to all the houses."

"Kid? The right way *is* this way 'cause this way is the way outta town."

Then he explains to Pooly that he's left a few of his reindeer back in Des Moines and he's got to go there and pick them up. But he's not so prepared for the next question.

"What's the money for?"

"What money???"

"Money you took outta the bank with you."

"Hmmm?"

"Money in your bag."

"Money? Right. That money. Uh . . . pay off the elves, kid—and keep the wolves away from the door."

Now Pooly's tugging on his sleeves. "Orphanage is over there, remember?"

Two of the most precious doleful eyes look up at him, and even Whiffy's heart begins melting.

So he promises one quick stop at the orphanage. Figures no one's out looking for him anyway since he is this 'Norson' fella the men at the tavern were talking about anyway.

Pooly pushes him through a back door, and suddenly all the lights in the orphanage snap on, and Whiffy (alias Santa) is surrounded by a pack of astonished children.

The mistress of the house thanks 'Mr. Norson' privately, makes him some hot tea, and then sends him off with a kiss on his cheek. "Everette?" She muses. "That beard of yours is just like real."

Off Whiffy heads again, and this time makes it to the train depot only to be stopped by Pooly.

"Kid? You got jets in your pants? I ain't never seen anybody move as fast as you before."

"What about the other houses?"

Once again, Whiffy is heading back to town, making stop after stop, dropping toys on doorsteps, getting kissed by townspeople at the front porch who offer him a gift in return, and, "Everette? What would we ever do without you."

A few hours later, Whiffy heads back to the depot, with Pooly tagging right along.

Maybe it's the fact that Whiffy never knew his parents, the way all the kids were hanging all over him back in town, the way everybody made him feel like a somebody, a feeling hoboes rarely have, but when he sees her again, he sits Pooly down and begins talking to her.

And the more he talks to her and the more he stares in those doleful eyes, the more guilt attacks his heart.

"Do elves need that much money, Santa?"

"Well, inflation has hit the North Pole, too."

"I betcha Mister Dalpeter will give you lots more if you need it."

Whiffy chokes. "You know Dalpeter?"

"Uh huh. The orphanage building is on the farm Mister Dalpeter use to own, and then he sold it to the county so they could have a place for kids like me."

Whiffy sighs deeply at the sack with all that green stuff stuffed inside.

Somehow he has the feeling those doleful eyes of Pooly's are looking right through him.

"How well did you know Mister Dalpeter?"

"Pretty good. He stops by every once in a while. And I also know Mister Norson but when I tug at his beard like this," she does, "it falls off, and yours doesn't so I know you're not Mister Norson. You just gotta be Mister Santa Claus."

"Would that make you happy if I told you that I was?"

"Uh huh. Very happy." She snuggles up next to him.

A few hours later Whiffy's back at the bank. He tells Pooly to keep staring at the north star because he expects his reindeer from Des Moines to be landing any minute, probably out looking for him by now.

"You just keeping looking up. I'll be right back."

Whiffy enters the bank again, puts the money back in the vault, says goodbye to retirement fit for a king, and walks back outdoors.

"See 'em yet?"

"Oh yes. They passed by while you were away."

One more stop. The Tavern where Dalpeter lies fast asleep. Whiffy places the bank's keys in his pocket, and then notices a note addressed to Norson. In it a ten dollar bill. Whiffy figures taking it isn't stealing since he *did* work for it. And leaves the same way he came in. On his way from someplace to somewhere.

Pooly's very teary eyed when she says goodbye to "Santa," and Whiffy's got to blow his nose, too, and wipe the tears away from his cheeks.

He grabs her up in his arms, squeezes her one more time real strong, watches her close the door to the orphanage, and then disappears back into the night.

The day after Christmas Everette Norson limps into the bank. Dalpeter is glowing. "Norson, you have never, I mean never, been as good as you were Christmas Eve."

"Dalpeter, what are you talking about?"

"I mean, everybody in this town has been saying you were one terrific Santa Claus."

And by the people coming up to him and slapping him on the back like McCitrich, the druggist, and Culdank, the barber, and Stein of the department store, Norson is flabbergasted.

"Now wait a minute. What are you talking about. I came in here to tell you I was sorry I couldn't make it Christmas Eve. Been in the Farmington Hospital with my darn rheumatism."

"Are you saying that wasn't you on Christmas Eve?"

"Yes sir. I'm saying that. I was in bed with a heating blanket on. Tried calling you but the phone lines were still down from the storm."

Every face in the bank registers the same expression: "Well, then, who was it?"

And each face slowly forms the same conclusion—Santa Claus, himself, in the flesh?????

That moment inside a freight car travelling somewhere north, Whiffy sits against a pile of hay, stirring some hot tea, and stretching his legs out. He's humming to himself.

Whiffy's pleased, sighs, smiles to himself, and then closes his eyes to sleep.

FADE OUT . . .

appendix E
A Story Concept

Some ideas for film and television, fiction and nonfiction, are sold on two-page outlines or even on an oral presentation to a producer. But even if the story is presented on just a few pages, the story itself is developed enough to whet the appetite of the buyer(s) and show them the potential for a powerful, exciting drama or documentary.

The following example is a complete story concept. The paucity of pages doesn't detract from the fact that the *story* stands out with action adventure potential and inherent jeopardy.

SUNBURST
Story Line by Paul Max Rubenstein

What would happen if the earth had 72 hours of sunlight left . . .

The year is sometime in the future. The earth's resources have been depleted. The only source of energy that gives heat to our planet is the SUN.

Until . . .

GORMAN SPACE COMMUNICATIONS CENTER, the most technically elaborate facility in the world which monitors every inch of the Sun's fireball.

The huge UPDATE SCREEN suddenly posts bright ORANGE WARNING LIGHTS.

Activity on the Sun is causing increased disturbances. These have been tracked for months. But not what is being read from the computers now.

The same disturbances are being recorded inside a SPACE ORBITING LABORATORY which circles around COLONY AMERICAS, a domed space village, completed recently by NASA. Again the orange warning lights flicker on their screen, too, sending scientists in a scramble to punch in all computers checking for some error. Some mistake.

2100 Hours. The bursts of gases spewing from the Sun's corona are now pouring violent hues which can be seen across space.

SUNBURSTS.

By midnight, all the computers both on earth and in our space-orbiting laboratories reach the same conclusion. The Sun is exploding. Going dark. The Sun which has warmed the earth and nurtured all living things on its energy for billions of years is coming to an end.

PROFESSOR JOSHUA ALFRED COLES, an eminent astronomer and solar specialist, can only surmise that something is "sucking" energy from the other side of the sun. Some force.

Computers spew out new times . . . 124 hours . . . updates to 100 hours . . . 80 hours . . . and now 72 hours left until the Sun burns itself out.

Something is draining the helium which keeps the star alive.

72 hours to launch a manned solar probe from space and effect a landing on the Sun's side our tracking capabilities can't see.

72 hours to discover who or what is reducing the Sun to what it was like when it was formed billions of years ago.

appendix F
A Television
Pilot Script

In the past it was relatively rare for an unknown writer to make a television pilot sale unless that person first brought in a seasoned television writer with substantial credits to participate in the initial development. But times have changed and recently networks have begun recruiting ideas for television series from outside the normal channels. Because of this, independent companies are sometimes formed with the expressed intention of trying their luck at a pilot sale.

The following half-hour sitcom television pilot is an example of such a venture. We have included the complete script in this section for two reasons: One, because we think it is a good first draft, recognizing the fact that it also needs some polishing. Two, because new writers and development companies who are signators of the Writers Guild should be encouraged to create properties in a climate that allows outsiders to come in.

BUMSTEERS was developed by the Three Marketeers, a midwest based independent television company.

BUMSTEERS

ALAN SCHILLER

Principal owner of Schiller and Schiller—stock brokers. There's really no second Schiller but Alan felt that you must have at least two names on a business to make a go of it.

A widower with four children ages 10 to 16, the 39 year old Alan who looks much younger, sometimes forgets to take his kitchen apron off when he opens up the office in the morning.

Independent, feisty and always getting himself fixed up by well meaning friends, he'll sometimes bring his oldest son along on dates when he wants to cut the evening short.

MRS. MARION MACKENZIE

Big mouth—soft heart. One of the most superstitious people in the world. Always asks every doctor who walks in for one "free question." Loves Alan like a son since she has three daughters, all married. And is loved by everyone who walks in. A mother to Alan and den mother to the office.

ANTHONY J. CARNUZZI

Short, stocky, hands always in jacket pocket like Napoleon; unlike Napoleon his is there to make sure his checkbook and wallet are safe.

He pontificates, because he sits on a cushion for his hemrroids. (sic)

TONY CARNUZZI, JR.

Frail, meek looking. Nice, actually cuddly. Looks younger than he is. Let's say he is in his early 30's, but you could almost mistake him for a teenager.

FRANK GITTLEMAN

Very big. Big, and tall, and raspy voiced. Constantly chews on a cigar. If England needed another Churchill they could call on Frank. Anything to sell a stock. And he would.

He is a garish dresser. Always compliments himself on the way he dresses because no one else does. Hyper salesman. Very frenetic. He wants the brokers not only to sell stocks but to get into insurance, tax shelters, investments. Once Frank forgot to take out his loose change, mostly in fives and tens from his jeans he wears on the weekends, and they were washed by mistake. He was accused of "laundering money."

VIVIAN WOLANSKY ("APPLE ANNIE")

Nicknamed "Apple Annie" by the office because that's what she brings in. Apples, stale cookies, week old sponge cake. "Do you think I want to eat this stuff. Why should I? I'll give it to you." In fact everything Apple Annie wears looks stale. A four dollar sweater off the rack of K-Mart which she complains doesn't wear right. Shoes from Kinney—and they're seconds. Once on Christmas Eve while she was standing for a bus five people walked over to her and handed her money. Crinkled dollar bills they pressed into her palm. Before she could object her benefactors split.

It's too bad. Because at 60 Apple Annie is worth around half a million dollars. It's just that dressing and eating well are low on her list.

EVELYN BAUM ("EVE")

There is nothing Evelyn Baum has offered a man that has ever been refused . . .

She is the Eve of the Twentieth Century. She has left her teeth marks on more than just apples.

Evelyn walks . . . let's put it this way, when Evelyn walks a head that doesn't turn in her direction belongs to a dead body.

Currently she's running a service called "Electra" where people send away for horoscopes. But these horoscopes are X-rated.

DONALD

There's rich—and then there's rich. Donald is rich. Once when Donald was getting ready to leave for the night he cleared off his desk and tossed into his garbage can along with everything else a check for six thousand dollars made payable to him. Mrs. McKenzie found it the next day looking for a trade that Donald also tossed out by mistake.

When Donald was younger nobody ever wanted to play baseball with him because he wasn't that good. So when Donald grew up he used part of his inheritance to buy into a National Football League franchise. Now he doesn't have to worry about finding someone to play with him.

He also happens to hold the United States title of Sports Trivia champion.

He will tell you what Irving "Lefty Shrimp" Gomez batted for the New Orleans Creoles in 1922. He will also tell you Irving "Lefty Shrimp" Gomez wasn't really his name. Irving "Lefty Shrimp" Gomez's real name was Titus "Banana Nose" Morton.

RALPH BONASIS

Loud, boisterous, optimistic, energetic, athletic, always on the run. His voice is as thick as his neck. He can stand on his head for five minutes but then all the loose change he jingles in his pockets falls out.

Every time Ralph sees a trade go up on the board he calls it out like a sportscaster doing color commentary for a football game. That's what Ralph should have been—a coach.

But he chose the law instead. Ralph defends the defenseless. The flagrantly guilty murderers, hit and run drivers, molesters.

Sometimes when he's in a rush to a trial but has to stop off at the office to trade he will bring in one of the defenseless with him.

He will even practice his summation on the staff during a slow period in the office. Usually the verdict is "guilty."

And his memory . . . his acquittal rate may be low but his memory is fantastic. He can remember the price of every stock he has purchased since he has been buying.

His brain is a digital computer. He quotes prices faster than they appear on the closed circuit screens. As a matter of fact he *was* the office's screen once when the machines conked out. Ralph got up on a chair and began quoting prices and highs and lows until the screen could be fixed.

DAVID

Donald's leg man. A tireless worker with a relentless amount of energy. Incredible because he really is Donald's leg man and he really has one leg shorter than the other and every morning he really does jog five miles and he jokes that he runs on the side of a hill to even things out.

You know the joke about Sam who knows everybody—Presidents and Popes? David does! The President has slept over at David and Ruthie's home.

When David flies to Washington it's because the President wants to see him. David is also a Russian scholar. He knows the language fluently; reads it fluently, writes it fluently, has published in Russian, a feat few other Americans share—and impresses his clients most of whom are affluent.

The President calls David so many times during the week that he has recorded "Hail to the Chief" on a cassette and puts it on when the operator says, "The President is calling."

With Donald's money and David's mind the combination is unbeatable.

SEYMOUR MOSHEN AND LILLIAN MOSHEN

The first and probably only mother and son stock buying team.

Seymour who is 46 still lives with Lillian who is 66. He is the neatest, fussiest person you can imagine second to his mother who takes a little hankie and cleans off a chair before sitting even though her son, Seymour, already has taken his little portable brush out of his pocket and swept clean, much like an umpire cleaning home-plate.

Seymour is so particular he arranges all his money with the President's picture up.

TEASE

FADE IN:

INT. ALAN SCHILLER'S BROKERAGE OFFICE—DAY

A hundred year old former bank building, partially restored. Alan occupies the first floor. On the second floor is a Summer Youth Employment Agency, an accountant's office, Electrolysis by appointment only, and Marvelous Comics, a two room office specializing in buying and selling rare comic books.

As you walk into the first floor ALAN SCHILLER'S desk is in the center. He is in his 30's, a trim, boyish friendly face . . . A widower with four sons whose sense of humor and hope just won't give up. MRS. MARION MACKENZIE, 50's, has the desk next to him. She's like a mother to Alan and den mother to everyone else.

BEN POMERANTZ, 70's, works in the backroom. Occasionally he walks into the front office. Mostly his presence is known through the intercom.

Then there's DONALD, 30's or 40's, who inherited a million dollars from his parents, graduated law school, gave that up to become a part-time broker, and owns an interest in a National Football League franchise.

The other part-time broker is DAVID, 40's, an MA in History and Slavic languages. He helped elect a United States President who slept in his house and commutes often to Washington D.C., to advise his Chief on foreign policy.

And MORRY GORDON, the accountant who has his one-man office upstairs of the brokerage firm. He is also a client who is more like an uncle to Alan, and has a solution for everything.

ANGLE FAVORING

DR. MILES NELSON walking up to MRS. MACKENZIE. He is a psychiatrist and more than once he has said he needs his head examined doing business here.

> DR. NELSON
>
> I'm really in a hurry. Just tell Alan I needed to see him for a few seconds.
>
> MRS. MACKENZIE
>
> Just one question, doctor?
>
> DR. NELSON
>
> It's always just 'one free question' Mrs. Mackenzie.
>
> (beat)
>
> My friend Darik, the orthopedic man, you hit for at least two back questions a week.
>
> (beat)
>
> Dr. Sanders says he gets one gum and one root canal question a week—
>
> (beat)
>
> Burton the Radiologist you hit for a lung question and a colon question and he has to draw you pictures yet—
>
> (beside himself)
>
> Okay, Mrs. Mackenzie—you get one head question—
>
> MRS. MACKENZIE
>
> My six year old grandson still tinkles in his pants.
>
> DR. NELSON
>
> So tell him unlike plants, pants don't grow.
>
> (beat)
>
> You don't have to water them.

ANOTHER ANGLE FAVORING

A CANNONBALL MESSENGER who comes in the office to deliver documents that Alan impatiently waits for—they are merger papers with the large downtown Chicago investment firm of CARNUZZI, SCHWARTZ, O'MALLEY, and CARNUZZI.

Cannonball which prides itself on speedy deliveries is represented by an old man who looks like he is 122 and talks so slowly that it takes an equal amount of years to get the sentence out.

                    MESSENGER

          C a n n o n B a a a a a l l l l l ...
          E x p r e ... s s s s s s sssss
          (beat)
          S i g n r i g h t o v e r ...

He runs out of breath before he can get the word "here" out.

                    ALAN

          (stammering excitedly)
          These are the merger papers!

                    MRS. MACKENZIE

          (holding up the old man)
          Sign the papers, I'll give him mouth to mouth!

FADE OUT:

                    END TEASE

FADE IN:

INT. THE NEW YORK STOCK EXCHANGE—FLASHBACK SIX MONTHS BEFORE

Mid-day, lots of trading. Men and women hurrying about. We hear more of the commotion than we see it. And someone else is doing a "live" remote for a local radio station located in a suburb of Chicago.

                    ALAN SCHILLER

          Hi, this is Alan Schiller broadcasting to you live from the New York
          Stock Exchange.

We PULLBACK to see ALAN SCHILLER broadcasting live all right—inside a pay telephone booth looking down at some wire copy.

                    ALAN (CONT'D)

          ... The Noon Dow Jones Averages ... Endicott Copper up ...

CUT TO:

EXT. JET PLANE—DAY

Streaking across the sky from New York back to Chicago.

CUT TO:

INT. SCHILLER AND SCHILLER STOCK BROKERAGE—DAY

A small cramped one man stock brokerage office. The place is a mess. Nothing is filed. Books are stacked at one corner of the room. THREE OLD MEN from the Convalescent Home across the street are stacked at another corner of the room, sleeping.

We see ALAN standing on a stool looking at an early afternoon edition of the newspaper and copying the latest stock quotes down on a blackboard which lists the well known stocks.

ALAN is announcing the old quotes to what looks, from his POV, a circle of listeners . . . but when we PULL BACK all we see is one customer, MORRY GORDON, who often comes in to kibbitz with Alan.

                                  ALAN

Commercial Airlines is up an eighth.

                                  MORRY

I should hope it's up more than an eighth. That's a stock you really hope should take off!

                                  ALAN

AT&T is up a quarter.

                                  MORRY

My quarter too probably.

(beat)

That pay phone outside keeps stealing my money.

(beat)

Why doesn't the phone company make the pay phones like slot machines. They take enough of our money anyway, they should at least give odds for an occasional jackpot.

                                  ALAN

And WYCO Jeans announces a split.

                                  MORRY

Yes, because my wife who doesn't belong in a pair, bought a pair!

                                  ALAN

Morry, what's the use. I can't keep up this charade any more. How am I going to compete with all these big firms moving in.

(beat)

I wanted to be a small broker not a lot broker!

(beat)

My two part-time salesmen are talking like they're going to leave all together.

                                  MORRY

Alan, I know, I know. But you're still new. You've been here, what? A year? My brother when he started his automobile agency, if it weren't for his family, all his cousins, aunts and uncles who bought the same cars from him, he would have gone broke.

(beat)

Only problem is every time he has a party people keep getting into the wrong cars when they leave.

ALAN looks at his watch and realizes that he is late for his noon stock report which he gives at a radio station across the street on the second floor on top of the theatre. So he asks his temporary secretary to finish writing the quotes.

MRS. NEIBERT

But I'm allergic to . . .

FLIP SCREEN

INT. RADIO STATION—A FEW MINUTES LATER

ALAN inside a small studio talking into a desk mike . . .

ALAN

Industries up for a new Mid-day high of thirteen point five nine.

As he leaves the door, the GENERAL MANAGER stops him.

GENERAL MANAGER

Good job at the New York Stock Exchange last week, Alan . . . I was thinking maybe next time we can do it from the World Trade Building . . . What do you th. . .?

FLIP SCREEN

To ALAN running back into his office looking for MRS. NEIBERT whom he finds gasping for air on the floor while poor MORRY tries his best to help her.

MRS. NEIBERT

I'm allergic to chalk . . . the dust gives me asthma. I can't write the stocks on the blackboard with chalk.

WIPE TO:

INT. ALAN'S OFFICE—SOMETIME LATER—DAY

DAVID and DONALD, his two part-time stock brokers, are there. DONALD who has inherited a million dollars and owns part of the Chicago Bears, doesn't really have to work, and DAVID who was Illinois Campaign Manager for the President of the United States doesn't work because he flies to Washington all the time to help the President, because DAVID is also an expert on Russian affairs.

ALAN is busy working on the books the Securities and Exchange Commission agent is supposed to review.

DONALD

I think I know what we should give Mrs. Neibert for her going away present. One of those cards you get in the bank with slots for a row of nickels, dimes and quarters.

ALAN

And we'll all pitch in and fill the whole card for her.

DONALD

Who's talking about filling it in.

(beat)

That takes away incentive.

The man from the SEC walks in back up to Alan's desk.

> SEC MAN
>
> Mister Schiller, we try to be a sympathetic as we can.
>
> (beat)
>
> But you *are* running a business.

> ALAN
>
> I lost my girl the other day.

> SEC MAN
>
> I lost my girl too, Mr. Miller. Twenty years ago to a plumber.

DIFFERENT ANGLE as BEN POMERANTZ walks in. He was forced to retire from Lupple, Gornischt, and Buffone. He was the best order man in the business. Somehow you look at him with his shock of white hair, and listen to his booming voice and you feel that he's been referred to in the Bible but by a different name. Quickly he sizes up Alan's predicament.

> BEN
>
> Excuse me but in section 296 paragraph ten of the Securities and Exchange Commission's bylaws, a brokerage house which has been in business for less than twelve months can apply for an automatic 90 day extension to get their books in order.
>
> (beat)
>
> We should have our business in order in less time that that if you'll let Mr. Schiller and I prepare the documents. Of course they'll be in triplicate, certified, notarized and I'll face the west and bow three times before I mail them.

The SEC MAN is flustered not expecting such efficiency.

> SEC MAN
>
> Yes of course . . . ninety days . . . triplicate . . . certified . . .
>
> (realizing what he is doing)
>
> don't have to bow . . . why am I bowing?

As he walks into the door narrowly missing the three old men sleeping, and then leaves.

> ALAN
>
> Mister Pomerantz? You're hired!

> BEN
>
> But I haven't even shown you my resume or my driver's license . . . references . . . my ninety year old mother spent a week writing this paragraph.

ALAN

A son should always have his mother's love in writing.

(beat)

Please don't say "no" to me. I'm getting the walls done over, we'll have rugs finally in two weeks and you can have the whole back room to yourself. A separate entrance. A space to park in back. I've got another person coming in for Mrs. Neibert's job . . .

FLIP SCREEN—A FEW HOURS LATER

MARION MACKENZIE walks in. She looks like an organizer, well dressed, stylish with a tinge of well meant sarcasm.

MRS. MACKENZIE

I'm sorry I'm late but my hair dresser was breaking in a new man and he sprayed his eyes shut by mistake.

(beat)

How do you like it? My husband preferred Farrah Fawcett.

(beat)

My grandson Morris the Cat.

(beat)

I wound up with this. I know it's a little short. From the back I look like Roger Staubach.

(beat)

Tell me something. How much experience are you looking for?

ALAN

How much do you have?

MRS. MACKENZIE

Including my last job?

ALAN

Yes.

MRS. MACKENZIE

None. But my husband wrote you this letter. He's a broker for Bacon, Porker, and Ham—you know. The ones who are piggish on America . . .

(beat)

Dear Mister Schiller. My wife knows nothing about the stock brokerage business. She has no experience but please give her a job. She can type seventy words a minute, take dictation and will occasionally do windows.

ALAN

Your husband wrote this?

MRS. MACKENZIE

Yes. He writes a lot of things. He wrote me a long letter when he wanted to have children.

ALAN

That's very beautiful. He was in the service . . .

MRS. MACKENZIE

No. He was on the other side of the bed. He loves memos!

(beat)

Mister Schiller, I could really use the work. I've got two kids all grown, and they got kids starting to grow. You know, and grandma here needs something to do with her time now.

ALAN

I'm going to be honest with you Mrs. Mackenzie. I don't know how long I can keep you.

(beat)

I lost my wife last year. I've got two girls and two boys to raise. That's also four sets of braces at the orthodontist, eventually. Eight arms or legs that will probably wind up in a cast the way they play football and basketball.

(beat)

And if I can't get this business going soon my kids the way they're growing will be able to cut telephone lines with their overbite.

(beat)

I need more money to run this place right.

MRS. MACKENZIE

I was reading . . . can I call you Alan?

ALAN

Yes.

MRS. MACKENZIE

I was reading, Alan, that our bodies have gone up in value thirty dollars in just ten years because of all the new chemicals we're absorbing.

(beat)

Honey, if things got really bad you could always sell your chemicals.

(beat)

Now do I get the job or do my varicose veins start singing the National Anthem from all this standing?

ALAN

When can you start?

MRS. MACKENZIE

Singing the National Anthem?

ALAN

No the job, the job.

MRS. MACKENZIE

As soon as you tell me I'm hired.

ALAN

Mrs. Mackenzie if you want to be my private secretary in sickness and in health for richer or poorer . . . to love honor and obey . . .

MRS. MACKENZIE

I never loved, honored, and obeyed my Bertram so why should I start with you—

ALAN

Then you're hired.

DISSOLVE TO:

INT. SCHILLER AND SCHILLER—A MONTH LATER

The place looks cleaner. More organized. MARION MACKENZIE seems to be everywhere at once. She's what's keeping the place together.

A few clients have walked in. APPLE ANNIE, a millionaire dowager who dresses like she is on welfare or worse. Actually she is wearing rags from the recent ORT sale and she is carrying a box which holds a birthday cake inside of it. She gives a piece to MARION and another to JERRY.

APPLE ANNIE

Last year's surprise party.

(beat)

I didn't come home in time.

(beat)

Have one. I thawed it out yesterday.

ALAN is with RALPH BONASIS, a criminal lawyer. He defends the "defenseless," and he also owns a travel agency where some of the defenseless go to book passage in a hurry to get out of the country.

APPLE ANNIE interrupts what appears to be a serious conversation. At least RALPH has a serious look on his face.

APPLE ANNIE chewing on a dried apricot.

APPLE ANNIE

Alan, how come my stocks are going down and your commissions are going up.

ALAN

I have to make a profit too.

                                    APPLE ANNIE

(musing)

Profit? What is a profit? Funny but no one in this office has ever used that word on me before.

                                       ALAN

Annie, I can't help it if the stocks you buy have a tendency to go down.

                                    APPLE ANNIE

My stocks go down, Alan. My stockings go down, Alan.

(wrinkling her brow for affect)

I want some "up" in my life.

(beat)

You know that retirement home. They won't let me in.

(beat)

They refused my application.

                                       ALAN

Annie, you could *buy* that building.

                                    APPLE ANNIE

Sweetie, what do I want with a building full of old people!

(beat)

Here, have a piece of cake, and give your friend one too. It's frozen but it's not bad.

(beat)

I couldn't eat it all and one way to get rid of it was to come over here.

RALPH shakes his head "no" he doesn't want any.

                                    APPLE ANNIE

What's the matter with him. The cost of sugar is rising—and he's refusing a piece of cake. He's lucky to get a crumb.

(beat)

Alan, put an order in for a thousand shares of Canning Copper. You'll call me with the details later. I gotta go, that thrift shop has a sale on. Instead of factory seconds they're selling factory thirds, fourths, fifths, and I can't say the next number because my teeth are loose.

As she leaves she stops at Marion's desk.

                                    APPLE ANNIE

Have an apple, Marion. It fell off my son's tree.

                                  MRS. MACKENZIE

Sure it doesn't have worms?

Leaving a distraught and highly agitated RALPH BONASIS alone in the conference room with ALAN.

> **RALPH**
>
> Now, do you have a few seconds for me? I'm a client too.
> (beat)
> It's serious, Alan. Millie gave me an ultimatum. Either I give up the stock market or get a divorce.

> **ALAN**
>
> That's serious.

> **RALPH**
>
> Isn't there another way I can buy the stocks so she doesn't have to know about it?

> **ALAN**
>
> In jail.

> **RALPH**
>
> Alan, say, uh, I got this friend of mine. She had a pretty good business going on the streets, you know.

> **ALAN**
>
> Fruit stand?

> **RALPH**
>
> Not exactly, uh, she sells something else you squeeze . . .
> (beat)
> What if like business partners I would buy stocks but in her name . . .

> **ALAN**
>
> You know uh . . .

> **RALPH**
>
> (losing his patience)
> Yes, I know an *uh* . . . and that *uh* is a way for me to buy stocks without the other *uh* knowing about it.

> **ALAN**
>
> Ralph, two "uh's" don't make a right. That's breaking the law. You should know that.

> **RALPH**
>
> Of course I know that. So you find a way to break it for me and I won't tell.

> **ALAN**
>
> I'm sorry Ralph.

> **RALPH**
>
> Alan, Alan, Alan, look, I know you need the business. I'm willing to buy some big stocks, I'm talking bucco bucks.

ALAN

Try jogging or tennis or stuffing yourself. There's no law against eating, and you can do it in your own name.

(beat)

I'm sorry. No. If I have to close this place I'll close it before I cheat anybody.

WIPE TO:

INT. SMALL RESTAURANT—DAY

The Country House run by two spinster sisters who dress in Gay Nineties outfits serve pancakes, eggs and toasts and also want free tips from Alan.

ALAN is seated with MORRY.

MORRY

My great Aunt use to say always "look at the bright side of things"— of course she always wore sunglasses, she couldn't see too well.

(beat)

Alan, it could be worse you know.

ALAN

How could it be any worse than it is right now.

MORRY

You could be sitting across from my wife.

ALAN

Morry, I can't kid myself anymore. How am I going to compete with all those big brokerage firms opening up branch offices.

MORRY

So merge. Just like the rest of 'em.

(beat)

Alan, look, I buy all those crummy little telephone company stocks like Appalachia Telephone and Telegraph, Taos Telephone . . . and one of these days I'm going to use the telephone and call the president of AT&T and tell him to buy into Taos T and T—and you watch the explosion, my stock'll split two for one. You'll see.

(beat)

Merge Alan. Find a company. Tell them how great you are. Sell yourself!

(beat)

You got a good location. This is a rich area. The suburbs. Trees, coiffed ladies out of Vogue, husbands who smoke big fat cigars and got coughs too.

(beat)

Take advantage. Merge.

WIPE TO:

INT. THE OFFICES OF LUTZ AND LUTZ—SOMETIME LATER

A Business Management Consulting firm. ALAN sits in the office of JEFFREY LUTZ, JR., a smooth clean cut hair puffed blown and set management type wearing a pin striped suit and a pin stripe smile. A real high power high price know it all who on second reflection doesn't . . .

JEFFREY LUTZ, JR.

Before you can *even* consider *merger* you have to position your-self. And you can't position yourself until you define your com-ponents.

ALAN

I've got two speakers, a Gerrard turntable, and a Dobie tuner.

JEFFREY LUTZ, JR.

Mister Schiller. I'm afraid you don't understand. When we here at Lutz and Lutz talk about components, we mean all the parts that make up your business. Your office help, your brokers, your clients—all these parts.

ALAN

You look at their parts?

JEFFREY LUTZ, JR.

How they fit into the X factor.

(beat)

Look, you have two components who work for you as part-time brokers. Then you have a back room component who does your orders—and a secretarial component plus your client components.

(beat)

Now am I missing any more components?

ALAN

(getting upset at this impersonal management jargon)

Yes. I've got an Oriental component who delivers Chinese food for our lunch some times from his restaurant.

(beat)

I've got a Polish component who services our heating and air-conditioning.

(beat)

And I also have a Chicano component who takes care of the plumbing and heating.

(beat)

Mr. Lutz unless I'm mistaken the last time I looked at my com-ponents they all looked back at me like *people*.

(beat)

I came in here telling you that I needed a way to make more money and you've been telling me you want to check my parts and charge me two thousand dollars to look.

(beat)

I'll go to my cousin who's just out of med school. For a hot dinner he'll check my components.

(beat)

Mr. Lutz if I was bleeding would I go to the Red Cross and donate a pint?

(beat)

I'm bleeding and instead of offering me a band aid you want to stick me with more needles.

(beat)

I don't have to pay you two thousand bucks to hemorrhage.

(beat)

Now if you don't mind I think I'm going to leave before I become anemic.

JEFFREY LUTZ, JR.

Fifteen hundred?

ALAN

I'm turning *whi* - ite . . .

JEFFREY LUTZ, JR.

A thousand.

ALAN

(doing a Bela Lugosi imitation)

Let me suck "yur bloodt."

JEFFREY LUTZ, JR.

Five hundred.

ALAN slams the door on the guy's face.

As JEFFREY LUTZ, JR. presses the intercom button and whimpers into it.

JEFFREY LUTZ, JR.

Dad, what do you do when they say no . . .

WIPE TO:

INT. ALAN'S PRIVATE OFFICE—LATER

MORRY is in with him eating a corned beef sandwich on rye with a bottle of Camaalox next to him.

MORRY

Then take the bull by the horns.

ALAN

The kind of bull I take doesn't come with horns.

MORRY

The answer, Alan, is an agressive act.

ALAN

I should hire Linda Lovelace?

MORRY

> You should go out and find yourself a partner, a rich partner and
> you should make him think that you are also rich.

WIPE TO:

EXT. SOME FINANCIAL LOOKING BUILDING—DAY

In the middle of Wall Street or the Board of Trade Building in Chicago.

CUT TO:

ALAN looking at directory.

CUT TO:

INT. PLUSH OFFICE—IMMEDIATELY FOLLOWING

ALAN walks into a posh plush office. In here secretaries have their own secretaries and janitors have their own janitors who have their own mops.

RECEPTIONIST

Mister Carnuzzi will see you now.

CUT TO:

INT. THE OFFICE OF ANTHONY J. CARNUZZI

Now *this* is an office! First of all ANTHONY J. CARNUZZI has a massive desk
that rests on an elevated platform. To see Anthony J. Carnuzzi means to have to
walk up. Furthermore, Anthony J. Carnuzzi sits on a telephone book, although
you don't see the phone book for a moment.

ANOTHER ANGLE

Anthony J. Carnuzzi's walls look like they've been extracted from the Chicago
Art Institute, the New York Metropolitan Art Institute and the Los Angeles
Art Museum. Must be a million bucks work of paintings that decorate the walls.

His sculptures look like things and people who walked into his office and got
stoned quickly.

Seated on his right, TONY M. CARNUZZI, JR., a frail eternally young looking
man whose manners are exceptionally polite, and to his left FRANK S. GITTLE-
MAN, one of several vice presidents of the firm Carnuzzi, Schwartz, O'Malley,
and Carnuzzi, in the top ten of Brokerage Houses in Chicago, whose manners are
exceptionally "uneven."

ANTHONY J. CARNUZZI

> This country was founded by spirited men like yourself Mister
> Schiller who did the same thing you are doing now—finding rich men
> like me. And there's nothing wrong with that.

(beat)

Look at my son over there. *He* found me. and now he's rich.

ALAN

(trying to be cool)

Well I'm sort of looking around, in the market, of course I'm in the market, I mean the other market—expanding, possibly merging with another firm . . .

ANTHONY J. CARNUZZI

How's business in general?

ALAN

(swallowing hard)

Couldn't be better.

ANTHONY J. CARNUZZI

Sounds like you don't need us.

ALAN chokes on some cold steel he has just been handed to swallow by Mister Carnuzzi.

ANTHONY J. CARNUZZI

In fact . . . sounds like you're doing everything right.

ALAN

(beginning to hyperventilate)

Th . . . th . . . thanks.

ANTHONY J. CARNUZZI

We've enjoyed the chat Mister Schiller. Good to see what you bright young men are doing nowadays in the suburbs. Keep us boys in the big city on our toes.

(beat)

Yes sir Mister Schiller, keep up the good work.

(beat)

Make sure you leave your address with the receptionist so we can send you our calendar and a Christmas card next year.

WIPE TO:

INT. ALAN'S OFFICE—LATER THAT DAY

ALAN is coming apart in front of MORRY, BEN, and MRS. MACKENZIE.

ALAN

Then I started acting cool and independent just like you said, Morry.

MORRY

And he respected you for it, right. He looked up to you.

ALAN

No. For some reason I kept looking up to him.

(beat)

It was like he was sitting on a throne.

(beat)

Morry, Mrs. Mackenzie, Ben, I blew it. He thinks I'm doing so well, he wants to put me on his mailing list and send me a Christmas card and next year's calendar. That's how cool and independent I was.

(beat)

He should send me a get well card! I cooled myself right out of my business.

MRS. MACKENZIE

Listen, I can give you an advance on *my* next paycheck.

BEN

Maybe you should take it, Alan. I just looked at the books. We're not selling as much as we should.

MORRY

Look at all of you, everybody wants to run from the ship and it's just starting to sink. It isn't sunk yet. Now's the time to roll up your sleeves.

ALAN

'Cause the water's already up to our shoulders right?

MORRY

Wrong, it's only up to our knees.

(beat)

You give Mrs. Mackenzie a letter.

ALAN

Take a letter, Mrs. MacKenzie.

(beat)

Now what.

MORRY

In the letter you tell Mister Carnuzzi how much you enjoyed the meeting and invite him out to lunch on your turf.

(beat)

It's shuttle diplomacy.

ALAN

I'm not Henry Kissinger.

MORRY

What are you talking you're not . . . even Henry Kissinger started small. Do you think he graduated to negotiating peace in the Middle East from nothing?

(beat)

The first border dispute he negotiated was between Iowa and Nebraska—but nobody remembers him for that one.

WIPE TO:

INT. ANTHONY J CARNUZZI'S OFFICE—SOMETIME LATER

Mister Carnuzzi is beaming because he has a letter in his hand and is "I told you soing" all over the place.

>   ANTHONY J. CARNUZZI
>
> What did I tell you.
>
> (beat)
>
> He wants us for lunch.
>
> (beat)
>
> If I had been too eager . . . See Tony? You can never let the other guy know what you want.

CARNUZZI gets up from his chair and pulls out a telephone directory from under him which he uses to prop himself up higher. Then he plops the Yellow Pages down on his desk and starts thumbing through some listings.

>   ANTHONY J. CARNUZZI
>
> You got hundreds of little brokers like Schiller all over these suburbs—if we could make his into a profit center and still keep it a three man office we can use it as a model and develop a whole bunch all over the country.

When CARNUZZI sits down again he forgets he's left the phone directory still on the desk, and he sinks down into his chair, you can barely see him.

>   FRANK GITTLEMAN
>
> And have our own television commercials.
>
>   TONY JR.
>
> Frank, there's enough bulls on the beach already.
>
> (beat)
>
> Dad, let's not forget we're dealing with a human being, too. Alan Schiller is a nice guy.
>
>   ANTHONY J. CARNUZZI
>
> So is the guy who runs our private elevator but look what happens to him—just when things look up—he goes down.
>
> (beat)
>
> Who's forgetting Alan Schiller is a nice guy. I'm not forgetting.
>
> (shrugging his shoulders)
>
> So I'll change him. Toughen him up a little.
>
>   TONY JR.
>
> Dad, not everybody's like you.

ANTHONY J. CARNUZZI

I know. Isn't that a shame too.

(beat)

But even you, Tony. One of these days I'll make you into a tiger.

TONY JR.

What if I don't want to be a tiger?

ANTHONY J. CARNUZZI

Then I'll disown you.

TONY JR.

Dad, you can't. Remember you incorporated me. So you can't disown me. You can only disown the corporation.

ANTHONY J. CARNUZZI

(looking at Frank)

Is that true Gittleman?

Frank nods his head.

I must be slipping . . .

FADE OUT.

END OF ACT I

ACT TWO

FADE IN:

INT. ALAN'S OFFICE—A FEW DAYS LATER

Everybody in the office, brokers, BEN, MARION, MORRY, ALAN are busily making the place look like something. They are busy putting art prints up on the wall—just like in Carnuzzi's office.

MRS. MACKENZIE

Where'd you get these prints anyway, Alan.

ALAN

Walgreens.

MRS. MACKENZIE

This one says, Leonardo—does that mean Divinci?

ALAN

No, Lehrman. He's a local artist.

(beat)

I think maybe you should hang the prints on the far walls and up high so thay won't see they're not originals.

MORRY uncrates a weird looking "thing."

MORRY

What's this?

ALAN

My son and two of his friends did that in his art class.

(beat)

It looks just as strange as what Carnuzzi has in his office—so I'm sure he won't know the difference . . .

HENRY KAZERMERKWESKI who buys and sells rare comic books from his office on the second floor, walks in almost tripping over one of the sculptures in Alan's office. His head and neck are in a harness, and his arm is in a cast, but then he is always in an accident and suing somebody.

KAZERMERE

(angrily)

I can't believe it. Ten years. Ten years wearing this lousy brace everytime I think my court date is scheduled and then that guy's attorney gets a continuance.

(beat)

Ten years of continuances.

(beat)

The guy who hit me in the rear end of my car ten years ago was 68 years old.

(beat)

Now he's 78 and my attorney just told me he's also senile.

(beat)

He can't remember hitting me, and what's worse he can't even remember ever driving a car.

KAZERMERE walks over to the teletype machine, looks at a few stock listings, shakes his head agonizingly over what may be one of his other losses and then looks critically at what is being hung on the wall.

KAZERMERE

Your work, Alan?

ALAN

No.

KAZERMERE

You hired a monkey from the pet store down the block?

ALAN

Thanks!

KAZERMERE

What's going on in this place. What used to be the friendly neighborhood stock brokerage firm is turning into the Ritz.

MRS. MACKENZIE

We're changing our image.

MORRY

The price of success.

KAZERMERE

Since when have you been succeeding?

ALAN

Kazermere will you please get out of the way, you're in my light and it makes hanging these priceless treasures very difficult.

(beat)

Why don't you go back upstairs and sell some more comic books. There's got to be some moody person who wants to buy an issue of Smiling Jack.

(beat)

Go do something. Buy a stock. Take a loss.

KAZERMERE

Alan, do you think I should go into futures?

ALAN

With your luck?

RALPH BONASIS and the "CLIENT" he has brought in with him also have a hard time walking through the obstacle course.

RALPH

Alan, do you mind? I need a room with my client.

ALAN steps over a few boxes to get to him.

ALAN

(suspecting tone)

For what Ralph.

BONASIS takes him aside.

RALPH

Assault.

ALAN

Run of the mill kind?

RALPH

Not really. Hitting a police officer but I'm going to plea bargain—going for a lesser.

ALAN

How do you go "lesser" from hitting a police officer?

(beat)

Hitting his motorcycle?

  RALPH

So will you let me use an office.

                                                ALAN

Well Ben's up here so you could use his.

                                                RALPH

Is that where you keep some of your securities?

                                                ALAN

Yes, so what?

                                                RALPH

So my client has also been up on stealing them a few years ago.
(beat)
Anything safer around here?

                                                ALAN

Yeah, the safe. There's nothing in it.

RALPH shrugs why not and ALAN leads them into the safe, keeping the door
partially opened so they won't suffocate.

                                                RALPH

(shouting out)

Oh Alan? I like my pastrami on rye and Everett here likes his on
whole wheat.

(beat)

You can bring us lunch around one.

                                                ALAN

(peeved)

Anything else?

                                                RALPH

Yeah, tell everyone not to make so much noise.

                                                ALAN

Maybe I should shut the vault door and put the time lock on.
(beat)
How much time do you need?

                                                RALPH

For me a couple of hours.
(beat)
For him?
(pointing to his client)
Ten to twenty.

                                                ALAN

Minutes?

  RALPH

No years.

So RALPH shuts the door partially and ALAN goes back to supervising the
hastily decorated new look so that when Carnuzzi walks in the office will look
just like the big ones do in downtown Chicago.

                                                ALAN

(to Mrs. Mackenzie)

We need something more. Plants, potted things.

                                        MRS. MACKENZIE

You've got your clients, isn't that enough?

When in walks EVE BAUM in her twenties. EVELYN swings in. Nearly everything about EVE is X-rated including her new horoscope service which special-
izes in erotic predictions.

                                                EVE

Alan, can you stop long enough to transact some business?

                                                ALAN

(sounding like Groucho Marx)

What did you have in mind?

                                                EVE

Two hundred shares of American National Pictures.

(beat)

The star of the picture, Cindy Gotall, is in the Seventh House.

                                        MRS. MACKENZIE

She's slipping. I thought she'd broken up more than that.

                                                EVE

(upset)

Her sign Marion. Her sign is in the Seventh House.

                                        MRS. MACKENZIE

That's what I mean. She should just hang it in one place at a time.

(beat)

I saw her movie.

(beat)

I mean all you see is her undressed in bed all the time.

(beat)

Poor people who have less clothes on that that still get around more
than she does.

(beat)

Why should I pay three and a half dollars to see someone sleeping
with somebody else when I do the same thing for free every night
with my Bertram.

(beat)

At least he hangs his clothes up before he jumps in.

EVELYN walks over to the newly installed quote board which Alan has gotten on consignment. MILFORD DICKSON who believes he sees naked ladies on the quote board rather than stock averages sits smiling up at the sign.

EVE

Milford knows what I mean, don't you Milford.

MILFORD

Uh huh.

EVE

Who are you watching today?

MILFORD

Valerie Perrine.

MRS. MACKENZIE

Alan, if we're going to finish by tomorrow afternoon take Evelyn's order and let's get back to work.

(beat)

Tell Valerie Perrine to cover herself up.

WIPE TO:

INT. THE OFFICE OF CARNUZZI, . . . , AND CARNUZZI—SAME DAY

ANTHONY J. CARNUZZI is upset and blustering over some disturbing news which has ruined the rest of his day. His son TONY JR. and his lackey FRANK GITTLEMAN are in the adjoining room when CARNUZZI buzzes them in.

ANTHONY J. CARNUZZI

Frank! Forget about golf this afternoon!

(beat)

Dr. Krammer had a heart attack and they took him to the hospital this morning.

(beat)

There goes our foursome.

FRANK GITTLEMAN

(stuffing some peanuts from a jar)

How did he get it? Playing golf?

ANTHONY J. CARNUZZI

No. Playing with his wife. They're both into that group grope. And I guess last night she was groping around too much, and *he* keeled over into the rest of the group.

(beat)

So that meeting with Schiller we had for tomorrow. I want to change it to this afternoon.

(beat)

But I want to pay a surprise visit. I want to see things in his place, normally.

(beat)

Tony?

                              TONY JR.

Yes father.

                        ANTHONY J. CARNUZZI

We're on our way to becoming the largest investment firm in the country.

(beat)

Where people will look up to us.

On that line the phone book falls off his chair and he sinks down barely able to see over his desk again.

WIPE TO:

INT. ALAN'S BROKERAGE FIRM—LATER THAT DAY

The sidewalk sale going on outside is spilling into Alan's office because SVEN ANDERSON who owns the ski shop next door needs more room for customers to try on his skis which have gone on sale (fifty percent reduction). Sven doesn't sell too many skis in the summer.

                              SVEN

Are you shor?

                              ALAN

Use the front part of the office, should be enough room.

                              SVEN

Whit abit the ault men over der lyink on der flur?

                              ALAN

They won't get up until four this afternoon. That's when they have to get back to the convalescent home.

                              SVEN

How lung have they bin lyink ovur der?

                              ALAN

Since we opened up the place, two years ago.

Looking askew at the three old men, SVEN scratches his head and walks out, as MRS. MACKENZIE looks back and surveys their progress.

                        MRS. MACKENZIE

By tomorrow Alan this place should look like an art museum.

(beat)

Do you think maybe we should put on some classical music?

(beat)

Beethoven's fifth—or do you think we should just crack open a fifth of Beam instead?

But the place with KAZERMERE swaddled in a cast and neck brace, RALPH rehearsing his defense in the vault with his killer CLIENT, EVE reading BEN'S hand in the back room, MILFORD seeing all the nude ladies on the quote board, and APPLE ANNIE walking in with her factory sixth's on looking like a cleaning lady just after the blitz in England, looks less like an art museum and more like Marat Sade.

And the first few ski customers come tramping in trying on their skis or trying them out on the rug.

For a few seconds in all this commotion no one notices someone else trying to make it through the front door—ANTHONY J. CARNUZZI!—Followed by FRANK GITTLEMAN whose face looks screwed into eternal perplexity, and TONY JR. who stops to admire a set of skis. That's when MORRY walks up.

                              MORRY

You in here for an upward trend or a downhill race.

(beat)

Stocks over there. And skis over here.

Bewilderedly shrugging his shoulders, CARNUZZI pushes ski customers aside and makes it as far as MILFORD DICKSON who is blocking the way staring up at the quote board admiringly.

                             MILFORD

Isn't that something?

                            CARNUZZI

Why? It's a blue chip stock.

                             MILFORD

(perturbed)

What stock? I'm talking about Valerie.

                      ANTHONY J. CARNUZZI

(sarcastically and snobbishly)

What Valerie?

                             MILFORD

(as if anybody knows)

The one up there. See? She's smiling at us. Wave back. Go on, wave back to her.

                      ANTHONY J. CARNUZZI

Who is this fruit cake?! Give him back to the bake sale where you got him from!

APPLE ANNIE who is eating from her bag of month old cookies couldn't agree more.

APPLE ANNIE

You're right. I never went to a church bake sale in my life.

(beat)

I feel if you want to get religion it shouldn't be fattening.

(beat)

Have one of my cookies instead handsome.

(she winks at him)

I figure a month in the deep freeze and even a cookie should have a chance to thaw out.

They crumble in her hands before they ever get to his hands. Helplessly ANTHONY J. CARNUZZI looks for his son who is trying on a pair of skis.

ANTHONY J. CARNUZZI

(grabbing him)

Tony?! Put those poles down!

KAZERMERE limps over—overhearing the "poles down" part.

KAZERMERE

I beg your pardon.

And then he begins to scold him in Polish for putting down the poles.

When ALAN and MRS. MACKENZIE walk out of the back office, ALAN freezes and turns white.

ALAN

Mister Carnuzzi?

The room fills with "Hail to the Chief" then we hear a needle scratch, followed by the Overture of 1812.

ALAN lunges to an intercom . . .

ALAN

Ben, classical music. Soft, not this!

BEN'S VOICE O.S.

(sophisticated manner)

This happens to be classical music.

(beat)

It also happens to be a test. If this were an actual air raid, you would have tuned to . . .

ALAN

(panicking into the intercom)

Ben? Mister Carnuzzi's here now.

(singing it out)

A *sur PRI ise.*

Another needle scratch and then we hear the funeral march.

ALAN runs up to CARNUZZI puts his arm around his shoulder and offers him a cigar which when he pulls it out of his inside suit coat pocket turns out to be a sucker which he gives to the little ones who come into the office with their "stock raving" parents.

ALAN

Have a . . . cherry one.

ANTHONY J. CARNUZZI

Schiller, what's going on here. Halloween?

ALAN

No sir.

(sheepishly)

Business as usual.

ANTHONY J. CARNUZZI

Schiller! Show me the front door.

ALAN

That's going to be kind of hard too.

(beat)

They took it off this morning. The building's eighty years old. So are the doors. We bought new ones last week.

(beat)

If you still want I can show you the door, but it's downstairs in the basement . . .

Through the vents we hear someone singing "Oklahoma."

Where that's coming from. If the boiler man sings Oklahoma for some reason the rats down there get scared and won't bother him.

ANTHONY J. CARNUZZI

Rats, doors, cookies, skis, musical comedy . . .

(he throws up his hands)

TONY JR.

Dad, at least let Mister Schiller show you around.

FRANK GITTLEMAN

He's got a vault, Anthony. That means he must be selling something.

Before ALAN can stop GITTLEMAN, he's opened the vault revealing RALPH and his CLIENT, still in summation rehearsal.

RALPH

. . . So I ask you ladies and gentlemen of the jury . . . is this a man who could beat his wife?

(beat)

You're right. It isn't. Because he didn't.

(beat)

Your honor, ladies and gentlemen of the jury . . . My client is not an embezzler.

(beat)

A little eager maybe.

(beat)

A little hungry maybe. A little overextended but certainly not an embezzler.

RALPH has to cut short his summation for the moment when he sees his CLIENT reaching for something on the vault shelf.

For gosh sakes, can't you just keep your hands in your pockets without always stuffing something else inside with them, Everett.

(back to his summation)

The Bible says he who taketh shall also giveth.

(beat)

My client taketh only because he has nothing to giveth.

(beat)

But giveth he will if taketh you won't.

RALPH receives applause from everyone in the office but—

ANTHONY J. CARNUZZI

They ought to put all of you in jail . . .

EVELYN has grabbed his hand . . .

EVE

I see something happening . . .

(beat)

See that line in your palm is a happening line . . .

(beat)

Yea, a woman, a very attractive woman enters your life. I see her grabbing your hand, and leading you somewhere . . .

Then suddenly the bell on the teletype rings. When the bell rings something is happening to the market. MORRY is the first over there and screams out.

MORRY

Taos Telephone and Telegraph just merged with Monopolated Light and Power.

(beat)

Alan it worked. My phone call to the President of Monopolated Light and Power worked. He really thought I was a big stockholder . . .

Now there is a commotion in the office. And a rush is on for orders. But no salesmen to take the orders because DAVID and DONALD are just now walking in.

                                    DAVID

Alan, this is Captain Harrington from the Secret Service. The President's coming in tomorrow and he'd like to stop by so Captain Harrington has to check out the place for security.

                        ANTHONY J. CARNUZZI

(shocked)

Your broker *knows* the President of the United States?

                                    ALAN

Yes. He ran his campaign in Illinois and is one of his closest friends— and advisors!

But whom DONALD strolls in with blows CARNUZZI's mind even more. It is a well-known pro football player.

                        ANTHONY J. CARNUZZI

Bull Kadofsky?

                                    BULL

Why not? My last quarters earnings were in excess of what they should have been to put me at a point where my gross profits would put me into a higher tax bracket so I'm going to sell off my interest and take a loss to offset the capital gains.

(beat)

Besides, Donald here is my broker—he also owns part of the team so I guess that makes him one of my bosses, too.

TONY JR. has to hold his father up. He slowly staggers to a chair, and ALAN remembers to prop it up first with a telephone book before he sinks down.

                              APPLE ANNIE

Wait a minute!

(a beat)

I *am* insulted.

She hands a cookie to BULL KADOFSKY who thanks her.

His royal highness the shrimp over there with the skinny kid he calls his son and the big burly one he calls his ape, thinks we're not good enough for him, huh?

(beat)

Because he thinks we're as stale as the cookies I bring in.

(beat)

He thinks we don't have a pot to—

ALAN

(covering up his ears)

Don't say it!

APPLE ANNIE

To put our pits in.

Just then SEYMOUR and LILLIAN MOSHEN walk in. Possibly the only mother and son stock buying team in the country whose combined ages equal 112. SEYMOUR still lives with "mother," who is fastidious second only to SEYMOUR.

They make their way to Alan's desk and virtually ignore Anthony J. Carnuzzi whose mouth has just dropped.

SEYMOUR takes out a small hand brush and sweeps one chair clean for himself before he sits down, another for his mother who still elects to place a small dainty handkerchief on it before she sits down.

LILLIAN

Alan?!

(in ever so proper tones)

I have been looking over my portfolio and think it's time to make some major moves.

SEYMOUR

What mother is trying to say Alan is that she's getting bullish in a bearish market.

LILLIAN

Shut up Seymour.

(beat)

I read the news over my private teletype at home.

(beat)

I want to purchase a thousand shares of Taos Telephone and Telegraph and I want you to buy another five hundred of Monopolated Light and Power.

ANTHONY J. CARNUZZI

Lillian?

(beat)

Don't you even want to say hello?

SEYMOUR

Mother? Mister Carnuzzi is inquiring whether you'll acknowledge his presence.

LILLIAN

Tell Anthony J. Carnuzzi I have no intention of ever saying hello to him again because his presence isn't *felt* by me!

ANTHONY J. CARNUZZI

She's one of your clients?!

ALAN

For about a year.

(beat)

Misses Moshen and Seymour only live a few blocks away.

MRS. MACKENZIE

Walk in trade, you know.

ANTHONY J. CARNUZZI

Lillian, you left *me* about the same time.

SEYMOUR

That's right, Mister Carnuzzi. Mother left you on the very day she let me have my first private telephone number all my very own.

LILLIAN

(snapping)

I still list it as a "child's phone" in the directory so don't get so smart, Seymour.

(beat)

And Anthony J. Carnuzzi, I didn't leave you. You shunned me. Because you grew to big for your own britches.

(beat)

Of course you growing big is like a raisin thinking tall.

ANTHONY J. CARNUZZI

Shunned? Lillian, my Lillian, you were one of our best customers. How could I shun you. I *loved* you Lillian. Loved, adored, there wasn't anything I wouldn't have done . . .

LILLIAN

For my money. That's why I like Alan. He's still poor enough to count his friends rather than his friends' cash.

(beat)

Alan write me up that order.

SEYMOUR

Me too mother?

LILLIAN

My son here is popping for it out of his allowance.

APPLE ANNIE

If Lillian wants to swing with Monopolated Light and Taos Telephone and Telegraph, so do I.

(beat)

A thousand Taos and two thousand Monopolated, Alan.

RALPH yells out that he wants a couple of "hundred years," his CLIENT turns green and RALPH quickly corrects himself and orders—

RALPH

A couple of hundred shares.

KAZERMERE who is screaming over the phone to his lawyer because of another continuance drops it long enough to order.

KAZERMERE

Three hundred shares.

EVE pops for two hundred shares—

MILFORD has stopped watching the naked ladies to speculate on—

MILFORD

Two hundred shares.

One of the OLD MEN still with his eyes closed raises his hand with three fingers up while the other two from the convalescent home sleep peacefully. That means he is in for three hundred shares as well.

SVEN ANDERSON stops waiting on a customer trying on skis long enough to order

SVEN

A hundred shares.

While FRANK GITTLEMAN who has whipped out his pocket calculator computes the transactions wiping the perspiration off his brow when he sees the numbers—

FRANK GITTLEMAN

Monopolated at sixty bucks a share and Taos Telephone and Telegraph at 15 no wait a minute, it's jumped to nineteen . . .

(beat)

That's nearly a quarter of a million dollars of business boss, in a few minutes.

APPLE ANNIE

(smiling slyly at Anthony J. Carnuzzi)

You wanna cookie now sweetheart.

ANTHONY J. CARNUZZI

(the last evidence of a steel exterior gone for the moment)

Yes, yes, yes. Cookies. Give me all your cookies.

(pulling up a chair for Apple Annie)

Sit down. Please. All of you sit down.

(beat)

Do you want some coffee? Frank? Tony? Make them coffee.

(back to business)

Of course you'll have to change the lettering on the front window outside. I think Carnuzzi, Schwartz, O'Malley and Carnuzzi should be in larger letters than Schiller, and you should have the words, 'A Division of' in bold letters just before your name.

(beat)

Then there's stationery, and I want the phone answered differently.

LILLIAN

(sternly)

Alan?! I may just decide to reconsider.

Catching on to LILLIAN'S strategy quickly the others, APPLE ANNIE, SVEN, EVE, RALPH, MILFORD and

BEN'S VOICE O.S.

(through the intercom)

And my ten shares too—

LILLIAN

Unless—

ANTHONY J. CARNUZZI

(knowing he is outnumbered)

But not right away, Schiller.

(beat)

We can hold off on the sign for a while, and the stationery, and answering the phones the new way—

(beat)

Consider this a period of transition.

MRS. MACKENZIE

How long will *that* last?

LILLIAN

(chiming in)

Until *I* say the word—

She gives MISTER CARNUZZI a raspberry.

SEYMOUR

(shuddering how unlady like)

Mother! Really!

She blows a raspberry in Seymour's direction, too.

FADE OUT:

END OF ACT TWO

TAG

FADE IN:

INT. ALAN'S BROKERAGE FIRM—A FEW WEEKS LATER

It is the end of the day. Everyone has gone except for MRS. MACKENZIE, MORRY, and BEN who is still in the back room.

The office is beginning to look a little different. More plants. Some better pictures are now hanging but a lot of the "old" is still there.

Alan's desk for example. Still messy, as ALAN tosses a behind the back lay up shot of a wad of paper which drops into a waste paper basket about ten feet away.

MORRY

(happily)

Taos Telephone and Telegraph merges with Monopolated Light and Power—

(beat)

And Schiller merges with Carnuzzi, Schwartz, O'Malley, and Carnuzzi.

(beat)

Now if I could just get my daughter to merge with that doctor she's been dating . . .

(beat)

I mean how many more "examinations" by *him* does it take for *her* to say "yes."

MRS. MACKENZIE

Just don't forget us, Alan.

ALAN

(putting his arms around Morry and Mrs. Mackenzie)

Never.

MRS. MACKENZIE

Good. Then I can ask you for something.

(beat)

Now that you're part of a conglomeration, maybe I can glom fifteen bucks out of you that you still owe me from last week's salary.

BEN'S VOICE O.S.

(intercom)

Fifteen dollars and seventy-five cents, Mrs. Mackenzie—to be exact.

ALAN digs into his pockets and pulls out a candy bar, a tube of Clearasil, baseball cards, and a half stick of Bubble Gum when he realizes—

ALAN

I put on Peter's pants by mistake.

(beat)

Marion, will you settle for two Reggie Jackson's, one Artis Gilmore, and three Joe Namaths instead?

MRS. MACKENZIE

Don't you have someone more my speed like one Bobby Riggs?

(then she gets a little serious for the moment)

Alan, are you sure you want to go through all this?

ALAN

I've got bills for basketball, football, baseball, books, and braces.

(beat)

It's either merging or applying for foreign aid.

MRS. MACKENZIE

(picking up a framed picture of his late wife)

She'd be proud of you, Alan.

ALAN

(sighing)

Yeah . . .

(then his spirits pick up again)

Well? What do you think? Do I buy suits from Saks? Or do I stick with chinos from the surplus store?

BEN'S VOICE O.S.

(intercom)

Stick with the Army and Navy Surplus. In case there's ever a war you'll be dressed for it.

MORRY

Alan, Alan . . . don't be so worried about how you look—clothes don't make the man.

ALAN

What does?

MORRY

In this business—a hot tip.

At that moment a bedraggled disheveled CANNON BALL DELIVERY SERVICE MESSENGER, the same old who came in earlier, shuffles back in slower than a turtle.

OLD MAN

G o t . . . l o s t . . .

(wheezing)

C a n ' t t e l l y o u r "N's" f r o m y o u r "S's" . . .

(handing Alan the envelope containing the original merger papers back)

Does this mean ... South Michigan Avenue?
(beat)
Or North Michigan Avenue?
(beat)
People ought to know that old age doesn't slow you down ...
(beat)
just bad directions do!

FADE OUT

THE END

appendix G

A Television

Documentary Script

The following example is part of a half-hour television special, *THE ART INSTITUTE: A SELF-PORTRAIT* which starred Vincent Price and was aired on *WBBM* TV, the *CBS* affiliate in Chicago.

VIDEO	AUDIO
DISSOLVE TO:	MUSIC: UP AND HOLD THEN FADE TO B. G. FOR NARRATION
49. MCU SELF PORT OF RENOIR (#19 in the exhibit stay in this shot to establish)	*VINCENT PRICE: VO* Pierre Auguste Renoir was born in Limoges, France in 1841. His family managed on the money his father made as a tailor. The thought of attaining wealth was never even dreamed about because his family realized it would never happen.
	Like most young boys, Renoir's childhood was one adventure after another. And each experience rested somewhere in the back of his mind to be recalled later on. He had a fine voice as a youngster and could have turned out to be a fine baritone singer. Instead, he turned out to be
SLOWLY PULL BACK	one of the greatest painters in Europe. Life touched Renoir like ink touches a blotter— Renoir absorbed life like a sponge. Whatever he saw found its way to his soul.

PULL ALL THE WAY BACK TO
REVEAL VINCENT PRICE

VINCENT PRICE STRAIGHT ON
Some men try to control their own destiny
Renoir lived his. Wherever it led him. And it
led him everywhere. One discovery after
another, each having a connection with a new
moment. Maybe he never got out of the stage
of a child who views each new experience with
astonishment and intense curiosity. It was this
fascination with people, places, and things
which pushed him further into the unpredictable world around him. Renoir never stopped
learning. Never felt so confident in his craft
that he could relax and live off his accomplishments. He was his worst critic—although early
in his career he has other critics like his friend
Edouard Manet, who told another painter,
"Renoir has absolutely no talent, tell him to
give up painting." Fortunately, Renoir didn't
listen.

THEN DISSOLVE TO:

51. 4. MERE ANTHONY'S CABARET
    MS. VINCENT PRICE
    (HE'LL BEGIN HIS DIALOGUE
    OVER THE DISSOLVE AND
    THEN WE'LL PICK HIM UP
    STRAIGHT ON)

VINCENT PRICE VO
(THROUGH THE DISSOLVE)
Renoir visited Mere Anthony's Cabaret often
usually with his friends Monet, Sisley, Frank
Lamy and sometimes with Pissaro . . .

52. 9. MATCH CAMERA ANGLE AND
    CUTS TO PRICE'S STORY

VINCENT PRICE STRAIGHT ON THEN VO
The Cabaret was in Marlotte on the south side
of the Forest of Fountainbleau. There were
only a few houses and properties along the
crossroads and the forest came almost up to the
first group of houses.

The painting represents an early period in
Renoir's life. His beginnings in a community of
artists who freed themselves from the traditional way of painting. We can see that he
already uses a loosely handled paint with every
brushstroke employed to describe his surfaces
as he renders them.

53. CAMERA CONTINUES TO MATCH
    PRICE'S DESCRIPTION PICK UP
    SHOTS, CUTS, ANGLES, ETC WILL
    FIT THIS SECTION OF DIALOGUE.

VINCENT PRICE VO
And each touch makes a delicate pattern itself.
Sisley is standing up, and Pissaro has his back
turned to us. The man with the clean shaven
face is Frank Lamy. Mother Anthony can be

seen in the background. Nana, the maid, is picking up the coffee cups, and the mongrel dog lying on the floor is Toto. He had lost one of his paws in a carriage accident. Renoir tried to make him a wooden leg but Toto who managed very well with three legs refused the gift . . .

54. MOVE IN ON THE CLOWN #5

    CAMERA MOVEMENT HERE SHOULD
    BE SLOW, CAREFUL

    CUT TO:

55. #82 IN THE COLLECTION
    PORCELAIN DISH

    SLOW DISSOLVE TO:

56. #68 LANDSCAPE AT BEAULIEU.

    DISSOLVE TO:

57. #64 YOUNG GIRLS AND LITTLE
    BOY IN LANDSCAPE
    DISSOLVE TO:

58. #37 VENICE FOG
    CUT TO:

59. #78 PAUL DURAND — RUEL
    CUT TO:

60. #80 FRAU THURNEYSSEN AND HER
    DAUGHTER
    CUT TO:

61. #68 LANDSCAPE AT BEAULIEU
    SLOWLY DISSOLVE TO:

62. #6 PONT-des-ARTS

    DISSOLVE TO:

63. SLOW PAN OF PONT-des-ARTS

*MUSIC: UP HOLD AND THEN FADE TO
BG.*

VINCENT PRICE VO
Renoir never took painting seriously until he was around twenty . . .

VINCENT PRICE VO (CONTINUES)
Before that he had painted porcelain dishes, window shades, and murals in cafes . . .

VINCENT PRICE VO
In Renoir's world mind is liberated from matter just as a rush or surge of water is freed from its holding dam. The blossom of the linden tree and the bee sipping the honey from it follow the same rhythm as the blood circulating under the skin of the young girl sitting on the grass.
Like the flight of a butterfly which changes its composition but not its soul as it soars from seas, to cities, to mountains . . . to man—

—woman and child . . .

. . . the wind, trees, and then to appear as the butterfly again.
For Renoir, the world was one.

VINCENT PRICE STRAIGHT ON
In this painting, Pont-des-Arts, Renoir isolated an event, a moment in life but you must remember it took a long time to paint this scene. So he was recording a concept as well as an observation.

We can sense the feelings Renoir had for the

CUT ACCORDING TO THE FEELING
OF THE PAINTING

city of Paris. The colors are fresh. The scene is natural. And Renoir masterfully draws us in to his point of view. What is surprising is that it is not a large work. It's relative smallness magnifies the brilliance of the effect which is almost the same kind of effect you would achieve through the use of a reducing glass. And yet if you were standing on the pier with your distance equal to that of Renoir's point of view, the people in the painting would have the same size relationship in real life.

DISSOLVE TO:

64. #21 THE GARDEN IN THE RUE
CORTOT, MONTMARTRE

A SERIES OF SLOW DISSOLVES,
WHICH ARE MOVING PANS, PULL
IN, PULL OUT, SO WE HAVE A
FEELING OF MOVEMENT DELICATE
MOVEMENT

*MUSIC: UP THEN HOLD TO ESTABLISH
THEN FADE TO B. G.*
VINCENT PRICE: VO
Renoir always dreamed of a world in which neither animals nor plants would be harmed by man's needs. That all living things would thrive untouched by selfish imposition or profit. And that man himself would follow a path untouched by humiliation or demeaning tasks . . .

Renoir once said, "An artist under pain of oblivion must have confidence in himself, and listen only to his real master: Nature."

SLOW DISSOLVE TO:

*SOUND: OUTDOORS BIRDS—ESTABLISH
THEN SLOWLY FADE UNTIL
OUT.*

65. #17 MONET PAINTING IN HIS
GARDEN AT ARGENTEUIL
CAMERA FOLLOWS WHAT PRICE
TALKS ABOUT. (RICHIE—TREAT IT
THE WAY YOU SEE IT)
WE PULL OUT OF THE PAINTING
FAR ENOUGH TO REVEAL
VINCENT PRICE TALKING AS HE'S
OBSERVING THE PICTURE

VO:
"It is the eye of the sensualist that I wish to open."

[portion omitted]

DISSOLVE TO:

71. #22 GIRL IN A BOAT

VINCENT PRICE VO
In Renoir's *Girl in a Boat,* he shows the truly individual painter he was. He has taken flat two dimensional patterns and combined them with three dimensional structure. There are three

things going on in this painting. Its charm, serenity—and Renoir's genius.

DISSOLVE TO:

72. #14 PARISIAN LADY

NOTE: MAYBE WE GO TO PRICE STRAIGHT ON AND ELIMINATE THIS PAINTING—

MUSIC: UP THEN HOLD THEN FADE TO B. G.

Renior never hid from life. Although at times life may have wanted to hide from Renoir. He had a running commentary on everything.

Once when Renoir was asked if he liked Rembrandt better than Rubens, his reply shot back quickly and sharply, "I don't give out awards." He thought Leonardo Da Vinci should have stuck to his flying machines . . .

DISSOLVE TO:

73. #71 VILLA DE LA

And yet he praised the teachings of the masters with one caution—never to copy them. "Only nature," he remarked, "should be copied." And nature was Impressionism.

DISSOLVE TO:

VINCENT PRICE STRAIGHT ON

For Renoir, color was not just an element it was energy, mist, softness, motive . . .

74. #24 TWO LITTLE CIRCUS GIRLS. DIFFERENT ANGLES CAMERA MOVEMENTS

VINCENT PRICE VO

Renoir's eyes were his skin. His eyes were his hands. His senses were magnetic. Nothing was ever disconnected or unrelated.

DISSOLVE TO:

75. #29 NEAR THE LAKE

VINCENT PRICE STRAIGHT ON

Feverishly looking for new methods of expression pushed Renoir to his limits. And during the autumn of 1881 this self-inflicted pressure finally got the best of him. Fatigue took hold and Renoir felt forced to leave Paris if for nothing more than rest and in search of fresh inspiration.

SLOW DISSOLVE TO:

76. #35 SAN MARCO
SLOW PANS DIFFERENT ANGLES

VINCENT PRICE VO

At the end of October, he left for Italy. But he carried with him the nagging fear that he was slipping as an artist.

77. #19 RENOIR SELF PORTRAIT WE NEED TO FRAME IN SUCH A WAY AS TO FEEL THE INTENSITY OF HIS EYES.

Renoir would suffer a number of crises in his career—and this was one of them. In Venice he looked to Raphael to lift him from his depression. But this only pushed him further into his malaise.

VINCENT PRICE VO

While in Naples he wrote a long letter to his friend Paul Durand-Ruel. His confidence was shattered and the letter was his means to understand why and then how to put the pieces back together again.

DISSOLVE TO:

VINCENT PRICE STRAIGHT ON

"I am like a schoolboy with a blank page that has to be neatly filled out and, bang! there's a blotchy mess. Here I am at forty and still at the blotch stage. I saw the Raphaels in Rome and found them really beautiful. I should have gone long before. They're full of knowledge and wisdom. He did not look for the impossible like I do, but it's beautiful."

DISSOLVE BACK TO:
78. #35 SAN MARCO
DISSOLVE TO:
79. #3 LANDSCAPE

Soon he was back in Paris with a renewed spirit and an eagerness to plunge back into his work with all the fury and passion which had temporarily left him before.

DISSOLVE TO:
80. #51 MADAME RENOIR

He was also in love. And this time he was sure it was love. He married Aline Chagrot in May of 1882. Before marriage, Renoir was always restless, unable to remain long in one place. But now his life with Aline had changed him. Aline was a lovely blond. Her skin as delicate as silk. She realized the happiness of her husband depended on his paintings so she saw to it that he was allowed to paint in peace.

VINCENT PRICE VO

His meals were regular, his socks were darned, the messy bed he never managed to straighten up was now made carefully—and to all these benefits a new dimension of marriage was added. Three children . . .

DISSOLVE TO:

81. #52 MADAME RENOIR WITH PIERRE

Renoir's eyes and his heart could never leave his children. The feeling of levity and pride which sweeps a father into new world caught hold of Renoir, never to leave him . . . Children, soft skin, dimpled and pure with a perfume no match to any other fragrance . . .

DISSOLVE TO:

82. #73 CLAUDE AND RENEE
    HOLD SHOT
    DISSOLVE TO:

Claude and . . .

(PAUSE)

Includes Jean . . . who is pictured here.

VINCENT PRICE STRAIGHT ON

For Jean to sit long enough for this portait was an exercise of will and determination. Jean's will—and his father's determination. For any little boy to sit long enough without moving surely must set some sort of record. Jean's performance fell short of that—and we can see the changes his father made to correct shifts in Jean's attention.

SLOW DISSOLVE

BACK TO

SHOT #83

VINCENT PRICE VO

The background is thinly painted, Renoir using his favorite blue, well scrubbed into the surface of the canvas. He added touches of green and yellow which achieves a sense of shimmering light. The picture was painted in a room in the Renoirs' home, near a window. And Renoir captured the light coming through which shines in on Jean.

DISSOLVE TO:

84. #78 PAUL DURAND-RUEL

VINCENT PRICE VO

Paul Durand-Ruel was an art dealer. A respectable middle class man. He was a good husband. He was also a great gambler. "Only he gambled for a good cause," as Jean Renoir said of the man who managed and exhibited his father's paintings.

SHOT 84 CONTINUES

VINCENT PRICE VO

In 1885 Durand-Ruel traveled from Paris to New York. Along with him were the works of Renoir.

CAMERA MOVEMENTS SLOW AND
SPECIFIED

CUT TO:

85. #62 PLACE de la TRINITE
DISSOLVE BACK TO:

86. VINCENT PRICE

VINCENT PRICE STRAIGHT ON
Renoir never cared that much for commissioned portraits; he had all the models he needed virtually under his roof. His wife, his children, his servants, and his friends who also had wives and children, and for those who could afford the extra help, servants too.

CUT TO:

87. #41 THE DAUGHTERS
DURAND-RUEL

VINCENT PRICE VO
And why not pick the daughters of his art dealer, to keep it all in the family. This portait may be one of the most important paintings in the exhibit.

DISSOLVE BACK TO:

88. VINCENT PRICE

VINCENT PRICE STRAIGHT ON
Women were sensual objects of admiration and Renoir left us a number of admiring examples of this view on canvas.

DISSOLVE TO:

89. #43 CITY DANCE
Here the CAMERA can slowly sweep and pan to take in the motion and form

VINCENT PRICE VO
Perhaps this painting is an example of the most solidly achieved painting Renoir ever did of the female form.
Every inch of this woman is precisely and beautifully drawn. Her skin, her arms, her back, the structure of her chin and head, the texture of her gloves and gown is all matched to achieve a sense of motion.

DISSOLVE TO:

90. #53 STANDING NUDE

VINCENT PRICE VO
And in this painting Renoir concentrated his interest on the beauty of the female figure in its textures, forms, and colors to suggest almost a fantasy . . .

DISSOLVE TO:

91. #47 THE AFTERNOON OF THE
CHILDREN AT WARGEMOUNT

VINCENT PRICE VO
And then, as if to break sharply from that style, Renoir almost prophetically styled this painting which could easily fit into a modern art exhibit held today.

DISSOLVE BACK TO:
92. ANGLE FAVORING VINCENT PRICE

VINCENT PRICE STRAIGHT ON
(TWO BEAT PAUSE)

Why is is that gifted men often fall to the cruelties of fate. Sometimes by a will greater than ours, sometimes by an assassin's bullet, and sometimes by a twisted sense of circumstance, an accident which has no grounds for reason or question . . .

DISSOLVE TO:
93. #54 ANTIBES

VINCENT PRICE VO

It was 1897 in Essoyes, France. Essoyes was far enough away to the east to escape from the effects of bad weather in Paris.

The countryside is rich in greens. The Seine river flows at the bottom of the valley and the meadows provide ample grazing for cows. The slopes above find home for woods and vineyards. And, it was in Essoyes, France where Renoir's world was to be shaken to its roots.

DISSOLVE BACK TO:
VINCENT PRICE

VINCENT PRICE STRAIGHT ON

Almost all the painters who came to see Renoir when he was working at Essoyes rode bicycles. And finally, Renoir was persuaded to try one, and so he asked cousin Parisot to send him one.

DISSOLVE TO:
95. ROAD AT WAIGEMONT

VINCENT PRICE VO

On that particular day, to the surprise of the entire household, Renoir was relaxing. It had been raining the day before but by the afternoon the rain had stopped. Renoir decided to ride his bicycle as far as Sévigné to see "what the tops of the poplars looked like under stormy skies." Sévigné was an enchanting place for Renoir.

96. #3 LANDSCAPE (REPEATED)

The surface was still slippery from rain when Renoir began bicycling down a path. He skidded in a puddle of water and fell on a mound of sharp edged stones . . . up—his right arm discolored—because it was broken . . .

DISSOLVE TO:
97. #77 SELF PORTRAIT

Renoir who was so fascinated by hands now

could not move his own . . . A physician who was in Essoyes put Renoir's arm in a plaster cast and six weeks later the cast was taken off . . .

[portion omitted]

DISSOLVE BACK TO:

99. ANGLE FAVORING VINCENT PRICE
MCU

VINCENT PRICE STARIGHT ON
Each year following, the accumulation of pain from rheumatism besieged him more. The ugly shadow of torment would follow him around because there was no possibility for a cure. Renoir had no choice. Either close his eyes and die. Or paint until the life he treasured would finally close . . .

The Renoirs moved to another home, a second floor apartment where the walk up wasn't so agonizing to his legs and back. He rented a studio on the same street which gave him a view of the Saint Denis plain so the outdoors he loved so much was still *in reach* of *his eyes.*

DISSOLVE TO:

100. #76 JEAN RENOIR

VINCENT PRICE VO
World War One broke out and his sons Jean and Pierre were seriously wounded.

CUT TO:

101. #79 MADAME RENOIR
LATER YEARS

VINCENT PRICE VO
His wife Aline who was a strong woman simply could not endure any longer. Her sons hospitalized, her husband now crippled, all the dreams she had, were now fragments no longer able to be put back together. Aline Renoir died on the 28th June 1915.

DISSOLVE TO:

102. #88 THE CONCERT
CAMERA MOVES SO SLOWLY

VINCENT PRICE VO
Renoir painted The Concert during the last months of his life. The paint brushes he used were strapped to his arms because he could no longer use his hands and fingers . . . .

STAY ON THIS SHOT FOR
A MOMENT LONGER THEN
DISSOLVE TO:

103. VINCENT PRICE

SHOT 103 CONTINUES

VINCENT PRICE STRAIGHT ON
Early in the morning of December third, 1919, Pierre Auguste Renoir was now barely conscious . . . Renoir died, but not his genius . . .

Renoir believed in something which is as universal now as it was when he was alive. That the chief function of a human being is to live . . . and his first responsibility—to have a respect for life . . .

DIFFERENT ANGLES SLOWLY
PULL IN ON VINCENT PRICE

This sense for life is shown not only by Renoir but by the other artists whose exhibits are inside this building. The Art Institute is a mirror which reflects feelings on many levels and in many dimensions. A sense of order . . . a cry for change . . . an editorial about the human condition . . . a sense of identity and a call for individuality. In short, a self portrait . . . .

104. VINCENT PRICE LEAVING THE
THE RENOIR GALLERY AS
WE ROLL:
CLOSING CREDITS

MUSIC: UP AND HOLD THEN FADE SLOWLY TO CONCLUSION

appendix H

A Treatment for an Industrial Film

Whether the treatment is fiction or nonfiction the same principles of good story telling apply: a beginning, a middle, and an end; conflict; character growth; resolution. The last example is an industrial film treatment on company safety.

TREATMENT: FILM ON ALCOHOLISM.
Producer: Gilbert Altschul Productions
Client: The National Safety Council.

Fred Dichter is 40 years old, married, with a son and daughter in high school. He operates a crane at the XCO Southside Plant, in Chicago. He has been a drinker since his teens, but in recent years his drinking has increased considerably and continues steadily through most of his waking hours. He probably consumes about a fifth of hard liquor a day. His wife, children, fellow workers and supervisor are of course aware of his drinking, but because he rarely seems drunk they do not regard him as a serious problem drinker. Also, there is the fact that most of the people he knows, his wife included, drink more or less regularly.

Fred himself is quite well aware that his drinking is, potentially at least, a serious problem. In his own mind he sees every day as a series of crises created in some sense by alcohol. He has learned to be extremely cautious, for example, in driving his car, in getting to work on time, in handling all the details of his job, and especially in his dealings with other people. The end of a day gives him a sense of profound relief if he can feel that he has not made any obvious mistakes or otherwise betrayed himself; the relief is always tempered by the realization that tomorrow he must do it all over again.

Fred's drinking is, of course, a matter of habit, but the fact is that, habit aside, he drinks for anesthesia. He can hardly imagine how to cope with work or other people or himself without being numb. In this sense his drinking is genuinely medicinal. He admits to himself that, with alcohol, his life is miserable, but he feels that, after all, he has survived this way, which may really be the only way left open to him.

(1) We begin the film with the accident, as shown from Fred's point of view. He has picked up a heavy load on his hook, and is moving it to a new position, following the hooker's hand signals. He makes a mistake—he misses or misreads one of the hooker's signals, or mishandles the controls in his cab. The result is that the load goes down, giving the hooker a possible fractured leg, and narrowly missing killing the man. Tumult; the injured man is checked, and an ambulance is summoned and takes him off to hospital. Fred is shocked and badly frightened; he knows the accident was his fault, but all his anger and fright are turned toward the injured man.

(2) When Fred reports to his supervisor, he tries unsuccessfully in a rather blustering way to blame the hooker. The supervisor, who has known Fred a long time, will have none of this. The question of Fred's drinking is not raised by either man, but the supervisor clearly suspects that this is the reason for the accident. However, he doesn't want to blow the whistle on Fred, so he finally accepts a partial and rather superficial account of the accident.

(3) Here we follow the supervisor to the plant hospital room, where he talks to the duty nurse about the condition of the injured man. While he is there, the safety director (or other appropriate person) comes looking for him. The SD is upset, possibly because he has been getting a series of near misses and potentially very dangerous accidents, and he wants to know what happened. The supervisor says he is just about to write his report. Reluctantly, he gives the SD an oral version of the story. The SD won't accept it, insists on knowing what's wrong. The supervisor finally mentions Fred's drinking, protesting as he does so that everybody drinks, Fred's a senior man with a generally good record, and so on. It turns out that Fred's record is somewhat marred by a series of near-accidents. The SD lectures the supervisor: It's your job to catch this sort of thing, heavy drinking isn't incurable, we can help him help himself, but we can't have a drinker in a job like this. Supervisor says, Sure, he'll have a talk with Fred.

(4) In the next scene, we open in a neighborhood tavern. It is just after the day shift is out. Enter Fred. He has gotten himself somewhat reorganized, and is able to talk to some of the other men from the plant, but he needs a drink badly, and is able to say so, with the accident for an excuse. Here we get the version of the accident which he has now worked out; the version absolves him of guilt, of course, but it is not the version he gave to his supervisor, nor is it the story he will later tell his wife. Quite possibly the bar version could turn on the fact that the hooker is a young man, likely to be a little careless, a little inexperienced. The conclusion is that he, the hooker, was lucky to get off so

easily. There is a good deal of sympathy for Fred, who really deserves better than to have to work with kids.

(5) The final scene is at Fred's home. He comes in, finds his wife getting dinner. Their son is at football practice, their daughter at a drama club meeting. Fred's pitch to his wife is for sympathy; he's had a bad day, and it wasn't his fault. Right now he needs to relax and have a couple of drinks. Possibly the story to his wife is that he always tries to help the young fellows at the plant, show them how to do things right, and today he failed. Afraid he's getting old. The wife tries to ressure him, cheer him up. She has a drink with him, then goes back to cooking. He has another on his own. In her final effort to cheer him, she says, "Well, tomorrow is another day." This is probably the worst thing she could say to him. We end on his reaction to this line.

Notes: (1) The opening sequence should certainly use subjective camera, and possibly the scene between Fred and the supervisor should. Scene three should have normal visual handling. But should we return to the subjective on scenes four and five? I'd appreciate your ideas on this.

(2) Should there be a scene after (3), in which the supervisor does talk with Fred? It would reinforce the "moral" of the script, but doesn't seem to me to be absolutely necessary.

(3) If we are to avoid completely any suggestion of the "open end" presentation of the topic, would you want any narration—say, voice over at the opening and closing of the film, to make the point(s) of the script?

(4) Finally, what would you think of "Another Day"—taken from the wife's closing line—as a title? It sounds a little soapy, but then, soap operas have pre-empted practically all human situations by now.

Index